A GALLANT
OF LORRAINE

FRANÇOIS, SEIGNEUR DE BASSOMPIERRE,
MARQUIS D'HAROUEL,
MARÉCHAL DE FRANCE (1579-1646)

BY
H. NOEL WILLIAMS

AUTHOR OF "FIVE FAIR SISTERS," "A PRINCESS OF INTRIGUE,"
"THE BROOD OF FALSE LORRAINE," ETC.

IN TWO VOLUMES

With 16 Illustrations

VOL. I

A GALLANT OF LORRAINE
VOL. I.

"C'étoit un homme de grande qualité, beau, bien fait, quoique d'une taille un peu épaisse. Il avoit bien de l'esprit et d'un caractère fort galant. Il avoit du courage, de l'ambition et l'âme du grand roi."

BUSSY-RABUTIN TO MADAME DE SCUDÉRY,
AUGUST 16, 1671.

FRANÇOIS, SEIGNEUR DE BASSOMPIERRE, MARQUIS D'HAROUEL, MARÉCHAL DE FRANCE.
From an engraving by Lasne.

PREFATORY NOTE

ALTHOUGH the *Mémoires* of the Maréchal de Bassompierre are acknowledged to be one of the chief authorities for the history of France during the early part of the seventeenth century, they have never been translated into English, nor, if we except the charming but all too brief sketch of the marshal by Comte Boudet de Puymaigre in his *Poètes et Romanciers de la Lorraine* (Paris, 1848), has any biography of their author yet been attempted. That such should be the case is certainly very surprising, since seldom can a man have led so eventful a life, or played so many different parts with distinction, as did François de Bassompierre. Soldier, courtier, diplomatist, gallant and wit, he was to the Courts of Henri IV and Louis XIII very much what the celebrated Maréchal de Richelieu was to that of Louis XV, and when on that fatal February day in 1631 the gates of the Bastille closed upon him, not to reopen for twelve long years, one of the most interesting careers in French history practically terminated. In my endeavour to give a full and authentic account of this career, I have naturally found my chief source of information in Bassompierre's own *Mémoires*, which he wrote, or rather arranged and revised, during his imprisonment in the Bastille; but I have also consulted a large number of other works, both contemporary and modern. Most of these are mentioned either in the text or the footnotes, but I desire to take this opportunity of acknowledging my great indebtedness to the admirable notes of the Marquis de Chantérac, who so ably edited the edition of the marshal's *Mémoires* published by the Société de l'Histoire de France.

H. NOEL WILLIAMS.

LONDON, *May*, 1921.

A Gallant of Lorraine

CHAPTER I

Birth of François de Bassompierre—Origin of the Bassompierre family—A romantic legend—His grandfather—His father—His early years—He and his younger brother Jean are sent to the University of Pont-à-Mousson, and afterwards to that of Ingoldstadt—Their studies at Ingoldstadt—Death of their father, Christophe de Bassompierre—Journey of the two brothers through Italy—Their return to Lorraine.

FRANÇOIS DE BASSOMPIERRE was born at the Château of Harouel, in Lorraine, on Palm Sunday, April 12, 1579, "at four o'clock in the morning." His family, which was one of the most ancient and illustrious of Lorraine, appears to have owed its name to the village of Betstein, or Bassompierre,[1] near Sancy, which formed part of its possessions until 1793, when it was confiscated and sold by the Government of Revolutionary France, with the rest of the Bassompierre property. If we are to believe the very confusing documents which François de Bassompierre collected about his family, it descended from the German House of Ravensberg, but, according to the learned genealogist, Père Anselme, its origin can be traced to the latter part of the thirteenth century, to one Olry de Dompierre, who became possessed of the fief of Bassompierre by marriage, and whose son, Simon, adopted the name, which became that of his descendants.

However that may be, it was undoubtedly a very old family indeed, as well as a distinguished one, and, like most old families, had its mysterious traditions; but, at any rate, the legend of the Bassompierres had nothing sinister about it.

The story goes that during the transitory reign of that Adolph of Nassau who lost his Imperial crown and his life at the Battle of Spire, there lived a certain Comte d'Angerveiller, or d'Orgeveiller. This nobleman, as he was returning home one evening from hunting—it was a Monday—stopped to rest at a summer-house situated in a wood a little distance from his château. There, to his astonishment, he found a young and beautiful woman—a fairy, it is said—(She must surely have been the last of the race!)— apparently awaiting his arrival. And the pair were so well pleased with one another at this first interview, that for two whole years they failed not to meet every Monday at the same rendezvous, "the count pretending to his wife that he had gone to shoot in the wood."

However, as time went on, the countess began to conceive suspicions, "and one morning entered the summer-house, where she found her husband with a woman of perfect beauty, and both asleep. And being unwilling to awaken them, she merely spread over their feet a kerchief which she was wearing on her head, which, being perceived by the fairy, she uttered a piercing cry and began to lament, saying that she must see her lover no more, nor even be within a hundred leagues of him; and so left him, having first bestowed upon him these three gifts—a spoon, a goblet and a ring, for his three daughters, which, said she, they must carefully preserve, as, if they did this, they would bring good fortune to their families and descendants."

Well, a lord of Bassompierre, an ancestor of the marshal, married one of the three daughters of the Comte Orgeveiller, who brought him as her dowry, together with certain fat lands, the spoon; and, in memory of this tradition, the town of Épinal, of which he had been burgrave, was obliged to offer to him and his descendants, on a certain day each year, by way of quit-rent, a spoonful from every measure of corn sold within its walls.

The ancestors of Bassompierre had served in turn the Emperors and great princes of Germany, the Dukes of Burgundy, the Kings of France and the

Dukes of Lorraine, and had ended by occupying the highest offices at the Court of Nancy. To go no further back than two generations, we find the marshal's grandfather, François de Bassompierre, high in the favour of the Emperor Charles V, to whom he was successively page of honour, gentleman of the Chamber, and Captain of the German Guard. In 1556 he accompanied his Imperial master to the gates of the Monastery of Yuste, where he witnessed Charles's last adieu to the world, and received from his hand a valuable diamond ring, which was ever afterwards religiously preserved in the Bassompierre family.

In 1552 Henri II, King of France, invaded Lorraine and established a protectorate over the duchy; and François de Bassompierre, who, some years before, had been sent by Charles V as Ambassador Extraordinary to Nancy to assist in the government of Lorraine, during the minority of its youthful sovereign, Charles III, was required to send his youngest son, Christophe, to the French Court, as a hostage for his good behaviour. The little boy—then about five years old—was brought up with the Duc d'Orléans, afterwards Charles IX, who "either on account of the conformity in their ages or some other reason, conceived a great affection for him," and admitted him to the closest intimacy. In consequence, when the Peace of Cateau-Cambrésis left Christophe at liberty to return to Lorraine, he preferred to remain in France, until, in 1564, when barely seventeen, he set off for Hungary to serve under one of his uncles, Colonel de Harouel, against the Turks. Here he made the acquaintance of Henri de Lorraine, Duc de Guise, who had also gone crusading on the Danube, and a warm friendship sprang up between the two lads, which lasted until Guise's tragic death in 1589. "My father," writes Bassompierre, "always preserved for him (Guise) his devotion and his service, and the said Sieur de Guise esteemed him above all his other servants and intimates, calling him '*l'amy du cœur.*' "[2]

Returning to France, after two years' service in Hungary, Christophe de Bassompierre was entrusted by Charles IX with the command of 1,500 *reiters*, at the head of whom he distinguished himself at the Battles of Jarnac and Montcontour, in both of which he was wounded. In 1568 he was sent by the King with a body of *reiters* to the Netherlands, to the assistance of Alva, and took part in the Battle of Gemmingen, in which Alva defeated the Duke of Nassau. On his return to the French Court after the

Peace of Saint-Germain, Charles IX proposed to reward his military services by marrying him to one of the two daughters of the late Maréchal de Brissac. Christophe, however, who was poor and a cadet of his House, represented to his Majesty that these damsels, who had little money and great pretensions, were ill suited to him who had none, and who needed it; "but that if he would do him the favour of marrying him to the niece of the said marshal Louise le Picart de Radeval,[3] who was an heiress, and whose aunt, Madame de Moreuil, intended to give her 100,000 crowns, it would do him much more good and make his fortune. And this the King did, in spite of her relations and in spite of the girl herself, who did not like him, because he was poor, a foreigner and a German."

Of this union, so inauspiciously begun, five children were born—three sons, of whom François was the eldest, and two daughters.[4]

Almost immediately after his marriage, Christophe was obliged to leave his bride, to take part in the siege of La Rochelle, which was interrupted by the news that the Duc d'Anjou (afterwards Henri III), who commanded the Catholic army, had been elected to the throne of Poland. Christophe was one of those chosen to accompany the prince to his kingdom, and set out for Poland, "with a great and noble retinue"; but, on reaching Vienna, he received orders from Charles IX to raise a levy of *reiters* for service against the Huguenots and *"Politiques"* and return to France with all speed. He performed a like service for Henri III in 1575, at the time of the revolt of Alençon, but in 1585 resigned his pensions and offices and threw in his lot with the Duc de Guise and the League, to whom his skill in recruiting mercenaries from Germany and Switzerland proved of great assistance.

After the King's surrender to the demands of the League, at the Peace of Nemours, in July of that year, Christophe's pensions and offices were restored to him, and in 1587, when the great army of *reiters* under Dohna and Bouillon invaded France, we find him commissioned by Henri III to raise a new levy of 1,500 horse. These troops were stationed with the main army, commanded by Henri III in person on the Loire, but Christophe himself preferred to serve under Guise on the Lorraine frontier. Here he was seized with a serious illness, which necessitated his return home and prevented him taking part in Guise's victories at Vimory and Auneau.

Christophe was at Blois at the time of the assassination of Guise in December, 1588, but, warned in time, he succeeded in effecting his escape from the town before the principal adherents of the duke were arrested, and, exasperated by the fate of his friend and patron, raised large levies in Germany for the service of the Leaguer princes. He fought under Mayenne against Henri IV at Arques and Ivry, in which latter engagement he was twice wounded and obliged to return to Lorraine. He returned to France in 1593, to assist, as representative of Duke Charles III, at the Estates of the League, where he offered very effective opposition to the proposal of the ultra-Catholic party to confer the crown of France on the Infanta Clara Eugenia. The conversion of Henri IV having caused him to abandon any projects which he might have had in France, he now devoted himself to re-establishing the affairs of the Duke of Lorraine, which were in sad disorder, and was appointed by that prince Grand Master of his Household and Superintendent of Finance. In July, 1534, he signed, on behalf of the duke, in Henri IV's camp before Laon, a treaty by which Charles III undertook to observe complete neutrality between France and Spain.

This gallant old warrior was an excellent father and spared no expense to give his sons the most thorough education which it was possible for them to obtain. François de Bassompierre's early years were passed at the Château of Harouel.

"I was brought up in this house," he writes, "until October, 1584, when I first remember seeing Henri, Duc de Guise, who was concealed at Harouel, for the purpose of treating with several colonels of *landsknechts* and *reiters* for the levies of the League. At this time I began to learn to read and write, and afterwards the rudiments. My tutor was a Norman priest, named Nicolas Ciret."

In the autumn of 1587, on the approach of the invading army of Dohna and Bouillon, Madame de Bassompierre and her children had to leave Harouel and take refuge at Nancy. The invaders burned the town of Harouel, but appear to have left the château untouched.

On the return of the family to Harouel, François and his younger brother Jean, who now shared his studies, were given another tutor, named Gravet, "and two young men, called Clinchamp and La Motte, the one to teach us to write, the other to dance, play the lute and music." They passed the next four years partly at Harouel and partly at Nancy, where, in the autumn of 1591, François saw for the first time Charles de Lorraine, Duc de Guise, who had recently effected his romantic escape from the Château of Blois,[5] and with whom he was to be on such intimate terms in later years.

In October, 1591, the two boys went, accompanied by their masters, to study at Freiburg, but only remained there five months, "because Gravet, our tutor, killed La Motte, who taught us to dance." In consequence of this unfortunate affair, they returned to Harouel, but towards the end of 1592 were sent to continue their studies at the University of Pont-à-Mousson, founded by Duke Charles III and his uncle the Cardinal de Lorraine, and early in the following year reached the first class. They passed the Carnival of 1593 at Nancy, where they took part in a tournament, "dressed *à la Suisse*." At its conclusion they returned to Pont-à-Mousson, where, shortly afterwards, their father brought them a German tutor, George von Springesfeld, in place of the homicidal Gravet. At the Carnival of 1594 they again went to Nancy, to assist at the marriage of William II, Duke of Bavaria, and Marie Élisabeth, younger daughter of the Duke of Lorraine, when it was decided that they should accompany the bridal pair back to Bavaria, and keep their terms at the University of Ingoldstadt. They travelled in the duke's suite by way of Heidelberg, Spire, Neustadt, Donauworth and Landshut, the party being splendidly entertained by the various nobles at whose houses they stopped; but the journey did not end without a tragic incident, in which François de Bassompierre had a narrow escape of his life.

At Donauworth, where they were delayed for two or three days by the swollen condition of the Danube, he went out in a boat with the duke and some of his attendants, to reconnoitre the passage of the river. As they were nearing the castle in which the duchess was lodged, William II ordered one of his pages to load and fire a pistol, in order to announce their approach to his consort. The pistol missed fire, and, while the page was examining the priming, it suddenly went off and killed an old nobleman of the prince's suite, who was sitting close to Bassompierre.

At Ingoldstadt the two brothers, and the elder in particular, would certainly not appear to have wasted much time:—

"We went on with rhetoric for a little while, and then proceeded to logic, which we studied in an abridged form, and in three months passed on to physics and occasionally studied the sphere. In the month of August we went to Munich, whither the duke had invited us to spend the stag-hunting season, which they call *Hirschfeiste*, with him. At the end of the hunting-season, which lasted a month, we returned to Ingoldstadt, and continued our studies until October, when we quitted physics, having got to the books *De Animâ*. And, as we had still seven months to remain, I set myself to study the institutes of law, in which I employed an hour; another hour I spent in cases of conscience; an hour in the aphorisms of Hippocrates; and an hour in the ethics and politics of Aristotle, upon which studies I was so intent that my tutor was obliged, from time to time, to draw me away from them, in order to divert my mind. I continued my studies during the rest of that year and the early part of 1596."

But what contributed a good deal more than this bizarre erudition to give to the future marshal that perfect aplomb, those graceful accomplishments and charming manners to which he owed his fortune, was the journey through Italy which he and his brother undertook after they had completed their course at Ingoldstadt and returned to Harouel, which was then a house of mourning, as their father, Christophe de Bassompierre, had died just before they left Bavaria.

In the autumn of 1596 they set out for the South, accompanied by the Sieur de Malleville, an old gentleman, who acted as their *gouverneur*, Springesfeld, their German tutor, and one of their late father's gentlemen, and travelled by way of Strasbourg, Ulm, Augsburg, Munich, Innsbrück and Trent to Verona, where they were the guests of the Counts Ciro and Alberto Canossa, the latter of whom had once been page to William II of Bavaria. From Verona they proceeded to Mantua and Bologna, and then, crossing the Apennines, arrived at Florence.

Here they received a gracious message from Ferdinand I, Grand Duke of Tuscany, who had married Christine of Lorraine, daughter of Charles III, inviting them to visit him at his country-seat at Lambrogiano, to which one of the prince's carriages would be sent to convey them. On the day following their arrival at Lambrogiano, the Grand Duchess invited the elder brother to walk with her in the gardens, where they met her niece Marie de' Medici, to whom she presented him. Bassompierre little imagined as he made his reverence that the young princess whom he was saluting was the future Queen of France. In the evening they left Lambrogiano and returned to Florence, where they remained for a few days and then set out for Rome, by way of Sienna and Viterbo.

At Rome they stayed a week, in order to perform the various devotions customary for good Catholics who visited the Eternal City, and waited upon several of the cardinals to whom they had letters of introduction, and also upon the Spanish Ambassador, the Duke of Sessa, who had been a friend of their father, and whose acquaintance they had made some years before when he passed through Lorraine on his way to France. The Ambassador provided them with passports and with letters of recommendation to the Viceroy of Naples, and they set out for that city, stopping on the road at Gaëta, Capua, and Aversa.

On their arrival at Naples, they lost no time in presenting the letters which the Duke of Sessa had given them to the Viceroy, Don Henriques de Guzman, Count of Olivares, "who, on opening them, inquired if we were the sons of that M. de Bassompierre, colonel of *reiters*, who had come to the succour of the Duke of Alva in Flanders, by orders of the late King Charles. And when we told him that we were, he embraced us most affectionately, assuring us that he had loved our father as his own brother, and that he was the most noble and generous cavalier whom he had ever known; adding that he would treat us, not only as persons of quality, but as his own children, which, indeed, he did, giving us all the proofs of affection and good-will possible to imagine."

At Naples, the brothers passed a considerable part of their time in practising equitation, under the guidance of two celebrated Italian riding-masters; but at the beginning of 1597 their course of instruction was interrupted by an attack of small-pox. On their recovery, they returned to Rome, where they remained until after Easter, the only incident of importance which marked their second visit to the Papal city being their rescue of a French gentleman named Saint-Offange, who had killed another in a duel, from the pursuit of the law.

From Rome they went to Florence, where they resumed the riding-lessons which the small-pox had interrupted at Naples.

"As for our other exercises," writes Bassompierre, "we had Messire Agostino for dancing, Messire Marquino for fencing, Guilio Parigi for fortification, in which Bernardo della Girandolla also sometimes assisted. We continued these lessons all the summer, and also witnessed the festivities of Florence, such as the *calcio* and the *palio*, the plays and some marriages within and without the palace."

While at Florence, they paid short visits to Pisa, Lucca, and Leghorn, and early in November left the Tuscan city and took the road to Bologna, whence they travelled by way of Faenza, Forli, and Ancona to Loretto. At Loretto, where they arrived on Christmas Eve, they were invited by Cardinal Gallio to stay at the Palazzo Santa-Casa. They spent the night in devotions in the chapel, and on Christmas Day the cardinal appointed the elder Bassompierre one of the witnesses to the opening of the alms-boxes, "which amounted to six thousand crowns for the last quarter of the year."

At Loretto our young travellers, inspired doubtless by their visit to that famous shrine with the desire to do and dare something for the sake of Holy Church, embarked in a strange adventure:—

"There were a great many other French gentlemen at Loretto, besides ourselves, and we all took the resolution to go together into Hungary to the wars before we returned home. Having mutually promised this, on the day after Christmas we all set out in a body, to wit: MM. de Bourlemont and d'Amolis, brothers; MM. de Foncaude and de Chasneuil, brothers; the Baron de Crapados and my brother and I. But, since the nature of Frenchmen is fickle, at the end of three days' journey some of us, who had not our purses sufficiently well-lined for a long journey or who had a stronger desire to return to our homes than the rest, began to say that it was useless to go so far in search of fighting when we had it near at hand; that we were in the midst of the Papal army, marching to the conquest of Ferrara, which had devolved on the Pope by the death of Duke Alphonso; that Don Cesare d'Este retained possession of it, contrary to all right;[6] that this was not less just and holy a war than that of Hungary, and that in a week we should be face to face with the enemy; whereas, if we went to Hungary, the armies would not take the field for four months.

"These persuasions prevailed on our minds, and we resolved that we would all go next day to Forli, to offer our services to Cardinal Aldobrandini,[7] legate of the army, and that I should speak in the name of us all, which I did, to the best of my ability. But the legate received us so coolly, and gave us so poor a welcome, that in the evening, at our lodging, we did not know how sufficiently to express the resentment and anger with which his indifference had inspired us.

"Then my brother began to say that in truth we had only got what we deserved; that, not being subjects of the Pope, nor in any way concerned in this war, we had gone inconsiderately to attack a prince of the House of Este, to which France had so many obligations, which had ever been so courteous to foreigners and particularly to Frenchmen, and which was so nearly allied, not only to the Kings of France, from whom that family was descended in the female line, but also to the families of Nemours and Guise; and that, if we were good for anything, we should go and offer our services to this poor prince whom the Pope wanted unjustly to despoil of a State possessed by so long a line of his ancestors.

"So soon as he had said these words, all the company expressed, not only their appreciation, but also their firm resolve to proceed on the morrow straight to Ferrara, to throw themselves into the town. I have related all this, first, to make known the volatile and inconstant character of Frenchmen, and, secondly, to show that Fortune is generally mistress and director of our actions, since we, who had intended to bear arms against the Turks, did, in point of fact, take them up against the Pope."

Travelling by way of Bologna, where their company was reinforced by the Comte de Sommerive, younger son of the famous Duc de Mayenne, of the League, the Chevalier de Verdelli, a friend of the Bassompierres, and several other adventurous young gentlemen, they arrived on January 3 at Ferrara. The duke received them with great honours and cordiality, but he was very irresolute on the question of the war, alleging that his coffers were well-nigh empty; that the King of Spain had declared for the Pope, and that the Venetians, who had encouraged him to resist the Pontiff, refused to assist him openly, and that the support that they were prepared to give him secretly was of very little account. In this state of mind he went, on the Feast of Kings, to hear Mass at a church near the palace, accompanied by a great retinue of lords and gentlemen, when the priests immediately quitted the altars, without finishing the masses they had begun, and retreated from them as excommunicated persons. This incident decided Don Cesare to send the Duchess of Urbino, sister of the late Duke Alphonso, to treat with the Legate;[8] and, accordingly, next day the band of young Frenchmen who had come to offer him their services took leave of him and went their several ways.

The Bassompierres went to Rovigo and thence to Padua, when Johann Tserclas, Count von Tilly, elder brother of the famous captain of the Thirty Years' War, who was then studying at the University of Padua, invited them to dinner, and the following day accompanied them on a visit to Venice, where they remained a week. On leaving Venice, they returned to Padua, and, after a short stay there, set out for Genoa, stopping on the way at Mantua. At Genoa they lodged at the house of the German consul, and "my brother and I both fell in love with the consul's daughter, whose name was Philippina, to such a degree that for some days we did not speak to one another." Which of the two brothers Philippina preferred, Bassompierre does not tell us.

Among the distinguished persons whose acquaintance they made at Genoa were the two brothers Ambrosio and Frederico Spinola, the former of whom, afterwards Duke of San Severino and Marquis of los Balbazes, was to earn such renown as a general in the service of Spain. Frederico, who also entered the Spanish service, was killed in a naval combat off Ostend in May, 1603.

From Genoa our travellers proceeded to Tortona, and thence to Milan, where they stayed for some days and were very hospitably entertained by the Spanish governor at the citadel. They then set out on their homeward journey, accompanied by the Chevalier de Verdelli and Don Alfonso Casale, Spanish Ambassador to Switzerland. They travelled by way of the St. Gotthard, stopping at Como, Lugano, Lucerne and Basle, and in the early summer arrived safely at Harouel, after an absence of more than a year and a half.

CHAPTER II

Visit of the Bassompierre family to Paris—François dances in a ballet before Henri IV at Monceaux—He is presented to the King, who receives him very graciously—He decides to enter the service of Henri IV—He escorts his Majesty's mistress, Gabrielle d'Estrées, Duchesse de Beaufort, to Paris—Sudden illness and death of the duchess—Extravagant grief of Henri IV, who, however, soon finds consolation in the society of Henriette d'Entragues—Affray between the Prince de Joinville and the Grand Equerry Bellegarde at Zamet's house, where the King is staying—Visit of Bassompierre to Lorraine—He returns to Paris.

IN September, 1598, the Archduke Albert, son of the Emperor Maximilian II, passed through Lorraine on his way to Italy, there to take ship for Spain to marry the Infanta Clara Eugenia, Philip II's daughter, by Élisabeth of France, and become through her the sovereign of the Netherlands.[9] The Comte de Vaudemont, younger son of Charles III of Lorraine, went to meet the archduke at Vaudrevange, and invited the brothers Bassompierre to accompany him. They were duly presented to the prince, who received them very cordially and "told them their name was very dear to all his House."

On their return from this little journey, the whole Bassompierre family began to prepare for a visit to France, Madame de Bassompierre, like a loyal

Frenchwoman, being anxious that her sons should be presented to Henri IV, in the hope that they might decide to enter his service. She was, however, at pains to conceal the real object of her journey from the Count von Mansfeld,[10] whom her late husband had associated with her in the guardianship of his children, and whose consent was required before they could leave Lorraine.

"The Count von Mansfeld," writes Bassompierre, "gave his consent very unwillingly, because he wished us to enter the service of the Catholic King [Philip III of Spain]; and it was only on condition that, after we had been some time at the Court of France and in Normandy (where my mother made him believe that we had some business affairs to transact), we should proceed from there to the Court of Spain, and should not commit ourselves until our return from both. He made us promise further that, when we wished to make our choice, we should follow the advice that might be given us in the matter by our principal friends and relatives."

At the beginning of October, the Bassompierres left Harouel and on the 12th of that month arrived in Paris, where they took up their quarters at the Hôtel de Montlor, in the Rue Saint-Thomas-du-Louvre.

Henri IV was then lying ill at the Château of Monceaux, near Meaux, which he had presented to his beloved Gabrielle d'Estrées, Duchesse de Beaufort, in 1595, and reported to be in considerable danger. The only courtier of Madame de Bassompierre's acquaintance who was with him at the time was Gaspard de Schomberg, father of the marshal, to whom she wrote to inquire when her sons could be presented to his Majesty. Schomberg replied that it was impossible to think of such matters as presentations in the condition the King was in, and advised her to remain in Paris until Henri IV was sufficiently recovered to return to the capital. This she decided to do, and meantime sent her sons to pay their court to Catherine de Bourbon, the King's sister, who was about to marry the Duke of Bar, eldest son of Charles III of Lorraine. The princess was very gracious to the young men, and, says Bassompierre, "had the intention of marrying me to Mlle. Catherine de Rohan,[11] in order to keep her near her when she went to Lorraine, but I had at that time no inclination towards marriage."

Several of Madame de Bassompierre's relatives and friends of her late husband came to visit the Bassompierres at the Hôtel de Montlor, amongst them being Charles de Balsac, Seigneur de Dunes—"*le bel Entraguet*"—the hero of the famous Duel of the Mignons; Jacques de Harlay, Seigneur de Chanvallon, a former lover of Marguerite de Valois, Queen of Navarre; Charles de Cossé, Maréchal de Brissac, and the Comte (afterwards) Duc de Gramont. One day, when Henri IV's health was beginning to mend, the Duc de Bellegarde, First Gentleman of the Chamber and Grand Equerry to the King—*Monsieur le Grand*, as he was commonly styled—arrived in Paris on a short visit, and Gramont presented François de Bassompierre to him. Bellegarde received the lad very cordially, and pressed him to dine with him, saying that he had invited some of the most brilliant gentlemen of the Court. During dinner a suggestion was made to organise a ballet to amuse their convalescent sovereign and to go to Monceaux to dance it, and was received with acclamation.

"They said," continues Bassompierre, "that I must be one of the party, but, thought I declared that I should be most delighted, I added that it appeared to me that, as I had not yet been presented to the King, I ought not to take part in the ballet. M. de Joinville[12] then said: 'That need not stand in your way; for we shall arrive at Monceaux early in the day, when you can be presented to the King, and in the evening we shall dance the ballet.' So I learned it with the others, who were MM. d'Auvergne,[13] de Sommerive, *le Grand*,[14] de Gramont, de Termes,[15]the young Schomberg,[16] Saint-Luc, Pompignan, Messillac and Maugiron, whose names I have decided to set down, since they represented a select band of persons so handsome and so well-made that it was impossible to find their superiors. At my suggestion, they made up as barbers, in order to poke fun at the King, who had placed himself in the hands of persons of that trade for the cure of a wart which he had."

After this aristocratic troupe had rehearsed the ballet to their satisfaction, they set out for Monceaux, but were met on the way by a messenger from the King, who expressed his regret that he was unable to lodge them at the château, where at that time there was but little accommodation, and desired them to stop at Meaux, to which he would send coaches that evening to bring them and their "props" to Meaux. Bassompierre was thus disappointed in his expectation of being presented to the King before the ballet. However, it was decided that he should take part in it all the same.

The party accordingly proceeded to Meaux, where they dressed for the ballet, and then bestowed themselves, with their pages, the musicians, and all their paraphernalia in six of the royal coaches, and set off for Monceaux, where they danced their ballet, which appears to have caused the good-natured monarch, who took the jest at his expense in excellent part, much amusement.

"After which," says Bassompierre, "as we were removing our masks, the King rose and came amongst us, and inquired where Bassompierre was. Then all the princes and nobles presented me to him to embrace his knees; and he received me most affectionately, and I should never have believed that so great a King would have shown so much kindness and familiarity towards a young man of my condition. Afterwards, he took me by the hand and presented me to the Duchesse de Beaufort, his mistress, whose gown I kissed; and the King, in order to give me the opportunity of saluting and kissing her, stepped aside."

Humility was certainly not a fault of this young gentleman from Lorraine, who had a nice appreciation of his own attractions. And he proceeds to relate with complacency how, a few days later, they danced again the same ballet at the Tuileries, for the diversion of

Catherine de Bourbon and Gabrielle d'Estrées, who, by permission of her royal lover, had come to Paris expressly to witness it again, and that "when the twenty-four men and women came forward to perform the dances, all the spectators were delighted to behold a selection of such handsome persons. So that, when the dances were over, they insisted on their being performed again, an incident which I have never seen happen since."

Undoubtedly, if we are to judge from his portraits, which belong, however, to the time of Louis XIII, that is to say, to a period when he had already passed the brilliant years of his youth, Bassompierre may be pardoned his satisfaction at his personal appearance. These depict him as of middle height and very well made, though his figure is a little inclined to *embonpoint*. The face is of an almost perfect oval, framed in long blond curls which descend to the richly-embroidered lace which covers his shoulders. The nose, which sinks a little in joining the forehead, dominates two small moustaches, separated above the mouth and ending in carefully-pomaded points. A *"royale"*—or, as it has been called since the time of the Second Empire, an *"impériale"*—extends from immediately under the lower lip to the extremity of the chin, and imparts to the whole physiognomy that intelligent expression which is to be observed in all the portraits of the time of Louis XIII. However, if Bassompierre had arranged his beard in quite a different manner, his features would not have been less intelligent or less pleasing; his agreeable smile and bright brown eyes would have always sufficed to animate his countenance and to denote a man made for successes of all kinds.

In December, Henri IV, being sufficiently recovered to leave Monceaux, removed for change of air to Saint-Germain-en-Laye, where he lodged at the Deanery, as did Gabrielle, and where he had his last natural son by the duchess—Alexandre de Vendôme, afterwards Grand Prior of France—baptised.[17] In the evening there was a grand ballet, in which Bassompierre took part, "dressed as an Indian."

The Court remained at Saint-Germain until after the marriage of Catherine de Bourbon with the Duke of Bar, which was celebrated on January 30, 1599, when it returned to Paris; but at the beginning of Lent the King set out for Fontainebleau. Bassompierre, however, remained for a few days longer in Paris, and was the last to bid farewell to that singular personage the Maréchal de Joyeuse, whom Voltaire has so well described in these two lines:

"Vicieux, pénitent, courtisan, solitaire,
Il prit, quitta, reprit la cuirasse et la haire,"

before he finally quitted the world for the convent.

"My cousin," Henri IV had remarked to Joyeuse a little while before, as they were standing one day on a balcony, beneath which a crowd had gathered, "those people down there do not appear very well pleased at seeing an apostate King and an unfrocked monk together." This pleasantry struck Joyeuse to the quick and this time he resumed the hair-shirt, not to put it off again. And as in those days people obeyed their religious convictions without deeming it necessary to advertise the fact to the public, Joyeuse, having spent the evening in the midst of the gayest company in Paris, withdrew to the convent where he had resolved to spend the remainder of his days, without saying a word of his intention to anyone.

"After we had supped together at the Hôtel de Retz," writes Bassompierre, "at midnight I bade him good night at the postern-door of his lodging, the threshold of which he merely crossed, and then repaired to the Capuchins, where he ended his days piously."

Bassompierre was by this time firmly established in the good graces of the King, for whom he had already conceived so warm an admiration and affection that he had decided to enter his service. We will allow him to speak himself on this occasion, inasmuch as he does so with a sensibility and gratitude very unusual with him, and which one does not find in his *Mémoires*, except when Henri IV is in question:

"Two days later I went to Fontainebleau, and, one day, as someone had told the King that I had some beautiful Portuguese pieces and other gold coins, he asked me if I would play for them against his mistress. On my agreeing to do this, he made me stay and play with her while he was at the chase, and in the evening he played too. This put me on terms of great familiarity with the King and the duchess, and when we were talking one day about the reason which led me to come to France, I told him [the King] frankly that I did not come with any intention of engaging in his service, but merely to pass some time there, and then to do the same at the Court of Spain, before I came to any determination as to the conduct of my future life; but that he had so charmed me, that, if he would accept my service, I would go no further to seek a master, but would devote myself to him until death. He embraced me and assured me that I should not find a better master than he would be to me, or one who would love me more or contribute more to my fortune or advancement. This was on a Tuesday, March 12 [1599]. Henceforth, I looked upon myself as a Frenchman; and I can say that, from that time, I experienced from him so much kindness, so much affability, and such proofs of good-will, that his memory will be deeply graven in my heart during the remainder of my days."

On the approach of Holy Week, Bassompierre requested the King's permission to go to Paris to perform his Easter devotions, when Henri IV informed him that he should go with him on the Tuesday to Melun, whither he proposed to escort the Duchesse de Beaufort, who also wished to perform her devotions in the capital, and next day continue his journey to Paris.

We must here explain that it had been for some months generally known that the Very Christian King, notwithstanding the strenuous opposition of his great Minister Sully and his faithful adviser Duplessis-Mornay, fully intended to marry his Gabrielle, as soon as he could obtain the dissolution of his marriage with Marguerite de Valois. Such a resolution aroused universal alarm. The duchess had many friends and few enemies, but not even her most devoted partisans could maintain that her birth and previous life fitted her to be the Queen of France, while it was obvious that the claims of her legitimated sons, and of those who might be born in wedlock, would add another element of discord to those already existing. After considerable difficulty, on February 7, 1599, Marguerite, who had declared that it was "repugnant to her to put in her place a woman of such low extraction, and of so impure a life as the one about whom rumour speaks,"[18] was at length persuaded to sign the necessary procuration, which Henri IV lost no time in sending to Rome. But Clement VIII disapproved of his Majesty's choice, less probably on account of Gabrielle's obvious unsuitability to share a throne than because she was the intimate friend of Catherine de Bourbon, Duchess of Bar, and Louise de Coligny, Princess of Orange. These two ladies were amongst the most stubborn heretics in Europe, and his Holiness did not doubt that, urged by them, Gabrielle would use all her influence with the King in favour of their co-religionists. He, therefore, refused to dissolve the marriage, sheltering himself behind the difficulties regarding the succession in which the new union which the King was contemplating would involve France. This paternal solicitude for his kingdom did not deceive Henri IV, who, impatient at the delay, instructed his representative at the Vatican to hint that, if the Holy Father continued contumacious, the eldest son of the Church might be tempted to behave in an exceedingly unfilial manner, and follow the example of his last namesake on the throne of England. Whether, with this threat hanging over him, Clement would eventually have yielded is a matter of opinion; but an unexpected event came to relieve the tension.

Bassompierre duly accompanied the King and the duchess to Melun, Gabrielle, who was in an advanced state of pregnancy, being carried in a litter. At supper Henri IV said to him: "Bassompierre, my mistress wishes to take you with her in her barge to-morrow to Paris. You will play cards together by the way." That night they slept at Savigny, about midway between Fontainebleau and the capital, and the following morning (April 6) the King accompanied the duchess to the bank of the Seine, where her barge was awaiting her, in which she embarked with Bassompierre, the Duc de Montbazon, Captain of the Guards, the Marquis de la Varenne and her waiting-women.

At the moment of parting from her royal lover, Gabrielle broke down and began to sob bitterly, declaring that she had a presentiment that she should never see him again. The King, after vainly endeavouring to console her, was on the point of yielding and taking her back to Fontainebleau. But, in view of their intended marriage, he attached great importance to the duchess performing her Easter devotions in the capital, and, after repeated embraces, he freed himself from her detaining arms and gave the signal for the barge to start.

About three o'clock in the afternoon, Gabrielle reached Paris, and disembarked on the quay near the Arsenal, where her brother-in-law, the Maréchal de Balagny, her brother the Marquis de Cœuvres, Madame de Retz, and the duchesse and Mlle. de Guise were awaiting her. She rested for a while at her sister's house, where a number of distinguished persons called upon her, and then went to sup at the house of Sebastian Zamet,—"the lord of the 1,800,000 crowns"—an Italian financier, who had risen from a very humble position to great wealth and the personal friendship of Henri IV. After supper she attended the *Tenebræ* at the Couvent du Petit Saint-Antoine, then renowned for its fine music. During the service she was taken ill and was carried to Zamet's house, where she recovered sufficiently to go to the apartments of her aunt Madame de Sourdes, at the Deanery of Saint-

Germain-l'Auxerrois, where she always stayed when paying a short visit to Paris, as she did not make use of her own house in the Rue Fromenteau, which communicated with the Louvre, except when the Court happened to be in residence. Next day, though still feeling far from well, she attended Mass at her parish church, Saint-Germain-l'Auxerrois. She was borne in a litter, by the side of which walked the Duc de Montbazon, in virtue of his position as Captain of the Guards, and escorted by archers; while the Lorraine princesses and a number of ladies of high rank followed in coaches. In the church she was again taken ill, and, on returning to the deanery, fell into violent convulsions. On the 9th—Good Friday—she gave birth to a still-born child, after which the surgeons who attended

GABRIELLE D'ESTRÉES, DUCHESSE DE BEAUFORT.

her proceeded to bleed the unfortunate woman four times. The consequence was that poor Gabrielle died the following morning (April 10); the only wonder is that she did not die before! The public, learning that she had been taken ill shortly after supping with Zamet, persisted in the belief that she had been poisoned—Italians bore a sinister reputation in those days, and, indeed, down to a much later period—but this theory is now generally discredited.[19]

"On Good Friday," writes Bassompierre, "while we were at the sermon on the Passion at Saint-Germain-l'Auxerrois, La Varenne came to tell the Maréchal d'Ornano[20] that the duchess had just died,[21] and that we ought to prevent the King, who was travelling post to Paris, from coming there; and he begged him to go and meet him, in order to stop him. I was with the marshal at the sermon, and he asked me to accompany him, which I did. We met the King beyond La Saussaye, near Villejuif, travelling at the top speed of his horses. When he saw the marshal, he suspected that he was the bearer of bad news, which caused him to weep bitterly. Finally, they made him alight at the Abbey of La Saussaye, where they laid him on a bed. He gave vent to every excess of grief which it is possible to describe. At length, a coach having arrived from Paris, they placed him in it to return to Fontainebleau, whither all the princes and nobles had hastened to find him. We went with him to Fontainebleau, and when he had mounted to the great Salle de la Cheminée, he begged all the company to return to Paris to pray God for his consolation. He kept with him *Monsieur le Grand*, the Comte du Lude, Termes, Castelnau de Charosse, Montglat, and Frontenac; and, as I was taking my leave with all those whom he had dismissed, he said to me: 'Bassompierre, you were the last who was with my mistress; stay with me to talk to me of her.' So I remained also, and we were eight or ten days without the company being augmented, if one excepts certain of the Ambassadors, who came to condole with him[22] and then returned to Paris immediately."

During this time the King remained prostrated with grief. "My affliction," he wrote to his sister Catherine, "is incomparable, like the person who is the cause of it. Regrets and tears will accompany me to the tomb. The root of my love is dead and will never put forth another branch."

But alas! how changeable are the affections of kings! Scarcely two months had passed[23] before his Majesty had embarked in a new love-affair, with

Henriette d'Entragues, whom he created Marquise de Verneuil, that ambitious, greedy, intriguing woman, who, later, was to conspire with the enemies of France against her royal lover. Nor did this attachment prevent him from seeking amusement in other directions and honouring with his fugitive attentions, not only divers beauties of the Court, whose names Bassompierre does not hesitate to hand down to fame, but even that vulgar class which the chronicler qualifies with a word so explicit that we dare not repeat it.

The following scene described by Bassompierre is too typical of the life of Henri IV and his immediate entourage to be omitted. It occurred during a flying visit to Paris which the King and a few of his favourites paid in July, 1599, while the Court was in residence at Blois:—

"The King had no retinue on this journey, and dined with a president and supped with a prince or noble as the humour took him. Mlle. d'Entragues was not yet his mistress,[24] and he used sometimes to pass the night with a pretty wench called la Glaude. It happened one evening that, after he had been supping with M. d'Elbeuf[25], the King came to pass the night with this girl at Zamet's house, and when, after we had undressed him, we were about to enter the King's coach, which was to take us back to our lodging, M. de Joinville and *Monsieur le Grand* quarrelled, touching something which the former pretended that *Monsieur le Grand* had told the King about him and Mlle. d'Entragues.[26] In consequence, *Monsieur le Grand* was wounded in the buttock, the Vidame de Mans received a thrust through the body, and La Rivière one in the stomach. After M. de Praslin had caused the doors of the house to be shut, and M. de Chevreuse [Joinville] had taken his departure, they asked me to go to the King and tell him what had occurred. The King rose, put on his dressing-gown and, taking up his sword, came on to the stairs, where the others were standing, while I preceded him, carrying a taper. He was intensely annoyed, and sent the same night to the First President[27] to command him to come to him on the morrow with the Court of the Parlement, when he directed them to investigate the affair and to show no favour to anyone. This they did, and proceeded to summon before them the Comte de Cramail, Chasseron, and myself to give evidence. And the King bade us go and answer the questions which the commissioners might put to us, which we did; and proceedings were instituted against the offender. But, by reason of the pressing entreaties which Monsieur, Madame, and Mlle. de Guise[28] addressed to the King, the affair went no further, and two months later the Constable[29] brought about a reconciliation at Conflans."

In November, Bassompierre obtained permission from the King to go to Lorraine, to persuade Charles IV to free him from the security which his late father had given for some 50,000 crowns which the duke had borrowed at the time of the marriage of his elder daughter to the Grand Duke of Tuscany, an obligation which had been causing him considerable uneasiness. In Lorraine he remained for some six weeks, "more for the love which I bore Mlle. de Bourbonne[30] than for the other affair."

Early in the New Year he returned to Paris, where the charms of Mlle. de Bourbonne were soon forgotten for those of a lady whom he calls la Raverie and who was presumably a star of the *demi-monde*. The courtiers of Henri IV were, however, quite capable of losing their hearts to two or more ladies at the same time, following the example of their royal master, who "fell in love that winter with Madame de Boinville and Mlle. Clin."[31] In addition to love-making, he danced in several ballets, one of which was appropriately called *le Ballet des Amoureux*.

CHAPTER III

Bassompierre accompanies Henri IV in his campaign against Charles Emmanuel of Savoy—His narrow escape at the taking of Montmélian—He goes with the King to visit Henriette d'Entragues, Madame de Verneuil, at La Côte-Saint-André, and reconciles Henri IV with his mistress—Marriage of the King to Marie de' Medici—Presentation of Madame de Verneuil to the Queen—Visit of Bassompierre to Lorraine—He returns to find the royal *ménage* in a very troubled state, owing to the jealousy of the wife and the mistress—He assists at a conference, in which the Chancellor recommends the King to get rid of Madame de Verneuil at any cost—He accompanies the Maréchal de Biron on a visit to England—He is present at the arrest of Biron at Fontainebleau, in June, 1602—Condemnation and execution of the marshal.

In February, 1600, Charles Emmanuel of Savoy paid a visit to the Court to negotiate personally with the King about the matter of the marquisate of Saluzzo, which, in 1588, the Duke, taking advantage of the internal troubles of France, had invaded and annexed, and the restoration of which Henri IV was now demanding. Charles Emmanuel offered to enter into an alliance with France against Spain, and assist her to conquer the Milanese, if only Henri IV would forgo his claims on Saluzzo, and lavished costly gifts and large sums of money upon the Ministers and the mistress in order to gain their support. But the King was adamant on the question of Saluzzo, and on February 27 the Duke was obliged to sign a treaty, whereby he engaged within three months either to surrender the marquisate, or, as compensation, the county of Bresse, the valley of Barcellonnette, the valley of the Stura, Pérousse, and Pinerolo.

Towards the middle of May, as Charles Emmanuel had as yet taken no steps to carry out his engagements, Henri IV began moving troops towards the frontier of Savoy, and he himself, accompanied by a few of his intimates, amongst whom was Bassompierre, set out for Lyons, having sent the rest of the Court on in advance to await him at Moulins. At Moulins, where he was the guest of Queen Louise, widow of the late King, he stayed for some little time "principally on account of la Bourdaisière, with whom he was in love"[32]; and it was not until the beginning of July that he arrived at Lyons. Here he remained three weeks, to see what action Charles Emmanuel proposed to take. That prince, however, had signed the treaty of February merely for the purpose of gaining time; and the promises of Spain, which feared, above all things, to see France once more in possession of Saluzzo, decided him to break his word. At the expiration of the three months he solicited a further delay or an amelioration of the conditions of the treaty, hoping that the expected rebellion of the Maréchal de Biron and the Comte d'Auvergne, whom, by specious promises, he had succeeded in seducing from their allegiance to their sovereign, would break out before Henri IV was ready to take the field.

Henri IV, however, was not deceived, and summoned the Duke to declare immediately what his intentions were. The latter, after many tergiversations, announced that he was prepared to surrender Saluzzo. But when the King despatched officers to take possession of the chief places in the marquisate, he refused to surrender them; and on August 11, Henri IV, at the end of his patience, declared war at Lyons.

Bassompierre has left us an interesting account of the campaign which followed—a campaign of invasion undertaken by an army scarcely more numerous than a brigade to-day; but which, thanks to the improvements in the artillery which Sully had introduced and the valour of the troops, proved entirely successful. He himself underwent his "baptism of fire" at the taking of the town of Montmélian, where he served with the regiment of the Sire (afterwards the Maréchal) de Créquy. His military career came very near to ending as well as beginning at Montmélian, for, in the darkness, he lost his way and was cut off from his comrades, "so that I was for more than an hour at the mercy of the fire from the citadel, at twenty paces from the ditch." By what seems like a miracle, however, he was not hit, and, at length a sergeant, whom Créquy had sent to find him, arrived and guided him to a place of safety.

Charles Emmanuel, for once entirely wrong in his calculations, was unable to offer any effective resistance to the invaders of his realm; France remained tranquil; Biron, traitor though he was, in spite of himself, mastered Bresse; Chambéry, the capital of Savoy, surrendered to Henri IV after but a show of resistance; the citadel of Montmélian, fondly deemed impregnable, fell before Sully's new siege-guns; and the Duke, seeing himself beaten, sued for peace, and, on New Year's Day, 1601, signed a treaty with France, by which he retained Saluzzo, in exchange for the cession of Bresse, Bugey, Valromey and Gex.

Whilst engaged in the conquest of Savoy, Henri IV went to visit Madame de Verneuil at Grenoble, as he had hastened at the peril of his life to throw himself at the feet of the Comtesse de Gramont (*"la belle*

Corisande") after the Battle of Coutras. The years had not changed him and he made these journeys as eagerly as a gallant of half his age.

"I had intended," writes Bassompierre, "to go with M. Lesdiguières to the valley of Marenne, which he was going to subdue, but the King ordered me to follow him. He went to sleep at La Rochette, and on the morrow dined at Grenoble. And having there learned that Madame de Verneuil was about to arrive at Saint-André de la Costé,[33] he set out to go to her and lent me one of his own horses to follow him. I rode the whole way at a trot, and was so tired that, when I arrived, I could scarcely stand. The King and Madame de Verneuil had a quarrel on meeting,[34] so that the King was going back in anger, and said to me: 'Bassompierre, order our horses to be saddled for us to return.' I told him that I would willingly order his to be saddled, but that, as for mine, I should declare myself on Madame de Verneuil's side and should stay with her. And, after going to and fro several times, in order to reconcile two persons who were well inclined to it, I made peace between them and we slept at Saint-André. The next day the King went to Grenoble and took Madame de Verneuil with him."

"No one," writes Boudet de Puymaigre, "makes us understand better than does Bassompierre the character of Henri IV, that extraordinary man, great on the field of battle, where his inspired language, in accord with his deeds, elevates him often to the sublimity of the epopee; skilful and even adroit in the government of his realm, causing at need acts which were merely the outcome of political necessity to be attributed to his clemency; in his private life, despotic and good-humoured at the same time, often duped by his mistresses and blinded by his passions. Such as he was, he remains the type of the popular king, and posterity has done honour even to his faults, for it has enshrined the name of '*la belle* Gabrielle' amidst the trophies of the Battle of Ivry. 'His tragic end,' remarks Chateaubriand, 'has contributed not a little to his renown; to disappear appropriately from life is a condition of glory.' "

Just a month before peace was signed with the Duke of Savoy, Marie de' Medici, whom the Duc de Bellegarde, acting as proxy for his master, had married at Florence on Oct. 6, 1600, arrived at Lyons. Henri IV joined her there a few days later, and on December 17 the marriage was celebrated with great splendour. On the arrival of the royal bride at

Nemours, the King caused Madame de Verneuil to be presented to her. As the sultana came forward, he explained who she was: "This young lady is my mistress; she will be your obedient and humble servant!" Then, as the scant curtsey which was all the salutation which Henriette vouchsafed the Queen appeared to hold out little hope of the fulfilment of this promise, he placed his hand on her head and bent it down, until she kissed the hem of her rival's dress.

It must be acknowledged that his Majesty could hardly have contrived an introduction better calculated to exasperate the temper of both women. Nevertheless, on this occasion, the Queen contrived to dissimulate her feelings, and, according to Bassompierre, gave Madame de Verneuil a very good reception—"*bonne chère*," as they said then.

In January, 1601, Bassompierre again went to Lorraine, to visit his mother, who was ill, and remained there three months. He returned in company with the Duchess of Bar and her father-in-law, Charles III of Lorraine, who were on their way to pay a visit to the Court, which was then in residence at Monceaux. The Château of Monceaux, so closely associated with memories of "*la belle* Gabrielle," had just been presented to the Queen by Henri IV, and Marie de'

Medici entertained her distinguished guests with lavish hospitality. The royal ménage was, however, in a very troubled state, for the wife and the mistress were already at daggers drawn, and between them the Very Christian King was having a decidedly unpleasant time of it. Matters, indeed, had come to such a pass that Henri IV was contemplating the advisability of marrying Madame de Verneuil, with a rich dowry, to some needy foreign prince, and thus removing her from his Court; and Bassompierre was called upon to assist at a sort of council between the King, Sully, and the Chancellor, Pomponne de Bellièvre, the last of whom strongly urged his Majesty to get rid of the lady at any cost:—

"The King inquired if he should give something to Madame de Verneuil in order to marry her to a prince, who she declared, was willing to espouse her, if she had 100,000 crowns. M. de Bellièvre (the Chancellor) said: 'Sire, I am of opinion that you should give 100,000 crowns to this young lady to procure a suitable husband.' And when M. de Sully made answer that it was very easy to speak of 100,000 crowns, but very difficult to find them, the Chancellor, without looking at him, rejoined: 'Sire, I am of opinion that you should take 200,000 crowns and give it to this young lady to marry her, and even 300,000, if you cannot do it for less. And that is my advice.' The King repented afterwards of not having approved and followed this counsel."

In September, 1601, Henri IV was at Calais, and Queen Elizabeth came to Dover, partly in the hope that her old ally would visit her to discuss the advisability of joint action against Spain. The King, however, was unwilling to alarm the Catholics or to do anything which might precipitate a renewal of the war with Spain, and he also perhaps feared that Elizabeth might seize the opportunity to demand the repayment of certain advances of money which she had made him during his struggle against the League, and which it would be highly inconvenient to refund just then. Accordingly, he dispatched the Maréchal de Biron to offer his excuses and regrets to the Queen; and Biron persuaded Bassompierre, who had just arrived at Calais from a journey to Verneuil upon which the King had sent him, to accompany him to England.

"We did not find the Queen in London," writes Bassompierre. "She was making a progress, and was at a country-house called Basin,[35] forty leagues distant, which belonged to the Marquis of

Vincester.[36] The Queen notified her intention of receiving us at another country-house, called The Vine, a league from Basin, whither M. de Biron was conducted. He was very honourably received by the Queen, who went a-hunting next day with fifty ladies on hackneys and sent for M. de Biron to join the hunt. On the morrow, he took leave of the Queen and returned to London, where, after remaining three days, he repassed the sea."

The first news which greeted Bassompierre and the marshal on their arrival at Boulogne, near which contrary winds had obliged them to land, was the birth of the Dauphin (afterwards Louis XIII), which had taken place on September 27, 1601.[37]

Bassompierre was present at Fontainebleau that evening in the following June, when Biron, after refusing Henri IV's magnanimous offer of pardon on condition that he would confess the truth concerning his treasonable dealings with the Duke of Savoy, was arrested by the Marquis de Vitry, Captain of the Château of Fontainebleau, as he was passing from the King's cabinet into the Chambre de Saint-Louis, and requested to give up his sword.

"I was in the Chamber," he writes, "having withdrawn to the window with M. de Montbazon and

La Guesle.[38] We approached the marshal, who asked M. de Montbazon to go and beg the King that he might be allowed to retain his sword, adding: 'What treatment, Messieurs, for a man who has served as I have!' M. de Montbazon went to the King and returned to say that the King desired him to give up his sword, upon which he permitted them to take it away."

Biron was conducted to the Bastille, where his captivity was shared by the Comte d'Auvergne, who had been arrested at the same time.[39] Later that evening, Henri IV sent for Bassompierre and other nobles, and placed before them the letters which La Fin, the instigator of the conspiracy, who had subsequently turned informer, had given him. They were all written in Biron's own hand.

The marshal was arraigned for high treason before the Parlement of Paris, the peers of the realm being summoned to take their places amongst the judges, as was the custom when one of their number was on his trial. The evidence of the accused's guilt was overwhelming, and he was unanimously sentenced to death. On July 31, 1602, he was beheaded in the courtyard of the Bastille, it having been decided to spare him the ignominy of a public execution in the

Place de Grève. The pusillanimous Comte d'Auvergne was pardoned and set at liberty in the following October, thanks to the intercession of his half-sister, Madame de Verneuil.

CHAPTER IV

Bassompierre sets out for Hungary to serve as a volunteer in the Imperial Army against the Turks—His journey to Vienna—He learns that the commander-in-chief of the army is General von Rossworm, a mortal enemy of the Bassompierre family—He is advised by his friends in Vienna to take service in the Army of Transylvania, instead of in that of Hungary, but declines to change his plans—He sups more well than wisely at Gran—His arrival at the Imperialist camp before Buda—Position of the hostile armies—Bassompierre is presented to Rossworm—He narrowly escapes being killed or taken prisoner by the Turks—He takes part in a fierce combat in the Isle of Adon, and has another narrow escape—He is reconciled with Rossworm—Massacre of eight hundred Turkish prisoners—Failure of a night-attack planned by the Imperialist general—Gallant but foolhardy enterprise of the Hungarians—The Turks bombard the Imperialist headquarters—Termination of the campaign—Bassompierre returns with Rossworm to Vienna.

PEACE having been concluded between France and Savoy, tranquillity reigned for the moment in Europe, except in Hungary, where the eternal conflict between the Cross and the Crescent continued to be waged as bitterly as ever. In those days, war, with very few exceptions, was the only road which led to honour and renown, and when Christians were at peace with one another, the Turks became the objective of all adventurous spirits, who went to fight the Infidel in

Hungary, Crete, or Malta as their ancestors flocked to the Crusades. Moreover, it was not without mortification that the German relatives of Bassompierre, who had seen all his family entirely devoted to the profession of arms, beheld him passing his youth at the Court of France in voluptuous idleness, and, to wean him from it, they obtained for him the offer of the command of a regiment of 3,000 men which the Circle of Bavaria had agreed to contribute to the Imperial Army in Hungary for the campaign of 1603. Bassompierre, however, though willing enough to go to Hungary, had the good sense to decline this post, "not deeming it fitting," he writes, "that, without any knowledge of the country, I should straightway take command of 3,000 men," and decided to serve as a simple volunteer.

Accordingly, about the middle of August, 1603, having obtained leave of absence from the King, he left Paris, and travelled by way of Nancy and Strasbourg to Ulm, where his attendants, whom he had sent on in advance, had procured two large boats for his passage down the Danube. In these he and his suite, which appears to have been quite an imposing one, as befitted a gentleman of such ancient lineage and one of the favourites of the King of France, embarked and proceeded to Neuburg, where he was very hospitably entertained by Duke William II, who, a few years before, had abdicated his throne in favour of his son, now Maximilian I. Continuing his journey, with stoppages at Ingoldstadt, Ratisbon, and Linz, at the beginning of the second week in September he arrived in Vienna, where he found the Prince de Joinville, who had been temporarily banished from France,[40] Frederick, Count von Salm, and several other gentlemen of his acquaintance, both French and German, most of whom were, like himself, on their way to win honour and glory, or peradventure to find a soldier's grave, on the plains of Hungary.

Some of these modern Crusaders came to dine with Bassompierre on the day following his arrival in Vienna, and from them he learned a most unwelcome piece of intelligence, namely, that the commander-in-chief of the Imperial forces in Hungary under whom he was about to take service was none other than General von Rossworm, a mortal enemy of the Bassompierre family.

It appears that some fifteen years before, in the time of the League, Rossworm had served in France under Bassompierre's father, by whom he had been placed in charge of the town of Blancmesnil.

Rossworm had taken advantage of his position to abduct a young lady of noble birth who had taken refuge at Blancmesnil with her mother, and whom he promised to marry, but subsequently discarded, after subjecting the poor girl to the most abominable treatment. On ascertaining the facts of the case, Christophe de Bassompierre, burning with righteous indignation, vowed that the German should pay for his villainy with his head; but the latter, warned in time, fled from Blancmesnil and for some little while succeeded in evading pursuit. Eventually, however, he was run to earth at Amiens, and would undoubtedly have been executed, had not the Sieur de Vitry, who commanded the light cavalry of the League, and who happened to be under some personal obligation to Rossworm, found means to enable him to escape. Rossworm subsequently returned to Germany and entered the Imperial service, and being, though a pretty bad scoundrel, even for a German soldier of fortune of those times, a very brave man and a most capable officer, rose step by step, until at length he was appointed to the command of the Imperial army in Hungary.[41] He had cherished the most implacable resentment against Christophe de Bassompierre, and while the two young Bassompierres were studying at Ingoldstadt, they received warning that Rossworm, in order to avenge himself upon the father, had actually planned to have the sons assassinated. On being informed of this, Christophe complained to the Duke of Bavaria, who had just appointed Rossworm to the command of the regiment of foot which Bavaria was about to send to Hungary. The Duke promptly deprived Rossworm of that post, a step which had served to incense that worthy still further against the Bassompierres.

Bassompierre's friends in Vienna, on being informed by him how matters stood, did not fail to represent to him the danger of placing himself in the power of so unscrupulous and vindictive a man as Rossworm had proved himself to be, and endeavoured to persuade him to renounce his intention of going to Hungary and take service instead in the Army of Transylvania, under its distinguished leader, George Basta. Finding, however, that the young Lorrainer, though he quite appreciated the risk he would be incurring, was indisposed to change his plans, they invited to meet him at dinner Siegfried Colowitz, an Hungarian colonel, who had just arrived in Vienna on a brief furlough, and laid the matter before him.

Colowitz, who had taken so great a fancy to Bassompierre that he had insisted on making *brudershaft* with him, expressed the opinion that Rossworm was too unpopular in the army to attempt any open violence against his new friend, and that, if he were so imprudent as to do so, he himself had 1,200 Hungarian cavalry under his command, and his brother Ferdinand 1,500 *landsknechts*, who would obey their orders without question. However, as it was possible that Rossworm might have recourse to some other means of injuring Bassompierre, he proposed that the latter should take up his quarters in his own part of the camp, where he would guarantee his safety.

Towards the end of September, Bassompierre having spent the interval in purchasing the tents, carts, horses, and other things which he required, left Vienna, in company with the Prince de Joinville, and continued his journey down the Danube. At Gran, the governor, Count Althann, came to meet them, bringing with him horses for them to ride to the citadel, where he informed them that he was expecting two other distinguished guests, in the persons of the Bishop of Erlau and Count Illischezki, one of the chief nobles of Hungary, whom the Emperor had appointed as deputies to treat, in conjunction with himself, for peace. At the citadel, the two young gentlemen appear to have supped more well than wisely:—

"He [Count Althann]," writes Bassompierre, "entertained M. de Joinville and myself to a most excellent supper, at which we drank in moderation. But, unhappily, the deputies having arrived, orders were given to serve it up again, and we remained at table until midnight; by which time we were so drunk that we lost all consciousness and had to be carried back to our boats."

On September 27th they arrived at Waitzen, on the left bank of the Danube, where they were met by Ferdinand Colowitz, who handed Bassompierre a letter from his brother Siegfried, in which he informed him that, at his request, the Count von Tilly, who, in his younger days, had served under Christophe de Bassompierre and was now a major-general in the Imperial Army, had broken the news of the coming of Christophe's son to the commander-in-chief, who had emphatically disclaimed any evil intentions towards the young man, although he would prefer to have no intercourse with him. Colowitz added that should Rossworm, despite what he had said, attempt any violence, half the army would rise against him.

Bassompierre was naturally much relieved at this news, and that afternoon he went with Joinville to Rossworm's head-quarters, where he was duly presented to the general and courteously, if somewhat coldly, received. Afterwards, he proceeded to the Isle of Adon, where Siegfried Colowitz's cavalry were posted, and where his servants had already put up his tent at a little distance from that of the Hungarian colonel.

It may be as well here to explain the situation of affairs at the moment when Bassompierre joined the army.

In the campaign of the preceding year, the Christians had captured Pesth and the lower town of Buda, situated on the opposite bank of the Danube. This year their army, which was composed of some 30,000 infantry and 10,000 cavalry, to which, as in the time of the Crusades, almost every country in Europe had contributed its quota, was encamped on the left bank of the Danube, covering Pesth and threatening Buda. The Turks were encamped on the right bank of the river, and their objective was the revictualling of Buda and the recovery of Pesth or Gran. Rossworm had strongly occupied the Isle of Adon, situated between the hostile camps, and it was in this island that most of the fighting took place. The Turks had occupied a small island, about 1,500 paces in circumference, which lay between the Isle of Adon and their own camp, and had built a bridge of boats from this island to the right bank. They had also made several attempts to construct another bridge from the little island to the left bank, but this was constantly broken by the fire of the Imperialist artillery. They, however, occasionally succeeding in crossing over to the Isle of Adon, and even to the Imperialists' side of the river, in caiques and on rafts, under cover of darkness, but had never yet succeeded in securing a footing there.

Hardly had Bassompierre finished supper that evening than a message arrived from Siegfried Colowitz to inform him that a reconnoitring party of the enemy had just landed on the island, and to request him, if he were in the mood for a little fighting, to put on his armour and have a horse saddled, as he was about to attack them. Shortly afterwards, Colowitz himself rode up, accompanied by a hundred or so of his Hungarians, one of whom he ordered to dismount and give his horse to Bassompierre, whose own charger he considered too heavy an animal for the work before them. They then galloped away, and, having come upon the Turks, charged them vigorously and forced them to beat a hasty retreat to their caiques and return to their own side of the river.

The following night, however, the Turks succeeded in landing on the island in considerable force from caiques and pontoons, on the same spot which they had just reconnoitred and began hurriedly constructing entrenchments, with the object of holding the Imperialists at bay long enough to enable the rest of the Ottoman army to be brought across. They were so fiercely attacked, however, that they were soon obliged to retreat.

A few days later, Bassompierre had a narrow escape of being killed or taken prisoner.

"At daybreak on September 29," he writes, "we issued from our great entrenchment with 200 Hungarian horse to reconnoitre the enemy; but we had not gone three hundred paces, when we perceived some hundred horsemen in front of us. The Hungarians, according to their custom, were dispersed in all directions, and we had not more than thirty with us, all of whom took to flight so soon as the enemy appeared. But I, who could not imagine that the Turks had advanced so far, and who could not distinguish them from the Hungarians, thought that they belonged to us, until an Hungarian fugitive called out to me: '*Heu, domine, adsunt Turcae!*' which caused me to retreat also."

At the beginning of October the Turks resolved upon a great effort to drive the Imperialists from the Isle of Adon. Rossworm, however, had received warning of the enemy's intention, and of the day and hour when the attempt would be made; and, though he might easily have prevented the Turks from reaching the island, he decided to allow them to pass the river and then to fall suddenly upon them. With this purpose, he brought, under cover of night, the greater part of his army over to the island, and placed in ambush a body of 4,000 infantry and 2,000 cavalry, the latter including the regiment of Siegfried Colowitz, to which Bassompierre and Joinville were attached. These troops swooped down upon the Turks before they had had time to form in order of battle after effecting their landing, and routed them with terrible slaughter, great numbers being cut down, while many more were drowned in the Danube, into which they had thrown themselves to escape the lances and sabres of the pursuing cavalry.

In this engagement Bassompierre again had a narrow escape. He was mounted that day on a magnificent Spanish stallion, for which he had given a thousand crowns; but he was a very mettlesome animal and by no means easy to ride, and, having been wounded below the eye by a javelin in the first charge, while, at the same time, his curb-chain broke, he became quite unmanageable and bolted after the flying enemy at breakneck speed. Bassompierre endeavoured in vain to stop him, and then, seeing that he had far outstripped his comrades and was alone in the midst of the fugitives, he bore hard on the left rein and succeeded in turning him in that direction. But he had only diverted the maddened animal's course, without checking his speed, and found himself being carried towards a body of some thousand Turks who had not yet been engaged and were retreating in good order. A few seconds more and he would have been in the middle of them, when, happily for him, his equerry Des Essans, who had been riding hard to overtake his master, came up and, seizing the runaway's bridle, managed to hold him long enough to enable Bassompierre to throw himself out of the saddle, within twenty paces of the Turks. The latter, though very reluctant to forgo the chance of killing and despoiling so magnificent a cavalier—for Bassompierre tells us that he was arrayed that day "in a suit of gilded armour, very beautifully chased, with a number of plumes and scarves upon himself and his horse"—were too hard pressed by their pursuers to turn aside, and continued their retreat, leaving him and

Des Essans unmolested. The faithful equerry had, however, not escaped unscathed, as, in seizing the bridle of his master's horse, he had been somewhat badly wounded in the leg by Bassompierre's sword, which was suspended from his wrist.

Having procured another horse, Bassompierre continued the pursuit of the enemy to the bank of the river, and then, accompanied by Joinville, made his way to the spot where Rossworm and his staff were gathered, "seated on some dead Turks." On seeing Bassompierre, the general rose and announced that he wished to say a few words.

"And, after having praised me for what he had just seen me do, and observed that I should not be a member of the family to which I belonged if I were not valiant, he continued: 'The late M. de Bassompierre, your father, was my master, but he wished to put me to death unjustly. I desire to forget that outrage and to remember only the obligations under which he had previously placed me, and to be henceforth, if you wish it, your friend and your servant.' Then I dismounted from my horse and advanced to salute him and thank him in the most suitable terms that I could think of. Upon which, turning towards the two princes, the Prince de

Joinville and the Landgrave of Hesse, and the colonels and other officers who were with him, he said: 'Gentlemen, I could not effect this reconciliation or offer these assurances of friendship to M. de Bassompierre in a better place, after a better action, or before more noble witnesses. I invite you to dine with me to-morrow, and him also, to confirm again what has just occurred.' And this we all promised to do."

After this victory the Imperialists returned to their camp on the left bank of the river, where Rossworm ordered all the Turkish prisoners taken in the battle to be put to death, "because they embarrassed the army." "It was a very cruel thing," adds Bassompierre, "to see more than 800 men who had surrendered slaughtered in cold blood." Nevertheless, the butchery of prisoners appears to have been an only too common practice in the wars between the Cross and the Crescent, which were conducted on both sides with the most pitiless ferocity.

Next day Bassompierre dined with the commander-in-chief and his staff, when they confirmed "with the bottle and a thousand protestations of friendship, the reconciliation which had been effected on the field of battle." To do Rossworm justice, he was perfectly sincere in his desire to terminate his feud with the Bassompierre family, and he and the young volunteer soon became firm friends.

The Turks still held the little island, and had preserved intact the bridge of boats by which communication with their army on the right bank of the Danube was maintained. They had mounted on this island six pieces of cannon, which completely commanded the approach from the left bank of the river, so that any attempt to capture it by day would have been out of the question, even if the bridge of boats had not enabled the enemy to hurry reinforcements across at the first alarm. Rossworm, however, considered that, if the communications of the garrison of the island with their army could be temporarily interrupted by the destruction of this bridge, a night attack might very well prove successful.

On the night of October 8-9 he determined to make the attempt, and accordingly dispatched engineers to blow up the bridge, while a large force was brought into the Isle of Adon, and boats and rafts collected to ferry them across. The engineers duly succeeded in destroying the bridge, but the Hungarians, who formed the advance-guard of the attacking force, remained inactive in their boats in the middle of the river, awaiting the arrival of a body of pikemen whom they had demanded as supports, in case there should be cavalry on the island. The consequence was that the Turks were given time to send over reinforcements, and the opportunity was lost.

Rossworm returned to his camp in great wrath, anathematizing the Hungarians, whom he accused of cowardice. The Hungarian chiefs indignantly repudiated such an aspersion, and, to redeem their reputation, volunteered to cross the river and construct a fort in the plain between Buda and the Turkish camp. Rossworm accepted this offer, though it is difficult to understand how he could have countenanced an undertaking which could have no other result than the useless sacrifice of gallant lives; and on the night of October 10-11, some 1,300 Hungarians landed on the right bank, unperceived by the enemy, and began to entrench themselves.

They worked desperately all night, but when morning dawned, a Turkish flotilla appeared upon the scene, and bombarded their hastily-constructed fort from the river; while the enemy in great force assailed it from the land side. After an heroic resistance, the

Hungarians were obliged to abandon it, with the loss of some 300 men, and retreat to the caiques which were waiting to take them off. So fierce was the pursuit that some of the Turkish cavalry spurred their horses into the water to attack the caiques, and two were made prisoners with their steeds.

Rossworm had placed a number of cannon in the Isle of Adon to cover the retreat of the Hungarians, but only two of these pieces appear to have come into action, which Bassompierre tells us the general ascribed to the fact that, the day being a Sunday, most of the artillerymen were drunk.

Shortly after this, the Turks brought up some twenty guns to a height overlooking the Imperialist headquarters, which they bombarded heavily and persistently. One day, whilst Bassompierre was playing cards with the general and two other officers, a shot passed right through the tent, whilst on another, when visiting Annibal de Schomberg, a shot struck the tent-pole and brought the whole tent down upon the heads of its occupants. Finally, after this unpleasant state of things had lasted for five days, Rossworm decided to remove his headquarters to a valley where cannon-shot could not reach him, upon which the bombardment ceased.

Towards the middle of November, the Turks, having succeeded in their main objective, that of revictualling Buda, struck their camp and marched back to Belgrade, where their army was disbanded. Rossworm, after leading a flying column along the river and capturing one or two not very important places, with the idea of showing that the campaign had not been wholly without results on the Imperialists' side, disbanded his troops likewise, and set out for Vienna, accompanied by Bassompierre.

CHAPTER V

Bassompierre goes to Prague, where the Imperial Court is in residence—He is presented by Rossworm to the lords of the Council—He dines at the house of Prestowitz, Burgrave of Karlstein, and falls in love with his widowed daughter, "Madame Esther"—Bassompierre and Rossworm engage in an amorous adventure, from which they narrowly escape with their lives—Bassompierre plays tennis with Wallenstein, with the Emperor Maximilian an interested spectator—He is presented to the Emperor, who receives him very graciously and commissions him to raise troops in Lorraine for service against the Turks. Bassompierre, Rossworm and other nobles parade the streets masked and have an affray with the police—Singular sequel to this affair—Bassompierre spends the Carnival with the Prestowitz family at Karlstein—Amorous escapade with "Madame Esther"— Bassompierre sets out for Lorraine—He engages in a drinking-bout with the canons of Saverne, which very nearly has a fatal termination—Death of his brother Jean, Seigneur de Removille, at the siege of Ostend—Grievances of Bassompierre against the French Government—Henri IV promises that "justice shall be done him" and invites him to return to his Court—Bassompierre renounces his intention of entering the Imperial service and sets out for France.

In Vienna, Bassompierre remained for six weeks, where he "passed his time extremely well," and about the middle of January, 1604, set out for Prague, where the Imperial Court was then in residence.

"At Prague," he writes, "I found Rossworm, who since our reconciliation had been on terms of the closest friendship with me. He came, the following morning, to my lodging in his coach to take me to the hall of the Palace of Prague,[42] where we walked up and down until the Council rose, when the lords of the Council came to salute Rossworm, whom they held in great respect, on account of his being commander-in-chief of the Army. He then presented me to them, begging them to honour me with their friendship and saying many kind things concerning me."

On leaving the Palace, Rossworm took Bassompierre to dine with an old Bohemian noble named Prestowitz, who occupied the post of burgrave of Karlstein, the fortress in which the Imperial regalia and all the charters of Bohemia were preserved. The burgrave had two sons, the elder of whom was Grand Falconer of the Empire, while the younger, Wolf von Prestowitz, had served with Bassompierre in the recent campaign, and aspired to the command of the cavalry regiment which Bohemia was to send to Hungary that year. For which reason the family were exceedingly civil to the great Rossworm, who could do much to obtain this post for the young man. The burgrave also possessed four young and pretty daughters. Rossworm, it appeared, was in love with the youngest girl, Sibylla; while Bassompierre promptly lost his heart to the third daughter, named Esther, "a young lady of excellent beauty, eighteen years of age, widow since six months of a gentleman called Briczner, to whom she had been married a year."

"We were nobly received and entertained at Prestowitz's house," he continues, "and after dinner there was dancing, when I began to fall in love with Madame Esther, who made me understand that she was not displeased with my design, which I revealed to her as I was leaving the house. For she responded in such a way as to afford me the means to write to her, and to tell me the places which she visited, so that I might go there. I went also to see her sometimes at her house, under cover of the friendship which had sprung up between her younger brother and myself, when we were in Hungary."

His new-born passion for "Madame Esther" did not, however, prevent our gentleman from indulging in other amorous adventures of a much less excusable character:

"On our return from dining with the Prestowitz family, Rossworm, thinking to oblige me, engaged me in a rather unfortunate affair. He had bargained with an innkeeper of the New Town that, for two hundred ducats, he should surrender to him his two daughters, who were very beautiful. I am of opinion, as will appear from the sequel, that he had taken advantage of this poor man when he was drunk to obtain such a promise from him. When we had arrived within some two hundred paces of this inn, we alighted from our coach, which we ordered to turn round and await our return; and Rossworm and I, with a page of his, who was to act as interpreter, went the rest of the way on foot.

"We found the father in the room where the stove stood, and with him his two daughters, who were going about their work. He was very astonished to see us, and still more so when Rossworm made him understand that each of us had brought him a hundred ducats for what the innkeeper had promised him. Thereupon the man cried out that he had never promised any such thing, and, opening the window, shouted twice: '*Mortriau! Mortriau!*' that is to say, 'Murder!' Then Rossworm held his poniard to the innkeeper's throat, and directed the page to tell him that if he spoke to the neighbours or did not order his daughters to do our will, he was a dead man, and told me to take away one of the girls.... But I, who had been at first under the impression that I was engaged in an affair in which all the parties were in accord, answered that I did not intend to touch the girls. Rossworm then said that, if I did not wish to do so, I must come and hold my poniard to the father's throat, and that he would take one of the girls away.... This I did very reluctantly; and the poor girls wept."

The odious Rossworm had already seized upon one of the unfortunate girls to drag her away, when a great shouting reached their ears, and looking out of the window, he saw a large and threatening crowd, which had come in response to the innkeeper's cries for help, gathered before the house. Thereupon he let his intended victim go, and told Bassompierre that they were in grave danger, and would need all their courage and presence of mind if they wanted to leave that house alive. Then, turning to the innkeeper, he told him—or rather made the page do so—that he would kill him, if he did not contrive their escape from the mob. Now, the innkeeper was wearing a long smock, under which Rossworm placed his poniard, pressing the point against the man's flesh, and told Bassompierre to give his dagger to the page, that he might do likewise. In this fashion they went out of the room and along the passage to the door of the inn, where the trembling Boniface gave some apparently satisfactory explanation to his neighbours, for the latter, who, of course, could not see the poniards pressed against his back, began to disperse.

Then Rossworm and the page, imagining that the danger was over, sheathed their poniards, and they and Bassompierre began to walk away in the direction of their coach. But they had gone but a few paces, when the innkeeper, recovering from his alarm, began to shout: "Murder! Murder!" again with all the strength of his lungs. They took to their heels and ran for their lives, pursued by an infuriated mob, who pelted them with volleys of stones, which they had apparently collected at the first alarm.

"Then Rossworm cried out to me: 'Brother, *sauve qui peut!* If you fall, do not expect me to pick you up, for each of us must look to his own safety.' We ran pretty fast, but the rain of stones incommoded us greatly, and one of them, striking Rossworm in the back, brought him to the ground. I, who did not wish to treat him in the manner in which he had just announced his intention of treating me, raised him up and helped him along for some twenty paces, when, happily, we reached our coach. Into this we threw ourselves, and were soon in safety in the Old Town, having escaped from the paws of more than four hundred people."

Next day, Rossworm, presumably out of gratitude to Bassompierre for having saved his life at the risk of his own, secured for him the high privilege of admission to the Emperor's ante-chamber, which was usually only accorded to princes and very great nobles. Here he appears to have met the Count von Wallenstein, the great captain of the Thirty Years' War, then a youth of twenty, who, a few days later, challenged him to a match at tennis. During the game the Emperor appeared at a window of the palace which overlooked the tennis-court, and remained there for some time, an interested spectator. The following morning his Majesty gave orders that Bassompierre should be presented to him, and received him very graciously indeed, observing that his family had always been faithful servants of the Imperial House, and that he had heard that he had conducted himself very well in Hungary. He added that, if he wished to enter his service and would inform him of what post he desired, he would be very pleased to appoint him to it. Maximilian spoke in Spanish and requested Bassompierre to reply in the same language.

Shortly after this, the Emperor sent the Count von Fürstenberg to inform Bassompierre that he proposed making certain changes in the cavalry of the Imperial Army, and that if he were willing to go to Lorraine and raise three new companies of light horse and three of musketeers for service in Hungary, he would appoint him colonel of a thousand horse. This offer Bassompierre accepted, "foreseeing," says he, "that France would remain at peace for a long while, and urged thereto by the intense love with which Madame Esther had inspired me."

His attachment to this young lady, however, made him far from anxious to hasten his departure for Lorraine, and he therefore decided to postpone it until after the Carnival, which "Madame Esther," who had returned to Karlstein, intended to pass at Prague. But, to his great disappointment, her father, the burgrave, fell ill and she was obliged to remain at Karlstein. However, notwithstanding the absence of his inamorata, he contrived to spend a very pleasant time, "with continual feasts and festivities and very high play at prime between five or six of us, to wit, Count von Stahrenberg, President of the Kingdom of Bohemia, Adam Galpopel, Grand Prior of Bohemia, Kinsky, Rossworm and myself. And there was not an evening in which I did not win or lose two or three thousand thalers."

On the occasion of the marriage of the Emperor's Grand Equerry, which took place during the Carnival, and the festivities in connection with which lasted several days, Bassompierre arranged with Rossworm and six other nobles to parade the town on horseback, masked and splendidly dressed. As they were passing the Town Hall, some constables came up to Bassompierre and Rossworm, who, preceded by their pages bearing their swords aloft, were riding at the head of the party, and informed them that the Emperor had forbidden anyone to pass through the town masked. They, however, pretended that they did not understand Sclavonic, and rode on. No attempt was made to stop them, but, on their return, they found chains stretched across all the streets leading to the square in which the Town Hall stood, except the one by which they entered, and, so soon as they had passed, chains were stretched across that also. Then a whole company of constables appeared upon the scene, and, beginning with the hindmost of the party, seized their companions, who, not having brought their swords with them, were unable to offer any resistance, and haled them off to prison. Meanwhile,

Bassompierre and Rossworm had taken their swords from their pages, but they did not draw them. However, when one of the constables attempted to seize the bridle of Bassompierre's horse, Rossworm struck him on the hand with his sheathed sword, and, the blade, breaking through the scabbard, wounded the man somewhat severely. They were immediately surrounded by more than two hundred police, but, drawing their swords, they contrived to prevent them from closing with them and dragging them off their horses, though not without receiving a volley of blows on their backs and arms.

"This went on for some time," continues Bassompierre, "until a chief justice came out of the Town Hall and raised his bâton (which they call *regimentstock*). Upon this, all the constables laid their halberds on the ground; and Rossworm (who knew the custom) threw down his sword and called out to me to do the same instantly. I did so, otherwise I should have been declared a rebel to the Emperor and punished as such. Rossworm asked me to answer when the judge began to question us, as he did not wish to be recognised. The judge inquired who I was, and I told him without disguising anything. He then asked the name of my companion, and I answered that it was Rossworm, whereupon he offered us the most profuse apologies. Rossworm, annoyed that I had given his name, when he saw that it was useless to deny it, fell into a rage and threatened the judge and the constables that he would complain to the Emperor and the Chancellor and have them severely punished. They tried every means to appease him, but he, as well as myself, had been too well beaten to be satisfied with words. They delivered up to us our six companions, who were more fortunate than ourselves, since they had suffered nothing worse than a fright, and we rode away. In the evening we attended the wedding festivities as though nothing had happened. But, next morning, Rossworm went to the Chancellor, to whom he spoke very arrogantly, and the Chancellor, to satisfy us, threw more than 150 constables into prison. Their wives were every day at my door to obtain a pardon for them, and I solicited Rossworm very earnestly to grant it. But he was inexorable, and made them lie a fortnight in prison during the rigour of winter, from the effects of which two of them died. Finally, with great difficulty, I contrived to get the rest set at liberty."

The imprisonment of these unfortunate constables, who had only done their duty, was indeed a singular way for a Government to encourage the faithful execution of its orders!

In the town of Prague the New Calendar was in use, but among the Hussites, in the country districts of Bohemia, it was not observed. In consequence, after the Carnival was over at Prague, it lasted another ten days in the country, and the Burgrave Prestowitz invited Bassompierre, Rossworm, and two Bohemian nobles named Stavata and Colwrat to come and spend a second Carnival at Karlstein, at which a large party of nobles and ladies were to assemble. Colwrat was a great admirer of the Countess Millessimo, the eldest sister of Bassompierre's inamorata, while Stavata was just embarking in a romance with her second sister, the not-too-devoted wife of a gentleman named Colowitz; and "on Ash Wednesday the four lovers of the four daughters of the burgrave travelled to Karlstein in the same coach."

At Karlstein Bassompierre appears to have spent an even more agreeable time than during the Carnival at Prague:

"We found there more than twenty ladies, including several who were very beautiful, and it is needless to say we were made welcome by the daughters of the house, but principally by my lady, who was enraptured to see me, as I was to see her. For I was desperately in love with her, and I can say that never in my life did I pass ten days more agreeably or better employed than those I passed there, being always at table, at the ball, in the sleigh, or engaged in another and better occupation. At length, the Carnival being over, we returned to Prague, with great regret on their part and ours, but very satisfied with our little journey."

Before leaving Karlstein, Bassompierre had extracted a promise from "Madame Esther" that she would take an early opportunity of coming to Prague; but, as the worthy burgrave fell ill again, very probably in consequence of the quantity of rich food and strong wine which he had consumed during the Carnival, she was unable to do this. However, she hastened to atone to her lover for his disappointment, for "she made him come in disguise to Karlstein, where he spent five days and six nights concealed in a chamber near her own."

On his return from this amorous escapade, Bassompierre prepared to set out for Lorraine, and, having received his despatches and an order on the Lorraine treasury for the payment of the troops which he had undertaken to raise in the duchy,[43] he left

Prague on Palm Sunday, accompanied alone by Cominges-Guitaut, Seigneur de Fléac, a French gentleman who had served with him in Hungary, and a German *valet de chambre.*

He spent the first night of his journey at Karlstein, ostensibly to bid adieu to the burgrave and his family, but, in reality, to take farewell of "Madame Esther," who was, of course, very disconsolate at the departure of her lover, though Bassompierre promised that, so soon as he had raised his levy, he would return to her side for a little while, before leading his horsemen into Hungary. As he was still *"éperdument amoureux,"* and to such a degree that he assures us that the charms of some very beautiful ladies whom he met at a country-house at which he stopped on the following day, and where, sad to relate, both he and his friend Guitaut got very drunk, were powerless to make the smallest impression upon him, he no doubt fully intended to keep his word; but, as events turned out, poor "Madame Esther" was never to see him again.

Travelling by way of Pilsen and Ratisbon, he arrived at Munich, where his friend William II. of Bavaria entertained him very hospitably and "offered him the command of the regiment of foot which Bavaria maintained in Hungary, in any year that he cared to accept it, provided he would notify him before Easter." The Duke also lent him one of his own coaches, which brought him to Augsburg, where he took horse to Strasbourg, and a few days after Easter reached Saverne, and put up at an inn, with the intention of continuing his journey early on the morrow.

At Saverne an adventure befell him which might very well have had a fatal termination:—

"I sat down to table to sup, before going to visit the canons at the castle; but, as I was about to begin, they arrived to take me to the château and lodge me there. They were the Dean of the Chapter, François de Crehange, the Count von Kayl, and the two brothers von Salm-Reifferscheid. They had already supped and were half-drunk. I begged them, since they had found me at table, to sit down with me, instead of taking me to sup at the castle. This they did, and in a short time Guitaut and I had contrived to make them so drunk, that we were obliged to have them carried back to the castle. I remained at my inn, and, at daybreak on the morrow, I mounted my horse, thinking to depart; but they had, the previous night, given orders that I was not to be allowed to pass, for they wished to have their revenge on me for having made them drunk. I was, therefore, compelled to remain and dine with them, which I had great cause to regret. For, in order to intoxicate me, they put brandy in my wine; at least, that is my opinion, though they afterwards assured me that they had not done so, and that it was only a wine of Leiperg, very strong and heady. Anyway, I had scarcely drunk ten or twelve glasses before I lost all consciousness and fell into such a lethargy that it was necessary to bleed me several times, to cup me and to bind my arms and legs with garters. I remained at Saverne five days in this condition, and lost to such a degree the taste for wine, that for two years I was not only unable to drink it, but even to smell it, without disgust."

So perhaps, after all, this very painful experience may have proved to be a blessing in disguise.

On his recovery, Bassompierre proceeded to Harouel, but learning that his mother was at Toul, set out thither, stopping for a few days on his way at the Abbey of Épinal, of which an aunt of his, Yolande de Bassompierre, was the Superior. Here he met again his cousin Yolande de Livron, with whom he had fallen in love two years before, and who happened also to be a guest of the abbess. This damsel had lately married the Comte des Cars, but this did not prevent her from being exceedingly agreeable to her handsome kinsman, and "the fires of their old passion blazed up again." However, perhaps fortunately for the young countess, Bassompierre was soon obliged to continue his journey to Toul, whence he returned with his mother to Harouel.

Their home-coming was a sad one, for, while at Toul, Madame de Bassompierre had learned that her second son, Jean, Seigneur de Removille, who towards the end of the previous year had quitted the service of France for that of Spain, had died from the effects of a wound which he had received at the siege of Ostend, and, the day after their arrival at Harouel, the poor young man's body was brought there for burial. Bassompierre was genuinely grieved at the death of his brother, to whom he had been much attached, and whom he describes as "a man of high courage and good sense, which, joined to a handsome presence, would have assured his fortune"; and he was greatly incensed against Henri IV, or, rather, against Sully, whom he regarded as indirectly responsible for the sad event.

This requires some explanation.

It appears that, during the Wars of Religion, the French Government had become indebted to

Christophe de Bassompierre for various large sums, amounting in all to about 140,000 crowns, which Christophe had paid the troops whom he had raised for their service. As it was not convenient for the Treasury to discharge the debt, it was decided that certain estates belonging to the Crown in Normandy— Saint Sauveur-le-Vicomte, Saint-Sauveur-Landelin, and the barony of Nehou, should be mortgaged to Christophe, the estates to be administered by persons appointed by him. It was anticipated that the revenues of these lands would be sufficient to pay the interest on the money which he had advanced; but this did not prove to be the case, and the arrears of interest continued to mount up, until at the time of his death they had reached a very large sum. However, being on the whole satisfied with the arrangement which had been made, Christophe does not appear to have taken any steps to press his claims upon the French Government, nor did his family do so after his death. But, in the autumn of 1601, Sully, seeing an opportunity of mortgaging these lands on more favourable terms, persuaded Henri IV to issue a decree which provided that the money advanced by Christophe should be refunded to his heirs, with the addition of a sum which represented less than half of the accumulated interest due to them. The King—or rather his Minister—defended this decision on the ground that of late years the Saint-Sauveur lands had become much more valuable, and had—or ought to have—produced a revenue in excess of the interest due.

Bassompierre protested warmly to the King against the injustice of this decree, and asked that it should be annulled; and Henri IV, a little ashamed of the shabby manner in which he had allowed his favourite to be treated, promised him, shortly before Bassompierre's departure for Hungary, that "within two months he should be satisfied."

However, as time went on, without anything being done, Removille, with whom his brother had left full authority to settle the matter with the Government, took upon himself to remind the King of his promise. Henri IV returned an evasive answer, upon which Removille, who was far less tactful than his elder brother, spoke to his Majesty "without that respect or restraint that he ought to have employed." This brought upon him a severe reprimand from the King, and, burning with resentment, the young man promptly quitted Henri IV's service and entered that of Spain, in which he met an untimely death.

Nor was this all, for, shortly before Removille's death, Henri IV, learning that he had been raising a regiment of foot in Lorraine to serve in Flanders, and that Bassompierre was raising a body of horse, concluded, not unnaturally, that the troops which the latter was recruiting were also destined for Flanders, and that he too had quitted his service for that of Philip III. Thereupon he seized the Château of Saint-Sauveur and ejected Bassompierre's servants.

This news, which reached him almost simultaneously with that of his brother's death, served to incense Bassompierre still further against Henri IV and his advisers, and it is very probable that the Court of France would have seen him no more, had not the King, ascertaining that the elder brother's levy was intended for service against the Turks in Hungary and that the younger was dead, hastened to make amends for his high-handed action, and directed Zamet to write Bassompierre a letter of explanation. In this letter Bassompierre was informed that his Majesty was greatly surprised and pained that he should desire to quit his service without cause; that he had not yet allowed the decree of the Council to be executed, and had only taken possession of the Château of Saint-Sauveur because Removille had become a Spanish subject and the château was Crown property; and that he fully intended to make an arrangement which would be satisfactory to him.

Bassompierre replied that nothing was further from his desire than to leave the King's service, but, unless the decree were annulled, he would be so impoverished that it would be no longer possible to live as befitted his rank at his Majesty's Court. This letter had the desired effect, for Henri IV was really much attached to the gay and lively Lorrainer, who was a man after his own heart; and, shortly afterwards, Bassompierre received a letter in the King's own hand inviting him to return to the Court, when "he would soon see how good a master he was."

Bassompierre, feeling sure that the King would keep his word, however much Sully might protest, decided to return to France forthwith, and accordingly sent a messenger to Vienna to inform the Emperor that he was summoned to France by private affairs of the highest importance, and that it would therefore be impossible for him to raise the troops which he had intended to recruit for his Imperial Majesty's service. At the same time, he returned in full the money which he had received for that purpose, although he had already disbursed a portion of it. This very honourable action served to mollify any resentment which the Emperor might otherwise have felt; and he replied, through Rossworm, that he should not appoint a colonel of his foreign cavalry for the present, but would keep the post open for Bassompierre, in case he desired to return to Hungary the following year.

CHAPTER VI

Bassompierre arrives at Fontainebleau and is most graciously received by Henri IV—He falls in love with Marie d'Entragues, sister of the King's mistress—The conspiracy of the d'Entragues—The Sieur d'Entragues and the Comte d'Auvergne are arrested and conveyed to the Bastille, and Madame de Verneuil kept a prisoner in her own house—Jacqueline de Bueil temporarily replaces Madame de Verneuil in the royal affections—The King, unable to do without the latter, sets her and her father at liberty—Bassompierre becomes the lover of Marie d'Entragues—He is dangerously wounded by the Duc de Guise in a tournament, and his life is at first despaired of—He recovers—Attentions which he receives during his illness from the ladies of the Court.

TOWARDS the end of August, 1604, Bassompierre arrived in Paris, where his numerous friends, he tells us, were so delighted to see him that it was three days before they would permit him to continue his journey to Fontainebleau, whither the Court had recently removed; and when he at last contrived to get away, so many of them desired to accompany him, that it required no less than forty post-horses to convey them.

At Fontainebleau he met with so warm a welcome both from the King and the ladies of the Court, that he thought no more of returning to Germany:

"The King was on the great terrace before the Cour du Cheval Blanc when we arrived, and awaited us there, receiving me with a thousand embraces. He then led me into the apartment of the Queen, his wife, who lodged in the apartment above his own, and I was well received by the ladies, who thought me not ill-looking for an inveterate German who had spent a year in his own country. On the morrow the King lent me his own horses to hunt the stag. It was St. Bartholomew's Day, August 24; and he himself would not hunt on a day whereon he had once been in such great danger. On my return from the chase I joined him in the Salle des Étuves, where we played lansquenet."

Henri IV lost no time in annulling the obnoxious decree concerning the Saint-Sauveur property and restoring it to Bassompierre, who was thus enabled to live "a most delightful life" at the Court, and indulge to the full his inclination for lavish display, gambling, and love-making:

"I then fell in love with Antragues, and was also in love with another handsome woman. I was in the flower of my youth, rather well-made and very gay."

The lady whom Bassompierre invariably refers to in his *Memoirs* as "Antragues," without any prefix, was Marie de Balsac d'Entragues, younger sister of Madame de Verneuil. Marie was quite as pretty as Henriette—indeed, by not a few she was considered the prettiest woman at the Court—and if she lacked something of the wit and vivacity which made the reigning sultana so attractive, she was not without intelligence. As one might expect in a child of Marie Touchet, she was wholly devoid of moral sense. But she was neither mercenary nor ambitious, or, at any rate, far less so than her sister; and several exalted personages appear to have sighed for her in vain, including Henri IV, who, like Louis XV, in later times, had not the smallest objection to the presence of two or more members of the same family in his seraglio.

At the time, however, when his Majesty appears to have made advances to the younger sister, his relations with the elder had been temporarily interrupted by the episode which is known as the Conspiracy of the d'Entragues.

In the summer of 1604, acting upon a warning received from James I of England, the French Government had caused one Morgan, an agent of Spain, to be arrested in Paris, and documents found upon this person indicated that he had relations of a highly suspicious character with François d'Entragues, his daughter, Madame de Verneuil, and his stepson, the Comte d'Auvergne. One fine morning, a party of the King's guards arrived at the Château of Malesherbes, where three moats and draw-bridges always raised protected its lord, as he fondly imagined, from surprise. Four of the soldiers, however, succeeded in gaining admission to the château, disguised as peasant-women with butter and eggs to dispose of, overpowered the sentries and admitted their comrades. D'Entragues was arrested and carried off to the Bastille, and with him a voluminous correspondence between the conspirators and the Court of Madrid, containing proposals for the assassination of Henri IV, and a promise signed by Philip III to recognise Henriette's son as heir to the French throne, in the event of the King's death. The Comte d'Auvergne once more found himself in the Bastille, while Madame de Verneuil was confined to her own house and strictly guarded. D'Entragues and his step-son were arraigned for high treason, convicted and sentenced to death; and Henriette was remanded until further evidence could be procured. The King's advisers were urgent that the law should be allowed to take its course; but Henri IV, though he had made a valiant attempt to overcome his infatuation for

Madame de Verneuil, and with the idea of driving out fire by fire, had taken unto himself a new sultana, in the person of Jacqueline de Bueil,[44] felt that he must have his Henriette back, and all the more because she affected to scorn him and refused to sue for his pardon. Dead though he might be to all sense of decency where his passions were concerned, he felt that, if he cut off her father's head, he could scarcely again be her lover, and that d'Entragues' life must therefore be spared. And if d'Entragues were spared, he could not well send his fellow-conspirator—the last scion of the House of Valois—to the scaffold, though, as this was Auvergne's second experiment in high treason, he was even more deserving of death. And so d'Entragues and his daughter were set at liberty; while Auvergne remained in the Bastille, nor did he emerge from it until more than ten years later.

Early in 1605 we find the King again in amorous correspondence with the woman who had been conspiring against him, entreating her to love him to whom all the rest of this world compared with her was as nothing; and, after keeping him at a distance for a little while, Henriette graciously consented to accord him her favours once more. Henceforth, Jacqueline de Beuil was merely retained as a refuge when the marchioness happened to be spiteful and the Queen sulky.

In those days rough horseplay was much in vogue, and during the Carnival of 1605, bands of young nobles rode through the streets of Paris, masked and arrayed in glittering armour. When two of these bands met, they charged vigorously and strove to unhorse one another, and though the points of the lances they carried were carefully padded, and they wielded heavy cudgels gaily decorated with crimson ribbons, instead of swords, very shrewd blows and thrusts were exchanged. On one occasion, Bassompierre, who was accompanied by his brother-in-law Saint-Luc, and two of their friends, met another party, headed by the Duc de Nemours and the Comte de Sommerive, who challenged him to a mimic combat later in the day in the Place de Cimetière Saint-Jean, it being agreed that both sides might bring as many supporters as they could get together. Both parties repaired to the field of battle in considerable force, but that of Nemours and Sommerive had the advantage in numbers. Nevertheless, victory rested with Bassompierre and his friends, who drove their opponents through the streets in disorder, and "he had the satisfaction of seeing one of his rivals in the affections of Mlle. d'Entragues soundly beaten before the eyes of that lady, who was watching them from one of the windows of her house." Nor was this all, for a day or two later Mlle. d'Entragues gave the victor a rendezvous.

This *bonne fortune* of Bassompierre, however, came very near to costing him his life:

"The Tuesday following, which was the first day of March, in the morning, the King being at the Tuileries, said to M. de Guise: 'Ah! Guisard, d'Entragues despises us all and dotes on Bassompierre. I don't speak without certainty.' 'Sire,' replied M. de Guise, 'you have means enough to avenge yourself. As for me, I have none other than that of a knight-errant. I will therefore break three lances with him this afternoon in open field, in whatever place you shall be pleased to appoint.' The King gave us permission, and said that it should be in the Louvre, and that he would have the court sanded. He [Guise] chose his brother M. de Joinville for his second and M. de Termes for third; while I chose M. de Saint-Luc and the Comte de Sault. We all six went to dine and arm ourselves at Saint-Luc's lodging; and, as we always kept armour and caparisons ready for all occasions, my friends and I wore silver armour, with silver and white plumes and silk stockings of the same colours. M. de Guise and his supporters wore black and gold, on account of the imprisonment of the Marquise de Verneuil, with whom he was at that time secretly in love. Then we repaired to the Louvre, preceded by our horses and attendants.

"My friends and I, who were the first to enter the lists, placed ourselves by the side of the old building; M. de Guise and his seconds took up their station beneath the windows of the Queen's apartment. Our course was the length of the Salle des Suisses. It happened that M. de Guise was mounted on a little horse called Lesparne, while I was riding a big charger which the Comte de Fiesque had given me. He took the lower ground, while I was on the wall side, so that I towered over him, and, instead of breaking his lance while raising it, he broke it while lowering it, in such a way that, after splintering it for the first time against my casque, he splintered it the second against my tasset; and the lance penetrated my stomach and lodged in that great bone which connects the hip and the loins. And there the lance broke again, and a stump longer than a man's arm remained attached to the thigh bone. I broke my lance against his breastplate, and, though I felt that I was mortally wounded, I finished my course, and they helped me to dismount near the King's private staircase, and *Monsieur le Grand* and the elder Guitaut aided me to ascend to M. de Vendôme's apartment, below the King's chamber."

Here someone, without awaiting the arrival of the surgeons, was so ill-advised as to pull the broken stump of the lance from the wound, with the result that part of the entrails came out with it; and, though the surgeons when they came contrived to replace them, Bassompierre seemed in desperate case:—

"The King, the Constable, and all the chief personages of the Court stood around, many weeping, as they thought that I should not live an hour. Nevertheless, I did not appear cast down, nor did I think I should die. Many ladies were there and helped to dress my wound, and, as I insisted on returning to my lodging, the Queen sent me the chair in which she was carried about, for she was then pregnant. The people followed me with many marks of sorrow. When I arrived at my lodging, I lost my sight, which made me think I was very ill, so that they made me confess and bled me at the same time. Yet I did not believe I should die, and laughed all the time.

"So soon as I received my wound, the King ordered the tournament to stop, and never permitted one afterwards. This was the only one in open field which had taken place in France for one hundred years, and they were never renewed."

Youth and a splendid constitution saved him, and the attentions he received from the ladies of the Court appear to have consoled him for the pain which he had to endure:

"I cannot say how much I was visited during my illness, and particularly by ladies. All the princesses were there, and the Queen sent on three occasions her maids-of-honour, who were brought by Mlle. de Guise to pass whole afternoons. This lady, who considered herself obliged to assist in nursing me, as it was her brother who had given me my wound, was there most of the time. My sister, Madame de Saint-Luc, who, so long as I was in danger, always slept at the foot of my bed, received the ladies, and, with the exception of the day after I was wounded, the King came every afternoon to see me, and partly also to see my pretty companions."

After being obliged to keep his bed for about a fortnight, he was allowed to get up and take the air in a chair, an object of sympathetic interest to all the ladies of the Court and town. His wound healed rapidly, and by Easter, though still somewhat lame, he felt sufficiently recovered to challenge the Marquis de Cœuvres, brother of Gabrielle d'Estrées, to a duel.

CHAPTER VII

Quarrel between Bassompierre and the Marquis de Cœuvres—Bassompierre sends his cousin the Sieur de Créquy to challenge the marquis to a duel—The King sends for the two nobles and orders them to be reconciled in his presence—Bassompierre and Créquy are forbidden to appear at Court, but are soon pardoned—Visit of Bassompierre to Plombières—He returns to Paris, and "breaks entirely" with Marie d'Entragues—The Chancellor, Pomponne de Bellièvre, ordered to resign the Seals—His conversation with Bassompierre at Artenay—Bassompierre wins more than 100,000 francs at play—He is reconciled with Marie d'Entragues—He joins Henri IV at Sedan—The adventure of the King's love-letter—Henri IV gives orders that a watch shall be kept on Marie d'Entragues's house to ascertain if Bassompierre is secretly visiting that lady—A comedy of errors—Madame d'Entragues surprises her daughter and Bassompierre.

ONE day, in the King's cabinet, Bassompierre, in taking his handkerchief from his pocket, drew out with it a *billet-doux* he had just received from Marie d'Entragues, which fell to the ground and lay there unperceived by him. An Italian banker named Sardini picked it up, and the Marquis de Cœuvres having told him that it was his, he gave it him. Cœuvres read the letter and then sent a message to Bassompierre, asking him to meet him that night before the Hôtel de Soissons and to come alone, as he had something of importance to communicate to him. Bassompierre, not a little surprised, since he and the marquis were on far from good terms with one another, kept the appointment and found Cœuvres awaiting him, in company with a friend of his, the Comte de Cramail, although in his letter he had given him to understand that there was to be no witness to their meeting.

The marquis began by reproaching Bassompierre with "certain bad offices which he asserted that he had rendered him," and then went on to say that, notwithstanding this, he esteemed him too much not to desire his friendship, and aspired to serve, rather than injure, him, in proof of which, although that morning a letter written to him by Mlle. d'Entragues had fallen into his hands, he had made no use of it, but sent it at once to the fair writer by the hand of Sardini. Bassompierre, believing that he was speaking the truth, "made him a thousand protestations of service and affection," after which Cœuvres informed him that the King was aware that he had found a letter written by some lady to him and had demanded to see it, and asked Bassompierre to send him as soon as possible one which he had received from another woman, to enable him to satisfy his Majesty's curiosity. Bassompierre complied with this request, which was an easy matter enough, as, like his royal master, he generally had more than one love-affair on hand, and, besides, was in the habit of carefully preserving all the epistles which he received from the fair. At the same time, he sent a message to Mlle. d'Entragues to apprise her of the mishap which had befallen her letter and to inquire if she had received it from Cœuvres.

"But, as she wrote that she had seen no one sent by the marquis, furious with anger and transported with resentment, I went straight to the marquis's house to recover the letter, or to punish him. On the way, however, I met M. d'Aiguillon[45] and M. de Créquy, who stopped me to inquire whither I was bound. 'I am going,' I replied, 'to the Marquis de Cœuvres' house, to get back from him a letter which Antragues wrote me and which he has found. And, if he does not give it up, I am resolved to kill him!' They remonstrated with me, pointing out that, in going to kill a man in his own house, amongst all his servants, I was running a great danger, without the means of escaping it; that he [Cœuvres] would be very cowardly if he surrendered the letter to me when I went to him in this manner; and that it would be better to send one of my friends. And Créquy offered to go."

Bassompierre reluctantly consented, and Créquy accordingly proceeded to Cœuvres's house. The marquis, at first, flatly refused to give up the letter, declaring that Fortune had brought it to him to enable him to avenge himself on Bassompierre for the ill that he had done him. Créquy pointed out that, if he were so imprudent as to do this, Bassompierre would certainly call him out, in which case one of them would probably be killed, while the victor would be sure to incur the severe displeasure of the King. Cœuvres thereupon began to waver, and finally told him to come back early on the following morning, when he would let him know his decision. When Créquy returned, the marquis, who, Bassompierre believes, had, in the meantime, sent La Varenne with the letter to the King and received it back again, told him that he would himself take the letter to Mlle. d'Entragues, if this would satisfy the lady's admirer.

"To this I agreed," writes Bassompierre, "resolved, nevertheless, to fight with this trickster, though I was anxious first to get Antragues out of the affair."

The marquis took the letter to the lady, and, shortly afterwards, Bassompierre received a message from his mistress, informing him that it was her good pleasure that he should be reconciled to Cœuvres, for which purpose he was to come to her house that afternoon at five o'clock, where he would find the marquis waiting to embrace him. Much against his will, he obeyed, and a formal reconciliation took place between the two gentlemen, who then separated, secretly hating one another more bitterly than ever. In the evening, as Bassompierre was leaving his lodging to go to the Louvre, the Grand Equerry, the Duc de Bellegarde, arrived and told him that the King, having learned that he had quarrelled with the Marquis de Cœuvres, forbade him, on pain of death, to call the latter out. Bassompierre replied, laughing, that it would be easy to obey his Majesty, as he and the marquis were now the best of friends.

Notwithstanding the royal command, Bassompierre was determined to fight the purloiner of his love-letter, though, as he did not wish Mlle. d'Entragues's name to be mixed up in the affair, he had decided to allow two or three days to pass and then to quarrel with him on some other matter. A pretext was easily found, and Créquy, who, now that the letter had been recovered, had altered his views on the question of a duel between them, repaired to Cœuvres's house as the bearer of a formal challenge.

The marquis, however, had no desire to oblige the fire-eating Lorrainer; possibly, he thought that he might get the worst of the encounter, but, more probably, since he appears to have been brave enough, he feared the displeasure of the King. Anyway, he refused to see Créquy, although the latter called on two or three occasions; and, meanwhile, Henri IV, having been warned of Bassompierre's bellicose intentions, again interfered, and, sending for him and Cœuvres, ordered them to be reconciled in his presence. He then told Bassompierre that he had gravely offended him by daring to call out the marquis in the face of his express command, and forbade him to come to the Louvre or to any place where the Court might be. His anger extended to Créquy, and, not only did he forbid him the Court, but even talked of depriving him of the command of the regiment of guards to which he had just been appointed. However, thanks to the solicitations of the ladies of the Court, the Queen interceded with the King on behalf of the offenders, and Henri IV, who had reasons of his own for wishing to keep his consort in a good humour, relented so far as to allow them to return. For some little time he pretended to ignore their presence, but he soon grew tired of this, and admitted them once more to his favour.

In May, Bassompierre went to Plombières, the baths of which had been recommended by the doctor, as his thigh was still causing him a good deal of pain. He travelled thither accompanied by several of his friends from the Court, and an imposing suite, which included a band of musicians whose services he had engaged, and remained there three months, enjoying "all the amusements which a young man, rich, debauched, and extravagant, could desire." His mother, his sister, Madame de Saint-Luc, his younger brother, who had assumed Jean de Bassompierre's title of Seigneur de Removille, and a number of friends from Lorraine joined him there, and he appears to have passed a very agreeable time, to which a love-affair with a Burgundian lady, named Madame de Fussé, contributed not a little.

About the middle of August, by which time he was completely cured, learning that Henri IV had set out at the head of a small army for the Limousin, where the friends of that incorrigible intriguer the Duc de Bouillon were threatening to cause trouble, and that there was a chance of seeing a little fighting, he returned to Paris to prepare to follow the King. On his arrival, he had a violent quarrel with Marie d'Entragues, and "broke with her entirely." What was the cause of the rupture he does not tell us; possibly, the lady may have been seeking consolation for his absence in the devotion of some rival admirer; possibly, she may have heard of the attentions which he had been paying to Madame de Fussé at Plombières and had taken umbrage. Anyway, complete as it may have been at the time, it was soon healed.

After spending a couple of days with a merry party at the Comtesse de Sault's château at Savigny, amongst whom he doubtless contrived to dissipate any inclination to melancholy which his breach with Mlle. d'Entragues may have caused him, Bassompierre set out for the South. At Artenay, he met the aged Chancellor, Bellièvre, who, to his profound mortification, had just been directed by the King to surrender the Seals to Nicolas Brulart, afterwards Marquis de Sillery, though Bellièvre was to remain Chancellor and head of the Council.

"I found him," writes Bassompierre, "walking in a garden with certain *maîtres des requêtes*, who were returning with him to Paris. He said to me: 'Monsieur, you behold in me a man who goes to seek a grave in Paris. I have served the Kings to the best of my ability, and when they saw that I was no longer capable, they sent me to take repose and to attend to the safety of my soul, of which their affairs had prevented me from thinking.' And when, a little later, I told him that he would continue to serve them and to preside at the Council as Chancellor, he replied: 'My friend, a Chancellor without seals is an apothecary without sugar."

Leaving the mortified Chancellor to continue his journey to Paris, where he died a year later, Bassompierre took the road to Orléans, where he found the Queen, whose pregnancy had prevented her following her husband to the Limousin, and Mlle. de Guise, who, while he was at Plombières, had married the Prince de Conti. From Orléans he proceeded to Limoges, which Henri IV had made his headquarters, and, though he was disappointed in his hope of seeing some fighting, since the rebels submitted without any attempt at resistance, he had no reason to regret his journey to the South, as he won at play more than 100,000 francs.

In November, he returned with the King to Fontainebleau, whither the Queen and the ladies of the Court had proceeded, and, shortly afterwards, followed their Majesties to Paris, where he and Mlle.

d'Entragues appear to have taken an early opportunity of making up their quarrel.

In the early spring, Henri IV, with a small army and a powerful battering-train, set out for Sedan, to teach the Duc de Bouillon a much-needed lesson. That troublesome nobleman, however, finding that neither the French Protestants nor Spain were disposed to move a finger to assist him, prudently decided to sue for pardon, and surrendered his impregnable fortress before a shot had been fired against it. The terms he obtained from the sovereign whose authority he had so long defied were favourable in the extreme, no punishment being inflicted upon him beyond the occupation of Sedan for five years by a body of the royal troops under a Huguenot commander.

Having settled with the Duc de Bouillon, Henri IV wrote to Bassompierre, Guise, and Bellegarde, ordering them to join him. On their arrival they found the King making preparations for his formal entry into Sedan, which took place the following day. In the morning Bouillon presented himself before his Majesty, who read to him his *abolition*, to which the duke listened with becoming humility. But the moment it was handed to him his manner changed, and he became as haughty and arrogant as ever, and even had the presumption to alter the order in which the King had marshalled his troops for the procession through the town.

After remaining a few days longer at Sedan, Henri IV went to Busancy, whence he despatched Bassompierre to Paris, to inquire, on his behalf, after the health of his former consort, Queen Margot, "who had lost Saint-Julian Date, her gallant, slain by a gentleman named Charmont [*sic*], whose head the King had caused to be cut off in consequence,"[46] and to carry letters to his two chief sultanas, Madame de Verneuil and the Comtesse de Moret.[47]

Bassompierre, impatient to see Marie d'Entragues, went first to the house of her sister, Madame de Verneuil, where he hoped to find her, and was not disappointed. Having saluted the ladies and executed his commission, he had the imprudence to mention that he was going to call upon Madame de Moret, for whom he had also a letter from the King. That was quite enough to pique the curiosity of the marchioness, who at once determined to see the correspondence which the Béarnais was carrying on with her rival, and asked Bassompierre to give her the letter. That gentleman naturally objected, but Marie d'Entragues joined her commands to the request of her sister, and he weakly allowed himself to be persuaded. Madame de Verneuil broke the seal, and having read the amorous epistle, handed it back to Bassompierre—presumably, it contained nothing of much importance, otherwise, she would have been quite capable of retaining

HENRIETTE DE BALSAC D'ENTRAGUES, MARQUISE DE VERNEUIL.
From an engraving by Aubert.

or destroying it—observing that in an hour he could get a seal made similar to that with which the letter was fastened, and that, when he had sealed it again, no one would suspect that it had ever been tampered with. Bassompierre, relying on this assurance, sent his *valet de chambre* with the letter into the town to get a replica of the seal made; but, as ill luck would have it, the man went to an engraver named Turpin, who happened to be the very same person who had made the original for the King. Turpin, recognising his handiwork and suspecting that something was wrong, seized the valet by the collar, with the intention of handing him over to the police. But the latter, who was a strong and active fellow, contrived to wrench himself free and hurried off to warn his master, leaving his hat and cloak, together with the King's letter, in the hands of the engraver.

Bassompierre, much disturbed by this misadventure, hid his valet, who, he tells us, would have been hanged within two hours if he had been caught, and then went to call on Madame de Moret. Having decided that his best plan was to brazen it out, he told the countess that having been entrusted by the King with a letter for her, he had unfortunately opened it, in mistake for a *poulet* which a lady had sent him; that, through fear of being suspected of having acted intentionally, he had, instead of coming to her at once to offer his apologies, as he, of course, should have done, been so imprudent as to try and get a similar seal made, and that his servant, having by ill chance gone to the King's engraver, the latter, his suspicions aroused, had retained the letter. If Madame de Moret wished to have it, she had only to send someone to explain the matter to Turpin, and no doubt the engraver would give it up. The countess believed, or pretended to believe, this not very probable story, and sent one of her servants to Turpin to claim her letter; but was informed that it was no longer in his hands, but in those of Séguier, President of the Tournelle, or criminal court of the Parlement of Paris, to whom the honest engraver had deemed it his duty to transmit it without delay.

Here was a fresh complication and one which caused Bassompierre no little disquietude, as he did not know Séguier personally, and the latter had the reputation of being a most austere magistrate, who would be certain to sift the matter to the very bottom. Resourceful though he was, he was for the moment at a loss how to act, but, finally, resolved to go and see Madame de Loménie, wife of Antoine de Loménie, one of the Secretaries of State, with whom he was on very friendly terms, and beg her to intervene in order to hush up this unfortunate affair, either by persuading Séguier to surrender the letter, or by writing to her husband, who was on his way to Paris with the King, to ask him to give some plausible explanation to his Majesty.

This time Fortune was on his side. He found the Minister's wife seated at her writing-desk and apparently very busy. She was engaged, she told him, in drafting a very important letter to her husband concerning a singular adventure. Bassompierre, having an idea that this singular adventure might well have some relation to his own, pressed her to tell him more, upon which the lady explained that an attempt had been made that morning to counterfeit the King's seal; that the man who had been sent to the engraver had unfortunately succeeded in effecting his escape, but that the letter of which he was the bearer had been seized, and that the President Séguier had just sent it to her, with the request that she would forward it to her husband, in order that he might lay it before the King, when perhaps they would be able to get to the bottom of the matter. And Madame de Loménie added that she would willingly give 2,000 crowns to solve this imbroglio.

Bassompierre, with a sigh of relief, offered to enlighten her for nothing, and proceeded to furnish her with the same explanation of the affair which he had already given Madame de Moret. Madame de

Loménie accepted it, and, after having given him a good lecture, promised to smooth things over for him, on condition that he would go on the morrow to Villers-Cotterets, where the King and her husband had just arrived, and take with him a report of the matter which she would draw up. Bassompierre agreed readily enough, as may be imagined, and, having called again upon Madame de Verneuil to obtain her answer to the King's letter, and also upon Madame de Moret, who wrote likewise to thank his Majesty, although she had not received the one intended for her, set out for Villers-Cotterets, where Henri IV laughed heartily over the adventure, of which he does not appear to have suspected the true explanation.

A few days later, Henri IV, in celebration of his bloodless victory over the Duc de Bouillon, made a sort of triumphal entry into Paris, where he was received with salvoes of artillery and loud acclamations from the populace. The effect of this ceremony, however, appears to have been somewhat spoiled by the extraordinary attitude assumed by the rebellious vassal whom he had just brought to heel, and who rode along bowing and smiling to the people who thronged the streets and the windows and roofs of the houses, for all the world as if he himself were the hero of the day and the object of all the acclamations.

"He [the King]," writes Bassompierre, "desired M. de Bouillon to march immediately before him, and this he did, but with such assurance and audacity, that it was impossible to decide whether it was the King who was leading him in triumph or he the King."

Henri IV only remained a few days in Paris, and then went to Fontainebleau; but Bassompierre did not accompany him, being desirous of enjoying the society of Marie d'Entragues, of whom, since their reconciliation, he was more enamoured than ever.

Bassompierre's conquest of Mlle. d'Entragues had naturally aroused a good deal of jealousy amongst the less fortunate admirers of that young lady, who were numerous and distinguished, and included both the King and the Duc de Guise. As yet, however, they had no actual proof of his *bonne fortune*, as the intrigue was conducted with unusual discretion. It was his habit, he tells us, to enter the house in the Rue de la Coutellière, where Marie lived with her mother, late at night, by a back entrance, "whereby I ascended to the third floor, which Madame d'Entragues had not furnished, and her daughter, by a secret staircase leading from her wardrobe, came to join me there, when her mother had fallen asleep."

Henri IV, piqued by the assurances of several of Bassompierre's rivals, and principally by Guise, that Marie d'Entragues made game of them all and preferred the handsome Lorrainer, gave orders, just before his departure for Fontainebleau, to have the house watched.

"As he was in love with Antragues, M. de Guise and several others also, who were all jealous of me, because they believed me to be on better terms with her than themselves, plotted together to have me spied upon, in order to discover if I entered her house, and if I saw her privately; and the King commanded those whom he had charged to watch it, to take their orders from M. de Guise and to report to him if they saw anything."

The sequel was a most amusing comedy of errors.

A day or two later, Bassompierre, who had an assignation with his inamorata that night, happened to sup with the Grand Equerry, the Duc de Bellegarde. During the meal it came on to rain heavily, and, as he had come unprovided with a cloak, he borrowed one from his host, and, wrapped in this, made his way, at about eleven o'clock, to the Rue de la Coutellière, without noticing that the Cross of the Ordre du Saint-Esprit, of which none but Princes of the Blood, very great nobles, and Ministers of State, were members, was attached to the cloak. The spies posted around Madame d'Entragues's house were more observant, and one of them at once hurried off to inform the Duc de Guise that they had just seen a young Knight of the Ordre du Saint-Esprit enter the house by a back door. Guise immediately sent two of his *valets de chambre* to identify the gentleman when he left, which did not happen until four o'clock in the morning. But Bassompierre caught sight of them before they saw him, and, recognising them as the duke's servants, pulled his cloak over his face, though he had little hope of escaping detection, since he was well known to them both. The valets, however, deceived by the Cross of the Saint-Esprit, reported to their master that Mlle. d'Entragues' midnight visitor was the Grand Equerry, since they were aware that there was no other Knight of the Order in Paris at the time in the least likely to have such a *bonne fortune*.

In the morning, Bassompierre wrote to Mlle. d'Entragues to inform her of the espionage of which he had been the object, and to urge her to be on her guard. On his side, the Duc de Guise went between nine and ten o'clock to the Grand Equerry's house, but was told that Bellegarde had given directions that he could see no one until the evening, as he had been kept awake all night by violent toothache. This seemed to confirm his suspicions in regard to the Grand Equerry, since a man who had not returned from an assignation until four o'clock in the morning would naturally desire to sleep until late in the day; and chuckling at the thought of Bassompierre's mortification when he learned that he had a successful rival, he made his way to that gentleman's lodging.

Bassompierre, like Bellegarde, was still in bed when the duke arrived, but, having told the servants that he had come to see their master on a matter of urgency, he was conducted to his room.

"I beg you to put on your dressing-gown," said he so soon as he entered; "I have a word to say to you."

"I felt quite sure," writes Bassompierre, "that he intended to tell me that I had been seen leaving Antragues's house, and determined to deny it positively. But, on the contrary, he continued: 'What would you say if the Grand Equerry were preferred by Antragues to you and everyone, and she were in the habit of receiving him at night?' I told him that I should decline to believe it, as neither he nor she had any inclination for the other. '*Mon Dieu*,' said he, 'how easy to deceive are lovers! I thought as you do; nevertheless, it is true that he went to her house last night, and did not leave until four o'clock this morning. He was seen to go in, and my *valets de chambre* themselves saw him come out, with so little care that he had not even troubled to wear a cloak without the cross of the Order, to disguise himself.'

"Thereupon, he called one of the valets, D'Urbal by name, and inquired whether he had not seen *Monsieur le Grand* leave Antragues's house. 'Yes, Monseigneur,' the man answered, 'as plainly as I see M. de Bassompierre there.' I dared not look in the face of this valet, who had seen me that same morning leaving the house, and believed that it was a trick to make game of me; but, as I turned away, I perceived on a chair *Monsieur le Grand's* cloak, which my valet had folded in such a way that the cross of the Order was visible, and ought to have been easily seen by M. de Guise, if he had not been so much occupied just then. I sat down upon it, fearing lest M. de Guise should catch sight of the cross, and pretending to be disconsolate as he was, I complained bitterly of the fickleness of Antragues. I refused to rise from my seat on the cloak, although M. de Guise invited me to go for a walk with him, until I had told my valet to take it away, when M. de Guise should be looking in another direction, and hide it in a wardrobe."

So soon as the duke had taken his departure, Bassompierre wrote to his mistress to inform her of this new incident. Marie d'Entragues had the caustic spirit of her family, and it pleased her, in order to perpetuate this comedy of errors and avert suspicion from Bassompierre, to show herself exceedingly gracious to the Grand Equerry when she met him that afternoon, so that Bellegarde, who was not without vanity, was himself deceived, and began to think he had made an impression upon the lady. The consequence was that when, on the morrow, Guise, who could not keep silent, although he and Bassompierre had agreed to say nothing to the Grand Equerry about it, began to rally that gentleman upon his supposed *bonne fortune*, the latter defended himself so feebly, that all the jealousy of Guise and of the King, when he heard of the affair, was turned in his direction, and the real gallant was able to continue his nocturnal visits to the Rue de la Coutillière with but few precautions.

However, they had warned Madame d'Entragues to take better care of her daughter—it was certainly high time that she did—and one fine June morning, happening to awake very early, she drew aside the curtain of her bed, and saw, to her astonishment, that that of Marie, who slept in the same room, was empty. She rose at once and went into her wardrobe, where she found the door leading to the secret staircase, which was always kept locked, open.

"She began to scream," relates Bassompierre, "and, at the sound of her voice, her daughter rose in haste and went to her. I, meanwhile, shut the door and took my departure, very troubled about what might come of this affair, which was that her mother chastised her, and caused the door of the room where we were that night to be broken open, so that she might enter, and was very amazed to find this apartment furnished with splendid furniture purchased from Zamet. Then all intercourse was broken off; but I made my peace with the mother through the intervention of Mlle. d'Asy, at whose house I saw her, when I asked her pardon so many times, coupled with the assurance that we had not gone beyond kissing, that she pretended to believe me. She went to Fontainebleau, and I went also, but I did not venture to speak to Antragues except secretly, because the King did not approve of it.[48] However, lovers are resourceful enough to find opportunities for occasional meetings."

CHAPTER VIII

A strange adventure—Bassompierre sent as Ambassador Extraordinary to Lorraine to represent Henri IV at the marriage of the Duke of Bar and Margherita di Gonzaga—He returns to Paris and orders a gorgeous suit, which is to cost fourteen thousand crowns, for the baptism of the Dauphin and Madame Élisabeth, though he has only seven hundred in his purse—He wins enough at play to pay for it—Charles III of Lorraine writes to request his presence at the Estates of Lorraine—Henri IV refuses him permission to leave France, but he sets out notwithstanding this—He is arrested by the King's orders at Meaux, but set at liberty on his promising to return to Court—He is allowed to leave for Lorraine a few days later—Affair of the Prince de Joinville and Madame de Moret.

ABOUT the middle of June of that year, Henri IV despatched Bassompierre as Ambassador Extraordinary to Lorraine, to represent him at the marriage of the Duke of Bar (whose first wife, Catherine de Bourbon, had died in 1604) to Margherita di Gonzaga, daughter of Vincenzo I, Duke of Mantua, and Eleanor de' Medici, sister of the Queen; and, at the same time to request the Duchess of Mantua to become godmother to the dauphin, and the Duke of Lorraine godfather to Madame Élisabeth, eldest daughter of the King.

Bassompierre accordingly left Fontainebleau for Paris, where he met with another love-adventure, which delayed his departure for Lorraine for several days, and which we shall allow him to relate himself, since—to borrow his own words—"though it was not of great consequence, it was, nevertheless, extravagant":

"For the past four or five months, every time I passed over the Petit-Pont—for in those days the Pont-Neuf was not built—a handsome woman, a sempstress at the sign of the Two Angels, made me deep courtesies and followed me with her eyes so far as she could. And, when I remarked her behaviour, I looked at her also and saluted her with greater care. It happened that, when I arrived in Paris from Fontainebleau, and was crossing the Petit-Pont, so soon as she saw me approaching, she placed herself at the door of her shop, and said to me as I passed: 'Monsieur, I am your very humble servant.' I returned her greeting and, turning round from time to time, I perceived that she followed me with her eyes so long as she was able. I had travelled post from Fontainebleau, and had brought one of my lackeys with me, intending to send him back to Fontainebleau the same evening with letters for Antragues and for another lady there. I made him alight and give his horse to the postilion to lead, and sent him to tell the young woman that, perceiving the care that she had to see me and salute me, if she desired a more private view of me, I was willing to meet her in whatever place she might choose to appoint. She told the lackey that this was the best news that one could have brought her and that she would go wherever I wished.

"I accepted this proposal and asked my lackey if he knew of some place to take her, which he did, saying that he knew a woman named Noiret, to whose house he would conduct her.... And in the evening I went there, and found a very beautiful woman, twenty years of age, who had her head dressed for the night, wearing naught but a very fine shift, and a short petticoat of green flannel and a *peignoir* over her. She pleased me mightily, and I can say that never had I seen a prettier woman....

"I asked her if I could not see her again, and said that I should not leave Paris until Sunday, this being Thursday night. She answered that she desired it more ardently than I did, but that it would not be possible, unless I stayed the whole of Sunday, in which case she would see me on Sunday night.... I was easy to persuade, and told her that I would remain all Sunday and meet her at night in the same place. Then she rejoined: 'Monsieur, I know well that I am in a house of ill-fame, to which, however, I came willingly, in order to see you, with whom I am so deeply in love.... Well, once is not habit, and though, urged by passion, I have come once to this house, I should be a public wanton if I were to return a second time. I have never surrendered myself to any man but my husband and yourself—may I die in misery if I speak not the truth!—and I have no intention of surrendering myself to another. But what would one not do for a man whom one loves, and for a Bassompierre? That is why I came to this house, but it was to be with a man who has rendered it honourable by his presence. If you wish to see me again, it must be at the house of one of my aunts, who lives in the Rue du Bourg-l'Abbé, next to the Rue aux Ours, the third door on the side of the Rue Saint-Martin. I will await you there from ten o'clock until midnight, and later still, and will leave the door open. At the entrance there is a little passage, through which you must go quickly, for the door of my aunt's room opens on to it, and you will find a stair, which will bring you to the second floor.'

"I agreed to this proposal, and, having despatched the rest of my suite on their journey towards Lorraine,

I came at ten o'clock to the door which she had indicated, and saw a great light, not only on the second floor, but on the third and first as well; but the door was closed. I knocked to announce my arrival, but I heard a man's voice asking who I was. I went back to the Rue aux Ours, and having returned for the second time, finding the door open, I entered and mounted to the second floor, where I found that the light which I had seen proceeded from the straw of the beds which they were burning, and two naked bodies lying upon the table in the room. Thereupon, I withdrew, greatly amazed, and, in going out, I met some 'crows,'[49] who asked me what I sought, and I, to make them give way, drew my sword, and so passed out and returned to my lodging, somewhat disturbed by the unexpected sight which I had beheld. I drank three or four glasses of neat wine, which is a German remedy against the plague, and then went to bed, as I intended to leave for Lorraine the following morning, which I did. And, although I afterwards sought as diligently as possible to learn what had become of this woman, I was never able to discover anything. I even went to the Two Angels, where she lodged, to inquire who she was, but the tenants of the house told me nothing, save that they knew that she was the former tenant. I have decided to relate this adventure, because, although she was a person of humble condition, she was so pretty that I have regretted her, and would have given much to see her again."[50]

At Nancy, Bassompierre, as the representative of the King of France and a personal friend of Charles III of Lorraine, was received with great honour and very sumptuously lodged and entertained. At the marriage ceremony and the *fêtes* which followed it he appeared in great magnificence, and this, in conjunction with his handsome face and ingratiating manners, without doubt made a deep impression upon the ladies of the Court. However, owing presumably to the official position which he occupied, he appears to have refrained from making any fresh conquests—at any rate, he does not record any; and, after having obtained the consent of the Duchess of Mantua and the Duke of Lorraine to stand godmother and godfather to Henri IV's children, he set out for Paris.

On his arrival, he found himself in sore distress of mind. The baptism of the Dauphin and Madame Élisabeth was fast approaching, and having imprudently worn all the new suits which he possessed at the marriage *fêtes* at Nancy, he had none in which to appear at it, or, at least, none which he considered worthy of so great an event. To appear in one which he had donned on some previous occasion was not to be thought of for a moment; his reputation as the most elegant and most recklessly extravagant gentleman of the Court would infallibly be lost. As well ask a modern professional beauty to wear the same toilette twice in a season! To add to his distress, he had spent so much money on his mission to Lorraine, for the post of Ambassador Extraordinary, in those days, though very gratifying to the vanity, was ruinously expensive to the pocket, that he had only a few hundred crowns in his purse, and the acolytes of Fashion were so overwhelmed with orders for the ceremony that they were actually impertinent enough to insist upon money down. Finally, they were reported to be so busy that, even if the financial difficulty were overcome, it was very improbable that he could get a costume of sufficient magnificence completed in time. Was ever so splendid a gallant in so sad a case?

However, Fortune once more came to his aid.

"Just as my sister (Madame de Saint-Luc), Madame de Verderonne,[51] and la Patière,[52] who had come to greet me on my arrival, had informed me that all the tailors and embroiderers were so busy that it was impossible to get a suit made, in came my own tailor, Tallot by name, and my embroiderer with him, to tell me that, on the rumours of the magnificence of the baptism, a merchant of Antwerp had brought a horse-load of pearls that are sold by weight, and that with these they could make me a suit which would surpass anything at the baptism; and my embroiderer offered to undertake it, if I paid him six hundred crowns for his work alone. The ladies and I fixed upon the suit, which required not less than fifty pounds' weight of pearls; and I decided that it should be of violet cloth-of-gold, with palm-branches interlacing. In short, before the tailor and embroiderer withdrew, I, who had only seven hundred crowns in my purse, had ordered them to undertake a suit which was to cost me fourteen thousand. At the same time, I sent for the merchant, who brought me samples of his pearls, and with whom I settled the price by weight. He demanded four thousand crowns earnest money, but for this I put him off till the morrow. M. d'Épernon[53] passed before my lodging, and, knowing that I had arrived, came to see me and told me that he had some good company coming to sup at his house and play afterwards, and asked me to be of the party. I took my seven hundred crowns and with them won five thousand. The next day the merchant came, and I paid him his four thousand crowns earnest money. I also gave something to the embroiderer, and went on to win at play, not only enough to pay for the suit and a diamond sword, which cost five thousand crowns, but had five or six thousand left wherewith to amuse myself."

Bassompierre accompanied the King to Villers-Cotterets to meet the Duke of Lorraine and the Duchess of Mantua. On the way the King turned aside to pay a visit to his former mistress, Charlotte de Essars, Comtesse de Romorantin, who was staying at the Abbey of Sainte-Perrinne, the superior of which was her aunt. Time seems to have dealt leniently with the fair Charlotte, who appeared, according to Bassompierre, more beautiful than ever.

The King conducted his distinguished guests to Paris, where they were magnificently entertained. But, as the plague was increasing in the capital, it was decided that the baptism should take place at Fontainebleau. So the Parisians were deprived of the opportunity of admiring Bassompierre's fourteen-thousand-crown suit and diamond scabbard, and he had to rest content with the sensation which they doubtless created at the Court.

In February, 1607, Charles III of Lorraine wrote to Bassompierre begging him, as a personal favour, to assist at the approaching meeting of the Estates of Lorraine, where his influence with the nobility of the duchy might serve to remove some of the difficulties which he feared that he might have with that body. Bassompierre, accordingly, requested leave of absence of Henri IV, but his Majesty was unwilling to let him go, because, he explains, he had been winning his money at play and he wanted to have his revenge, and put him off on two or three occasions. At last, in despair of obtaining permission, he determined to go without it, and one day, when the Court was at Chantilly, he slipped away unperceived and set out for Paris. On the road he met the Ducs d'Aiguillon and de Bouillon, and begged them not to tell the King that they had seen him; but the two dukes, probably supposing that he was bound on some amorous adventure which he wished to keep from his Majesty's knowledge, denounced him so soon as they arrived at Chantilly. The consequence was that when Bassompierre reached Meaux, he found the provost of that town and two exempts of the King's guards, whom his Majesty had sent to head him off, waiting to arrest him. In great indignation, he despatched one of his suite to Chantilly, with letters for the King and

Villeroy, one of the Secretaries of State, protesting against the indignity to which he was being subjected; and the following day the provost came to inform him that he had received orders to set him at liberty, provided he would give his word to return to the Court. On his arrival at Chantilly he was sent for by the King, who laughed heartily at his crestfallen demeanour, telling him that he had now had an opportunity of seeing the good order that he maintained in his realm, which no one could leave without his consent; but that he only wanted him to remain ten days longer, when he would give him permission to go to Lorraine. He added that his stay would not be unprofitable; and he was as good as his word, for during this time the vexed question of the Saint-Sauveur lands was finally settled, to Bassompierre's entire satisfaction.

Before leaving for Lorraine, Bassompierre endeavoured to do a good turn to his friend the Prince de Joinville and Madame de Moret, who had been so imprudent as to fall in love with one another, and warned them that the King intended to surprise them together, in which event he had vowed to make a public example both of the presumptuous noble who had dared to violate the sanctity of the royal seraglio and of his faithless sultana. The lovers, however, did not profit by his warnings, and, while on his way to Nancy, he learned that, though the King had not succeeded in surprising them, he had discovered enough to confirm his suspicions, and had banished Joinville from the Court for the second time. Bassompierre at once turned back and came to Paris incognito, "in order to see Madame de Moret and offer to serve her in her affliction"; but his presence was discovered and reported to Madame d'Entragues, who, suspecting that he had returned with the object of paying surreptitious visits to her daughter, promptly locked that flighty young lady up until he had taken his departure.

CHAPTER IX

Amusements of Bassompierre during the winter of 1608—His gambling-parties—Embarrassment which the fact of having several love-affairs on his hands simultaneously sometimes occasions him—Death of Charles III of Lorraine—Bassompierre goes to Nancy to attend the Duke's funeral—Gratifying testimony which he receives during his absence of the esteem in which he is held by the ladies of the Court of France—"The star of Venus is very much in the ascendant over him"—Marriage arranged between Marie d'Entragues and the Comte d'Aché, of Auvergne—The affair is broken off—Frenzied gambling at the Court: gains of Bassompierre—Secret visits paid by him and the Duc de Guise to Madame de Verneuil and Marie d'Entragues at Conflans—Visit of the Duke of Mantua to the Court of France.

BASSOMPIERRE begins his journal for the year 1608 in the following strain:—

"In the year 1608 I embarked in an affair with a blonde lady. I won a great deal at play that year, and gave away much at the Foire. We danced a number of ballets.... I had more mistresses at the Court, and was on excellent terms with Antragues. M. de Vendôme also danced a ballet, in which the King would have Cramail, Termes, and myself, who were called *les dangereux*, assist. We went to dance it at M. de Montpensier's, who rose to see it, though he was dying."[54]

After Easter the King went to Fontainebleau, where on April 25 the Queen gave birth to her third son, Gaston, Duc d'Anjou, afterwards Duc d'Orléans. Bassompierre, however, excused himself from accompanying his Majesty, apparently on the plea of illness, and remained in Paris, where, he tells us, he passed his time very agreeably.

"I pretended to be suffering from a weakness of the lungs, so that no one saw me until midday, when all the Court came to my lodging to pass the time until nine o'clock in the evening, when I made believe to retire, on account of my delicate state of health; but it was to pass the night in good company."

The "good company" he speaks of was a little coterie of gamblers, "eight or ten worthy men of the town, and of the Court, M. de Guise, Créquy, and myself," who played for tremendously high stakes, since Bassompierre had considerately introduced amongst them a Portuguese merchant named Fernandez, who came prepared to make good the losses of those upon whom Fortune happened to frown, in return for approved security. This kind of arrangement was so convenient that, when the King returned from Fontainebleau, he wished to be of the party, which met every day either at the Louvre,

Zamet's, or the Marquis de Roquelaure's; and doubtless the organiser of these *séances*, who appears to have been one of the luckiest gamblers who ever turned a card or rattled a dice-box, and the accommodating Fernandez, derived substantial benefits from them.

In July, Queen Marguerite gave a grand *fête* at the Arsenal, the principal feature of which was the then fashionable pastime of tilting at the ring. Bassompierre, of course, attended it, very splendidly arrayed, but also very reluctantly, since, as he naïvely explains, those gentlemen who, like himself, had several love-affairs on their hands simultaneously were often sadly embarrassed at these great assemblies, since all the ladies whom they professed to adore were sure to be present, and it was practically impossible to pay sufficient attention to one without giving umbrage to the others.

"I thought," he continues, "that I should experience great difficulty there; but Fortune came to my aid in such fashion that, without neglecting anyone, I contented all. For, in short, having stationed myself unintentionally beneath the Queen's stand, where Mlle. de Montmorency[55] was sitting, Pérault,[56] who had served with me in Hungary, insisted on my taking his place; and then, for the first time, I spoke to her and strove to insinuate myself into her good graces, little imagining what was to happen later. After the *fête* was over, I was delighted to see that I had contented all the ladies with whom I was on good terms, and that not one of them had had reason to be jealous of another, a thing which very rarely happened on such occasions."

On May 14, 1608, Charles III of Lorraine, who had been in bad health for some time past, died. Bassompierre went to Nancy to attend his funeral, and was away three weeks, during which, he tells us, he received the most gratifying testimony to the esteem in which he was held by the ladies of the Court of France:—

"It is impossible to describe how much care the ladies took to send me frequently news of themselves and to despatch couriers to me with letters and presents. The star of Venus was very much in the ascendant over me. I returned to Paris, and four ladies in a coach came beyond Pantin to meet me, making believe that they were merely taking a drive. They placed me in their coach and brought me to the Porte de Saint-Honoré, where I remounted my horse to enter Paris."

On his arrival in the capital, he learned that Marie d'Entragues had gone, with her mother and Madame de Verneuil, to Malesherbes, to marry a certain Comte d'Aché, of Auvergne; but, as may be supposed, his other lady-loves made every effort to console him for his loss, which, in point of fact, proved to be only a temporary one, since the parties were unable to agree about the marriage-articles, and the affair was broken off. In after years Bassompierre had good reason to regret that the projected marriage had not taken place, in which event he would have been spared great trouble and expense.

The King, learning that he had returned, wrote telling him to come at once to Fontainebleau, where the Court was then in residence, and informing him that, although he had until then been the greatest gambler in his circle of friends, since his absence in Lorraine a Portuguese gentleman named Pimentel had appeared upon the scene, who played much higher than even he did. He must lose no time in redeeming his lost reputation.

Bassompierre hastened to obey, and plunged once more into this ruinous amusement—ruinous, that is to say, to others, for, as we know, he was well able to take care of himself—with all the zest begotten of a three weeks' abstinence from the card-table. For, though he had probably gambled at Nancy, the stakes in vogue there must have seemed a mere bagatelle compared with those for which Henri IV and his intimates played.

"We remained some days at Fontainebleau," he says, "playing the most frenzied game that I have ever heard of. Not a day passed on which there were not gains or losses of 20,000 pistoles. The counters of the least value which were used were for 50 pistoles. The highest were worth 500 pistoles; so that it was possible to hold in one's hand at one time counters to the value of 50,000 pistoles. I won that year there more than 500,000 francs at play, notwithstanding that I was distracted by a thousand follies of youth and love. The King returned to Paris, and from there went to Saint-Germain. Play on the same scale continued, and Pimentel won more than 200,000 crowns."

In July, Madame d'Entragues and her two daughters returned from Malesherbes, and went to stay at Conflans, Madame de Verneuil in one house, and Madame d'Entragues and Marie in another. Marie, however, frequently found a pretext for spending the night with her elder sister, and on these occasions, says Bassompierre, "M. de Guise and I played the part of knights-errant and went to visit them." After a short stay at Conflans, the d'Entragues returned to Paris, where Marie and Bassompierre had another quarrel—for what reason he does not tell us— and "he broke entirely with her." Like the last, however, it would not appear to have been of long duration.

At the beginning of August, the Duke of Mantua came to the French Court, where, as the husband of the Queen's sister, he was magnificently entertained. His Highness, however, seems to have spent a considerable part of his visit at the card-tables, for, "being a great gambler, he was delighted to take part in the high play which went on, which was to him extraordinary." When the Duke took his departure, Bassompierre, who spoke Italian fluently, was deputed to accompany him on his homeward journey so far as Montargis.

CHAPTER X

Enviable position of Bassompierre at the Court of France—The Connétable de Montmorency offers him the hand of his beautiful daughter Charlotte, the greatest heiress in France—The marriage-articles are drawn up—The consent of Henri IV is obtained—The Duc de Bouillon, whom Bassompierre has offended, endeavours to persuade the King to withdraw his sanction and to marry Mlle. de Montmorency to the Prince de Condé (*Monsieur le Prince*)—Henri IV falls madly in love with the young lady—Singular conversation between the King and Bassompierre, in which his Majesty orders the latter to renounce his pretensions to Mlle. de Montmorency's hand—Astonishment and mortification of Bassompierre, who, however, yields with a good grace—Bassompierre falls ill of chagrin and remains for two days "without sleeping, eating or drinking"—He is persuaded by his friend Praslin to return to the Louvre—Mlle. de Montmorency is betrothed to the Prince de Condé—Bassompierre falls ill of tertian fever, but rises from his sick-bed to fight a duel with a Gascon gentleman—The combatants are separated by friends of the latter—Serious illness of Bassompierre.

BASSOMPIERRE had now fairly established his claim to be regarded as "the most amiable and elegant gentleman of the Court," and his position was in every way an enviable one. He was idolised by the ladies to a degree that no gallant has ever been either before or since his time, with the possible exception of the too-celebrated Maréchal de Richelieu, in the days of Louis

XV;[57] liked and admired by the men, who looked upon him as "the glass of fashion and the mould of form;" so great a favourite of the King that his Majesty grumbled whenever he absented himself from Court, and there seemed no rank or office, however high, to which he might not ultimately aspire; and, though not wealthy, as wealth was accounted in those days at the Court of France, enabled, thanks to his extraordinary good fortune at play, to vie with the greatest in the land in luxury and extravagance. "It would have been well," says a writer of the time, Tallemant des Réaux, "if there had always been at the Court someone like him; he did the honours and received and entertained foreigners. I used to remark that he was at the Court what *Bon Accueil* was in the romance of *la Rose*. People everywhere used to call a man a Bassompierre, if he excelled in good looks and the elegance of his appearance and manners."

But Bassompierre possessed more solid claims to the universal popularity which he enjoyed than these. He was not only an adept at all manly exercises, but a good musician, a sound classical scholar, and a master of four languages: French, German, Spanish, and Italian. Despite his follies, his innumerable gallantries, his gambling, and his prodigality, he possessed a vein of sound common-sense, which caused him to be consulted frequently by those who were in pecuniary or other embarrassments; and he was a kindly, good-natured man, who held aloof from the intrigues of the Court, never spoke ill of anyone, and was always ready to do a service to a friend who needed it. And he was now about to receive the most flattering tribute to his better qualities possible to imagine—one, indeed, which he could not have hoped for even in his fondest dreams—namely, the offer of a bride who was at once the most beautiful girl at the Court, the greatest heiress in France, and, with a single exception,[58] the young lady of the highest rank in the land after the daughters of the Princes of the Blood.

One day, in October, 1608, the old Connétable de Montmorency, with whom Bassompierre had always been a great favourite, invited him to dine with him on the morrow, at the same time impressing upon him the importance of not failing to be there, which was no doubt a very necessary precaution, in view of the frequency with which that young gentleman's love-affairs and gambling-parties must have necessitated the breaking of other social engagements. On his arrival at Montmorency's hôtel, he found that the Duc d'Epernon, the Marquis de Roquelaure, Zamet, and a *maître des requêtes* named La Cave, had also been invited, all four being intimate friends of both the Constable and himself; and from their presence he divined that some important matter which must concern him very closely was in the wind.

After dinner, Montmorency conducted his guests into his chamber, where they were joined by Du Tillet-Girard, his confidential secretary, and his physician Rancin, the latter of whom the Constable directed to station himself at the door and on no account to allow their privacy to be interrupted. Then, in a solemn speech, the old nobleman proceeded to inform them of the reason which had led him to invite them there that day.

Having, he said, arrived at the close of life, he had deemed it his duty to look around him for a man to whom he might give his youngest daughter in marriage—one who might be agreeable both to himself and to her; and, although he might choose amongst all the princes in France, he preferred his daughter's happiness to her elevation, and to see her, during the rest of his days, living in joy and contentment. For which reason, the esteem which he had so long entertained for the person and family of

M. de Bassompierre had decided him to offer him what others of far higher rank would most gladly accept. And he had wished to do this in the presence of his best friends, who were likewise M. de Bassompierre's, and to tell him that, having loved him as dearly as if he were his son, he desired to make him so by marrying him to his daughter, being assured that she would be happy with him, knowing as he did his good qualities; and that M. de Bassompierre, on his part, would hold himself honoured in marrying the daughter and grand-daughter of Constables of France; while he (Montmorency) would be happy the rest of his days if he saw them both living happily and contentedly together. He added that it was his intention to give his daughter a dowry of 100,000 crowns, while she would receive another 50,000 on the death of his younger brother;[59] and if nothing prevented M. de Bassompierre from accepting the offer which he now made him, he would instruct Du Tillet-Girard to draw up, in conjunction with whatever person he might choose to appoint, the marriage-articles.

"There were tears of joy in his eyes when he finished speaking," writes Bassompierre, "and, as for me, I was so overcome by an honour as unhoped for as it was dear to me, that words failed me to express what I felt. At length, I told him that this honour so great and so unexpected which he, in his generosity, designed for me deprived me of the power of speech; that I could only marvel at my good fortune; that it was above all my expectations, as it was above my deserts; that it could only be repaid by very humble service and infinite submission; that my life would be too short to requite it, and that I could only offer him entire devotion to his will; that it was not a husband whom he would give his daughter, but a being by whom she would be incessantly adored like a goddess and respected like a queen, and that he had not chosen a son-in-law so much as a domestic servant of his House, whose every action would be guided by his intentions and wishes alone; and that if anything abated the excess of my joy, it was the apprehension that Mlle. de Montmorency, who could choose from all the marriageable princes in France, might regret renouncing the quality of princess, of which she ought with reason to be assured, to occupy that of a simple lady; and that I would prefer to die and lose the honour which Monsieur le Connétable designed for me than occasion her the least regret or discontent. And upon that, as I occupied a rather low seat close to his own, I placed a knee to the ground, and, taking his hand, kissed it, while he held me in a long embrace. After which, he told me not to entertain any fear of that, as, before speaking to me, he had consulted his daughter, and found her perfectly disposed to fulfil all the wishes of her father, and particularly in that which was not disagreeable to her.

"MM. d'Épernon and de Roquelaure approved the choice which the Constable had made of my person, and said more kind things concerning me than I merited; as did also Zamet, La Cave, and Du Tillet-Girard; and they then all embraced me, praising the Constable's choice and felicitating me on my good fortune. After this, the Constable told them that it was not opportune to reveal this affair, and that he entrusted it to their discretion until the time came to divulge it; because he was not just then in the good graces of the King, since he had refused his consent to the marriage which the King had desired to bring about between M. de Montmorency[60] and Mlle. de Verneuil,[61] his daughter. This they promised him, and I likewise.

"The Constable requested me to come to him again in the evening, when Madame d'Angoulême, his sister-in-law[62] would be there, saying that he intended to speak before her

**CHARLOTTE MARGUERITE DE MONTMORENCY,
PRINCESSE DE CONDÉ.**

From an engraving by Barbant.

and his daughter of his decision to give the latter to me in marriage. On my arrival, he said to me before her: 'My son, here is a wife whom I am keeping for you; salute her.' This I did, and kissed her. Then he spoke to her and to Madame d'Angoulême, who seemed very content with the choice which her brother-in-law had made of me for her niece."

The following day, the Princess de Conti, who had been let into the secret, took Madame de Bassompierre to the Constable's hotel and presented her to the Duchesse d'Angoulême, who received her very graciously, observing: "We shall be the two mothers of our newly-married pair, and I know not whether you or I, Madame, will be the most rejoiced." Madame de Bassompierre then had an interview with the Constable, who impressed upon her the importance of keeping the affair secret for the present, and proposed that, meanwhile, their respective men of business should meet and draw up the marriage-articles. This was accordingly done, Du Tillet-Girard acting for the one side, and Bauvillier, Procurator-General of the Cour des Monnaies, for the other; and a draft was submitted to the Constable and Madame de Bassompierre, and duly approved by them.

Shortly after this, the Constable, who, Bassompierre tells us, did not seem able to see enough of his prospective son-in-law or to think of anything but advancing his interests, proposed to give him at once 50,000 crowns out of his daughter's promised dowry, to enable him to purchase the post of Colonel-General of the Light Cavalry, whose occupant, the Comte d'Auvergne, was then in the Bastille and likely to remain there indefinitely, though his wife, the Constable's eldest daughter, had been allowed to receive the salary attached to it. Madame de Bassompierre, however, offered to find this sum, and suggested that, in lieu of the dowry of 100,000 crowns, Montmorency should give her son the estate of La Fère-en-Tardenois, near Château-Thierry, with remainder to his daughter and any children which might be born of the marriage. To this the Constable readily agreed, and, at the same time, told Bassompierre to make ready to come secretly to Chantilly, where he intended that the marriage should be celebrated so soon as possible, in the presence of none but members of his family and a few intimate friends. However, their common friend Roquelaure, who was making great efforts to reconcile the King to Montmorency, sought to dissuade the latter from this step, pointing out that, if he gave his daughter in marriage without previously informing his Majesty and obtaining his approval, he would offend him still more; while the King would certainly be seriously annoyed if so great a favourite of his as Bassompierre were to marry without consulting him.

Now, Henri IV had, some time before this, expressed a desire that Bassompierre should become one of his First Gentlemen of the Chamber, in place of the Duc de Bouillon, whose haughty airs displeased his Majesty, and had promised to give him 20,000 crowns to assist him to purchase this coveted office from the duke. He had also sent a gentleman of his Household to Bouillon to sound him upon the matter, and the latter had intimated his willingness to resign his post, in consideration of receiving the sum of 50,000 crowns, though it was believed that he would accept a smaller sum. Anyway, he was coming to the Court almost immediately, for the purpose of settling the matter. Roquelaure, who was much attached to Bassompierre, and had himself suggested to Henri IV that he should aid him to purchase the post, told the Constable that the announcement of his approaching marriage would be an excellent opportunity for Bassompierre to obtain from the King the 20,000 écus he had been promised, for which otherwise he might have to wait long, since, where money was concerned, the Béarnais was far more ready to promise than to perform.

Bassompierre was of the same opinion, and, since the Constable was not just then on visiting terms with his sovereign, it was decided that he and Roquelaure should wait upon Henri IV that evening, and that, after the former had acquainted the King with his matrimonial intentions, the latter should inform him that he came on behalf of the Constable to demand his Majesty's consent to his daughter's marriage. This they did, and the King, not only expressed his warm approval of the marriage, but declared that, in view of such a happy event, he felt that he could no longer remain on bad terms with the Constable, and sent Bassompierre to tell the old nobleman to come and see him on the morrow, when he might rest assured that he would be well received.

The following day, after receiving the Constable, whom he treated very graciously, Henri IV, at Bassompierre's request, paid a visit to the Duchesse d'Angoulême, and told her that he had come, not as the King, but as Bassompierre's personal friend, to see the young lady whom he was about to marry and to rejoice with her that so admirable a husband had been chosen for her. And he said all manner of kind things about Bassompierre, and spoke much of the affection which he entertained for him.

So far everything had gone smoothly, but now an obstacle arose.

That same evening the Duc de Bouillon arrived at Court. The King at once spoke to him about the proposed purchase of his post of First Gentleman of the Chamber by Bassompierre, and he answered that he had come to arrange the matter. Bassompierre, who was present, with several other nobles and gentlemen, exchanged a few words with the duke, as did the rest of the company; but he forgot to pay him a visit on the morrow, as he most certainly ought to have done, seeing that Bouillon was the Constable's nephew,[63] and "for all manner of other reasons." His unfortunate omission appears to have wounded the pride of this most haughty of nobles, who was already none too well disposed towards the projected marriage, since he believed that it was the work of the Duc d'Épernon, of whom, Bassompierre tells us, he had been all his life intensely jealous. He therefore resolved to do what he could to prevent it, and that evening, when he was talking to the King, who had just returned from the Queen's apartments, "where he had seen Mlle. de Montmorency, whom he and everyone had found perfect in beauty," he told him that he was greatly astonished that his Majesty should have given his consent to the marriage, since the Prince de Condé, the first Prince of the Blood,[64] was of an age to marry, and that, while it was inexpedient that he should marry a foreign princess, there were no young ladies of sufficiently high rank for him to wed in France, with the exception of Mlle. de Mayenne and Mlle. de Montmorency. Well, no one who had his sovereign's interests at heart could possibly counsel his union with Mlle. de Mayenne, since the remnant of the League was still too powerful for it to be prudent to strengthen it by a marriage between the daughter of its former chief and the first Prince of the Blood. On the other hand, there could be no such objection to his marriage with Mlle. de Montmorency, which would give him no new connections, since he was already related to the Montmorencys on his mother's side.[65] And he besought his Majesty very humbly to weigh the counsel which he had had the honour to give him and to reflect well upon it. This the King promised to do, and the interview ended.

It happened that the next day had been appointed by the Queen for the rehearsal of a grand ballet entitled *les Nymphes de Diane*, which some of the ladies of the Court, carefully chosen for their grace and beauty, were to dance during the approaching Carnival, Mlle. de Montmorency being amongst the number. The rehearsal took place in the great hall of the Louvre, from which all the masculine portion of the Court, with the exception of the King, the Grand Equerry, the Duc de Bellegarde, and Montespan, the Captain of the Guards, were rigorously excluded. The sight of Mlle. de Montmorency, who, according to Mézeray, had been cast for the part of Diana, in the costume of ancient Greece, proved altogether too much for the susceptible monarch, and inspired him with sentiments very different from those which that chaste goddess was supposed to implant in the hearts of men. In a word, he straightway fell madly in love with her. "*Monsieur le Grand*," writes Bassompierre, "faithful to his habit of praising to excess anything new, and particularly Mlle. de Montmorency, infused into the excitable mind of the King that love which afterwards caused him to commit so many extravagances."

The same evening the King was attacked by his old enemy, the gout, in so severe a form that he was obliged to keep his bed for a fortnight; and, most unfortunately as it was to prove for Bassompierre, the Constable also fell ill of the same malady, so that the wedding, which it had been decided was to take place almost immediately at Chantilly, had to be postponed until the old gentleman was well enough to leave Paris.

Meanwhile, Bassompierre had learned that the Duc de Bouillon was endeavouring to prevent the marriage. That nobleman, it appears, had told Roquelaure, who lost no time in informing his friend, that "M. de Bassompierre wanted to have his office of First Gentleman of the Chamber, and said nothing to him about it; that he wanted to marry his niece, and said not a word to him upon the matter; but that he would burn his books if he had either his office or his niece."

Having already represented to the King the advisability of reserving the hand of Mlle. de Montmorency for the Prince de Condé, the duke sought an interview with Condé himself and proposed the match to him, pointing out that this alliance would give him for relatives all the grandees of France, who would become the very humble servants of a personage of his exalted rank, and that, if he did not marry Mlle. de Montmorency, he would probably have to spend the remainder of his days in single blessedness, because the King would not allow him to wed a foreign princess, and there was no other young lady in France of suitable rank, with the exception of Mlle. de Mayenne, and the King would never consent to his marrying her. These arguments were not without effect, and eventually Condé authorised him to approach the Constable on his behalf.

The Constable, warned by Bassompierre of his nephew's machinations, told him not to allow them to disquiet him, since whatever match was proposed to him he should refuse it, adding that he knew M. de

Bouillon's ways far too well to be persuaded by him. He was as good as his word, and when Bouillon spoke to him on the subject, he met with a sharp rebuff, the Constable telling him that he had no need to seek a husband for his daughter, as he had found one, and that he already had the honour of being *Monsieur le Prince's* great-uncle, which was enough for him.

During the illness of Henri IV, Bellegarde, Gramont, and Bassompierre took it in turn to sit up with him at night, the long hours being passed in reading to him d'Urfé's sentimental romance *Astrée*, which was then enjoying a great vogue, or in conversation, for the King suffered so much pain that sometimes he was unable to sleep at all. It was the custom of the Princesses of the Blood to visit the sick-room daily; and the Duchesse d'Angoulême on more than one occasion brought her niece with her. One day, while the duchess was talking to one of his gentlemen, Henri IV, who did not disguise the pleasure which Mlle. de Montmorency's visits gave him, called the girl to his bedside, told her that he intended to love her as if she were his own daughter, and that she should be lodged in the Louvre when Bassompierre was on duty as First Gentleman of the Chamber. He then desired her to tell him frankly whether she were pleased with the marriage which had been arranged for her, because, if it were not to her liking, he would soon find means to break it, and marry her to his nephew, the Prince de Condé. The damsel replied demurely that, since it was her father's wish, she would esteem herself very happy with M. de Bassompierre. And, writes that gentleman, "he [the King] told me afterwards that these words made him resolve to break my marriage, from fear lest, if I married her, she should love me too much to be agreeable to him."

"M. de Gramont," continues Bassompierre, "sat up with the King that night, during which he slept but little, for love and the gout keep those whom they attack very much awake. At eight o'clock the following morning he sent a page of the Chamber to fetch me, and, when I came, inquired why I had not sat up with him the previous night. I answered that it was M. de Gramont's night, and that the next was mine. He told me that he had not closed an eye, and that he had often thought of me. Then he made me place myself on a hassock by his bedside (as was customary for those who entertained him when he was in bed), and went on to tell me that he had been thinking of me and of a marriage for me. I, who suspected nothing so little as what he was going to say, replied that, but for the Constable's attack of gout, my marriage would already have been concluded. 'No,' said he, 'I thought of marrying you to Mlle. d'Aumale,[66] and, in consideration of this marriage, of renewing the duchy of Aumale in your person.'[67] I asked him if he wished to give me two wives, upon which, after a deep sigh, he replied:

" 'Bassompierre, I wish to speak to you as a friend. I am not only in love, but madly and desperately in love, with Mlle. de Montmorency. If she marries you, and loves you, I shall hate you; if she loves me, you will hate me. It is better that this should not be the cause of interrupting our friendly intercourse, for I have much affection for you. I am resolved to marry her to my nephew the Prince de Condé,[68] and to retain her about the person of my wife. She will be the consolation and support of the old age upon which I am about to enter. I shall give my nephew, who is young and cares more for the chase than for ladies, a hundred thousand francs a year, wherewith to amuse himself, and I do not desire any other favour from her than her affection, without pretending to anything further.' "

Bassompierre's astonishment and dismay at this announcement can well be imagined. But he was above all things a courtier, and, aware that opposition to the infatuated monarch's will would be worse than futile, he resolved to make a virtue of necessity, and proceeded to assure the King of his joy at being afforded an opportunity of showing his devotion to his Majesty, by cheerfully resigning to him what he valued more than his own life.

But let us allow him to continue his narrative of this singular interview:—

"While he was telling me this, I was reflecting that, were I to reply that I refused to abandon my suit, it would be but a useless impertinence, because he was all-powerful; and, having decided to yield with a good grace, I said:—

" 'Sire, I have always ardently desired a thing which has happened to me when I was least anticipating it, which was the opportunity of showing your Majesty, by some signal proof, the extreme and ardent devotion which I cherish for you, and how truly I love you. Assuredly, I could not have met with one more suitable than this—of abandoning without pain and without regret an alliance so illustrious, and a lady so perfect and so passionately beloved by me, since by this resignation which I am making I please in some way your Majesty. Yes, Sire, I renounce it for ever, and trust that this new love may bring you as much joy as the loss of it would occasion me distress, were it not that the consideration of your Majesty prevents me feeling it.'

"Then the King embraced me and wept, assuring me that he would make my fortune as if I were one of his natural children, and that he loved me dearly, of which I should be assured, and that he would recompense my honesty and my friendship. The arrival of the princes and nobles made me rise, and, when the King recalled me and told me again that he intended me to marry his cousin d'Aumale, I answered that he had the power to prevent my marriage, but, as for marrying elsewhere, 'that is a thing which I will never do.' And with that our conversation terminated."

That day Bassompierre dined with the Duc d'Épernon, to whom he related what the King had said to him. D'Épernon was disposed to make light of the matter. "It is merely a caprice of the King," said he, "which will pass as quickly as it came. Do not be alarmed about it; for when *Monsieur le Prince* understands what the King's intentions are, he will not commit himself." Bassompierre tried to persuade himself that such was the case, and, on the duke's advice, said nothing to anyone else about the matter.

In the evening, as he and two or three other gentlemen were playing at dice with the King at a table placed beside his bed, the Duchesse d'Angoulême entered the room with her niece, whom she had brought, it appeared, in response to a message from his Majesty. The King immediately ceased playing and had a long and earnest conversation with the duchess on the further side of the bed. Then he called Mlle. de Montmorency and spoke to her also for a long time. It was evident that he informed her that Bassompierre had renounced his pretensions to her hand, and that he intended to bestow it upon the Prince de Condé, for when the conversation came to an end and the girl turned away, she glanced in her unfortunate suitor's direction and shrugged her pretty shoulders.

"This simple action," writes Bassompierre, "pierced me to the heart and affected me to such a degree that, feeling quite unequal to continuing the game, I simulated a bleeding of the nose and left the first cabinet and the second. On the stairs the *valets de chambre* brought me my cloak and hat. My money I had left to take care of itself, but Beringhen[69] gathered it up. At the bottom of the staircase I found M. d'Épernon's coach, and, entering it, I told the coachman to drive me to my lodging. I met my *valet de chambre* and went up with him to my room, where I instructed him to say that I was not at my lodging; and I remained there two days, tormented like one possessed, without sleeping, eating, or drinking. People believed that I had gone into the country, as I was in the habit of playing such pranks. At length, my valet, fearing that I should die or lose my reason, acquainted M. de Praslin, who was much attached to me, of the state in which I was, and he came to see me, in order to divert my mind."

M. de Praslin succeeded in persuading Bassompierre that there was still something to live for, and brought him that evening to the Louvre, where "everyone was at first astonished to see that in the space of two days he had become so thin, pale and changed as to be unrecognisable."

A few days later, the Prince de Condé announced his intention of marrying Mlle. de Montmorency. The prince, who was by no means an amiable young man, had taken a dislike to Bassompierre, whose pretensions to the young heiress's hand would, but for the intervention of the King, have most certainly been preferred to his own; and happening to meet his discomfited rival, said to him with obvious malice: "M. de Bassompierre, I beg you to come to my hôtel this afternoon and accompany me to Madame d'Angoulême's, whither I propose going to pay my respects to Mlle. de Montmorency."

"I made him a low bow," says Bassompierre, "but I did not go there."

It is probable that the loss of Mlle. de Montmorency's dowry and all the advantages which his alliance with so illustrious a family would have brought him distressed Bassompierre a good deal more than the loss of the young lady herself.

"It is true," says he, "that there was not at that time under Heaven a being more beautiful than Mlle. de Montmorency, nor one more graceful or perfect in every respect. She had made a deep impression upon my heart; but, as it was a love which was to be regulated by marriage, I did not feel my disappointment so much as I should otherwise have done."

Nor had he far to look for consolation, and "in order not to remain idle and to console myself for my loss, I sought diversion in making my peace with three ladies, with whom I had totally broken in expectation of marrying—one of them being Antragues."

If, however, like a true courtier, he had been ready to bow to the caprice of his sovereign, and to make the best of the situation, his vanity had been wounded far too deeply for him to allow himself "to be led in triumph"—as he expresses it—by Condé, when that prince's formal betrothal to Mlle. de Montmorency took place:

"I was that morning in the King's apartments, when *Monsieur le Prince*, after speaking to several others, approached me and said: 'M. de Bassompierre, I beg you to come this afternoon to my hôtel and accompany me to my betrothal at the Louvre.' The King, seeing him speak to me, inquired what he had said. 'He has asked of me, Sire,' I replied, 'a thing which I am unable to do.' 'And why?' said he. 'It is to accompany him to his betrothal. Is he not sufficiently great to go alone, and can he not be betrothed without me being present? I answer that, if there is no one to accompany him but myself, he will be very badly escorted.' The King said that it was his wish that I should go, to which I replied that I begged his Majesty not to command me, for go I would not; that his Majesty ought to be content that I had renounced my passion at the first expression of his desires and wishes, without desiring to force me to be led in triumph, after having ravished away my wife and all my happiness.' The King, who was the best of men, said to me: 'I see well, Bassompierre, that you are angry, but I assure you that you will fail not to go when you have reflected that he who has asked you is my nephew, first prince of my blood.' Upon which he left me and, taking MM. de Praslin and Termes aside, ordered them to go and dine with me and persuade me to go, since duty and decorum demanded it of me. And this I did, after a little remonstrance, but in such fashion that I did not set out until the princesses were conducting the *fiancée* to the Louvre, and were passing before my lodging, which obliged me to accompany her with the gentlemen who had dined with me. And then, from the gate of the Louvre, we returned to find *Monsieur le Prince*, whom we met as he was leaving the Pont-Neuf to come thither. The betrothal took place in the gallery of the Louvre, and the King maliciously leant upon my shoulder and kept me close to the affianced couple during the whole ceremony."

Two days afterwards, Bassompierre fell ill of tertian fever, and one morning, while he lay in bed, he received a visit from a Gascon gentleman named Noé, who had, or imagined he had, some grievance against him, and who had come to inquire whether he might have the honour of fighting a duel with him, so soon as his strength would permit. Bassompierre replied that he had enough and to spare whenever it was a question of giving another gentleman satisfaction, and, rising forthwith, ordered a horse to be saddled, dressed, and rode off to the "field of honour," which M. de Noé had appointed at Bicêtre. It was hardly the kind of day which even a hale man would have chosen to indulge in one of these little affairs, as there was a thick fog, and the ground was two feet deep in snow. But he scorned to turn back, and at length reached the rendezvous, where he found his adversary awaiting him.

It had been agreed that, as Bassompierre was in no condition to fight on foot, the combat should take place on horseback; but just as it was about to begin, two Gascons, named La Gaulas and Carbon, with a third man called Le Fay, all of whom were apparently friends of Noé, came galloping up, with the intention of preventing the duel, and called out to that fire-eating gentleman: "You can meet some other time."

Bassompierre, however, having put himself to so much inconvenience just to oblige M. de Noé, was highly indignant at the interruption, and, resolved not to return to Paris without striking at least one blow, shouted to his adversary to mount his horse, and rode towards him. Noé, who was as anxious to get at Bassompierre as the latter was to get at him, threw himself into the saddle, and though his friends endeavoured to intercept him, he contrived to evade them; and he and Bassompierre were about to cross swords when Carbon urged his horse against the flank of Noé's with such force that he bore both the animal and its rider to the ground. Noé was soon in the saddle again, but the fog was now so thick that it was quite impossible for one man to recognise another, with the consequence that Bassompierre came near to killing La Gaulas, whom he mistook for Noé. This mishap put an end to the combat, and Bassompierre, who was feeling so ill that he could scarcely sit his horse, made his way to Gentilly, where fortunately he found some friends of his, who assisted him back to Paris.

One might suppose that, after this adventure, our gentleman would have been content to remain in bed for a day or two; but, since there happened to be a grand ballet at the Arsenal that evening, at which all the Court was to be present, and which he was particularly anxious to attend, he must needs array himself in all his bravery and go out into the snow and fog again. The result of this imprudence was that he fell dangerously ill and was at one time at death's door; and the spring had come before he was about again.

CHAPTER XI

The body of a man who has been assassinated opposite Marie d'Entragues's house mistaken for that of Bassompierre—Bassompierre wins a wager of a thousand crowns from the King—Marriage of the Prince de Condé and Mlle. de Montmorency—Henri IV informs Bassompierre of his intention to send him on a secret mission to Henri II, Duke of Lorraine, to propose an alliance between that prince's elder daughter and the Dauphin—Departure of Bassompierre—He arrives at Nancy and challenges a gentleman to a duel, but the affair is arranged—His first audience of Duke Henri II—Irresolution of that prince, who desires to postpone his answer until he has consulted his advisers—Negotiations of Bassompierre with the Margrave of Baden-Durlach—He returns to Nancy—Continued hesitation of the Duke of Lorraine—Memoir of Bassompierre: his prediction of the advantages which Lorraine would derive from being incorporated with France abundantly justified by time—The Duke gives a qualified acceptance of Henri IV's propositions—Difficulty which Bassompierre experiences in inducing him to commit his reply to writing.

SOON after Bassompierre's recovery an incident occurred which brought him and his love-affairs rather more prominently before the public than he altogether cared about.

In the same street in which Madame d'Entragues and her younger daughter were then living, there lodged an Italian equerry of the Queen, named Camille Sanconi. This Sanconi was in love with his landlady, and finding her one fine night in the company of a rival admirer, he or his servants gave the latter several sword-thrusts, and then threw him into the street in his night-attire. The unfortunate man's wounds were mortal, and he had scarcely managed to drag himself along for fifty paces, when he fell down dead, directly beneath the window of the room occupied by Marie d'Entragues.

"Some passer-by," writes Bassompierre, "seeing the dead body, believed that it was I, on account of the spot where it lay, and came battering at the door of my lodging, saying that I had been assassinated at Madame d'Entragues's house, and then thrown out of the window, and that my servants ought to go to succour me promptly, if I were still alive, or to bring me back, if I were dead. As chance would have it, I had left my lodging, in disguise, to visit a lady, a circumstance which seemed to my servants to afford such strong confirmation of this story, that they thoughtlessly rushed off to where the body which had been taken for mine was lying, and the more impetuous ones having thrown themselves upon it, prevented the more prudent from examining it closely; and all bore it away to my lodging. On the way thither they were met by other servants of mine who carried torches, by the light of which they perceived that the corpse was that of another man, upon which they carried it to the house of a surgeon, where the officers of the law soon came to take possession of it. This affair occasioned a rather great scandal, and my servants to become the laughing-stock of the town."

Early in May, the Court went to Fontainebleau, and Bassompierre followed it shortly afterwards. On his arrival, he found that the engineers had just begun to let the water into the canal which had recently been constructed there; and the King offered to wager a thousand crowns that in two days it would be quite full. Bassompierre took the bet and won it easily, as it was more than a week before the canal was full.

On May 17, the Prince de Condé and Charlotte de Montmorency were married at Chantilly, the wedding having been delayed until then owing to the necessity of awaiting the Papal dispensation for the marriage of blood relations. Shortly afterwards, the bridal pair joined the Court at Fontainebleau, but the young princess only remained there a week, and then went with her mother-in-law to the Château of Valery, near Sens, one of Condé's country-houses.

One day, while the Court was at Fontainebleau, the King sent for Bassompierre and announced that he proposed to send him on a secret mission of the highest importance to his Majesty's brother-in-law, Henri II, Duke of Lorraine. By his first marriage with Catherine de Bourbon, the Duke had had no children; but by his second marriage with Margherita di Gonzaga, at which, it will be remembered, Bassompierre had assisted in the quality of Ambassador Extraordinary, he had two daughters, the Princesses Nicole and Claude; and the chief object of the mission which he was now to undertake was to propose, on behalf of the King, an alliance between the elder princess and the Dauphin, and to employ all his powers of persuasion to induce the Duke to consent to it. These would be needed, for the Lorrainers, like the people of all small countries, were always exceedingly suspicious about the designs of their powerful neighbours; and, though the prospect of one of his daughters sharing the throne of France might flatter the pride of Henri II, his subjects would probably regard the affair in a very different light. However, the advantages to be derived from such an alliance were so great that the King was determined to spare no expense to bring it about, and, with the idea that corruption might succeed where other means might fail, he authorised Bassompierre "to offer pensions up to the value of 12,000 crowns to any private persons whom he should judge capable of assisting him in this affair." Finally, "in order to encourage him to serve him the more zealously on this occasion, he offered to marry him to Mlle. de Chemillé[70] and to re-establish in his favour the estate of Beaupreau into a duchy and peerage." "But," continues Bassompierre, "I was so over head and ears in love just then, that I told him that, if he desired to do me any favour, I begged that it might not be by way of marriage, since by marriage he had done me so much injury."

Henri IV was most anxious that Bassompierre should set out at once for Lorraine, and this the latter promised to do. But, on reaching Paris, he reflected that the marriage of the Duc de Vendôme, the King's son by Gabrielle d'Estrées, which was to be a very splendid affair indeed, was to take place at Fontainebleau in ten days' time, and that it would be a thousand pities to miss it, even if he had to go there in disguise. He therefore decided to postpone his departure until after the wedding and to spend the interval in Paris, confining himself, we may suppose, to the company of such of his friends as might be trusted not to reveal his presence there to the King, who, of course, imagined him to be well on his way to

Lorraine. He soon had reason to regret having disobeyed his sovereign's commands, for, during the ten days he spent in the capital, his usual extraordinary good fortune at play for once entirely deserted him, and he contrived to lose no less a sum than 25,000 crowns, which seems a somewhat exorbitant price to pay for the pleasure of attending even the most magnificent of weddings.

Having witnessed the ceremony, so carefully disguised that his identity would not appear to have been even suspected, he returned to Paris and started the same day for Lorraine, from which, after his mission had been accomplished, he had orders to proceed to Germany, to sound the Margrave of Baden-Durlach as to the attitude he was likely to assume in the event of a war between France and the House of Austria, for which Henri IV had long been making preparations.

The King had not failed to impress upon his emissary the importance of not allowing it to be suspected that he had come to Lorraine with any diplomatic object in view, and, faithful to these instructions, Bassompierre, instead of going at once to Nancy, proceeded to Harouel, where, in honour of his arrival, his mother kept open house, and he was visited by a great many of the nobles of Lorraine. At Harouel he remained for some days and then proceeded to Nancy, "just as if he had no other business there than to pay his respects to the princes and pass the time."

On the morrow of his arrival, one of his servants came to complain to him that he had been chastised by a gentleman named Du Ludre, whom he had in some way offended. Bassompierre at once sent that gentleman a challenge to mortal combat, apparently forgetting, in his indignation at the affront which had been offered him in the person of his servant, that if Du Ludre happened to be an expert swordsman and were to kill or even wound him seriously, there would be an end to the mission with which the King had charged him. Happily, however, the gentleman in question turned out to be a pacifist, who, though ready enough to cane insolent lackeys, had no desire to cross swords with their masters; and, calling upon Bassompierre, he offered him so many excuses and apologies that, instead of fighting, the latter ended by embracing him.

This incident, trivial in itself, had, nevertheless, an important consequence, since no one was now likely to suspect a gentleman so ready to seek the "field of honour" of having come to Nancy on an important diplomatic mission.

However, in order to leave nothing to chance, he waited nearly a week, and then asked for an audience of the Duke, who was greatly surprised when he presented his credentials, and still more when he learned the object of his mission. Henri II was a timid and irresolute prince, always profoundly suspicious of the great Powers on either side of him, and his first question to Bassompierre was whether he were to understand that the troops which the King of France had lately assembled on the Lorraine frontier were intended to act against him, in the event of his being unable to comply with the wishes of his Majesty. Bassompierre hastened to assure him that they were assembled for a very different purpose, namely, to prevent the annexation of the duchy of Clèves by the House of Austria, a step which would be so detrimental to the interests of France that the King was determined not to permit it.[71] The prince, evidently much relieved, then said that the proposition which had just been made him was of such importance that he must have time to consider it and to consult his advisers, and inquired how long Bassompierre could give him. The latter replied that his Highness might take so long as he pleased, and said that he would go and visit some of his relatives in Germany and return for his answer in a fortnight's time. He begged him, however, to refrain from admitting anyone to his confidence upon whose discretion he could not implicitly rely, as it was of the utmost importance that the matter should be kept secret. The Duke said that he proposed to consult Bouvet, President of Lorraine, to which Bassompierre, who was on friendly terms with the President, readily agreed.

In the course of the day, Bouvet came to visit Bassompierre and told him that he had never seen the duke in such perplexity before. He himself seemed not unfavourably disposed to the French alliance, and Bassompierre seized the occasion to hint that, if he could persuade his Highness to consent to it, he would not find the Very Christian King ungrateful. But the President, who was an honest man, indignantly repudiated such a suggestion, observing that "he was a good servant of his master, who was able to make him and all his family wealthier than they had any desire to be." Bassompierre hastened to offer his apologies, and they parted very amicably.

Next day Bassompierre set out for Germany, accompanied by an old friend, the Count von Salm, whose sister was married to the Margrave of Baden-Durlach, to whom, as we have mentioned, he was also accredited. He was at pains, however, not to allow the count to suspect that his intended visit to the latter's brother-in-law was other than a friendly one.

With this object he travelled leisurely, stopping at Strasbourg, Saverne and other places, to visit people whom he knew. At Saverne, where he had such a painful experience five years earlier, he was again entertained by the canons of the Chapter, but on this occasion appears to have risen from table in a condition to which no one could take exception. He made up for this moderation, however, a day or two later, at a supper-party to which he was invited by the Count and Countess von Hanau, relatives of Salm, where all the company, including apparently the hostess, got "terribly drunk."

Having ascertained that the Margrave of Baden-Durlach was at one of his country-houses near Lichtentau, he and Salm proceeded thither and were very hospitably entertained. He refrained from saying anything about the object of his visit until the day of his departure, when, as the company rose from the dinner-table, he said, in a low voice, to the Margrave that he had a message of importance to deliver to him, at the same time giving him a significant look. The Margrave thereupon inquired, in a loud tone, whether M. de Bassompierre were proceeding direct to France after his return to Nancy, and, on being told that such was his intention, asked him to step into his cabinet, since, if he were disposed to do him a kindness, he had a little commission for him to execute there.

So soon as they were alone, Bassompierre showed the Margrave his credentials and informed him that he had been sent by his master to ascertain if he could reckon upon his support, in the event of a war between France and the House of Austria. The Margrave replied that the King could certainly count upon him, adding, however, that he by himself could do but little. If his Majesty would do him the honour of following his counsel, he would at once enter into communication with his relatives, the Duke of Würtemberg, the Margrave of Anspach, and the Landgraves of Hesse and Darmstadt, all of whom he would find very disposed to serve him.

Bassompierre now had an opportunity of showing that he had in him something of the stuff whereof successful diplomatists are made, and he did not fail to seize it. Although he had received no instructions whatever from Henri IV in regard to any of the princes mentioned, whose attitude the King had probably considered far too doubtful to justify him in disclosing to them his plans, he did not hesitate to assure the Margrave that he had been charged to visit them all, as well as the Elector Palatine, provided he could do so without exciting suspicion. Unfortunately, however, this condition could not be fulfilled, as the Duke of Würtemberg, whom he had intended to visit at Stuttgart, had gone to Anspach to attend the wedding of its ruler, and to follow him there would be too risky a proceeding; the Elector Palatine had gone to the Upper Palatinate to hunt, and he could find no pretext sufficiently plausible for approaching the Landgraves of Hesse and Darmstadt. He had, therefore, he continued, written to the King to explain the difficulties with which he had to contend and to ask for fresh instructions, and had received orders to confine himself to visiting the Margrave, and, if he found him as well-disposed towards the cause of his Majesty as the latter hoped and believed him to be, to request him to undertake the chief direction of his negotiations with the princes of Germany, and to advise him as to which of them would be most inclined to aid him, by what means they ought to be approached, what letters ought to be written to them, which of their Ministers it would be advisable to gain over to his interests, and so forth.

The Margrave, little suspecting that the young diplomatist before him was acting entirely on his own responsibility, and highly flattered by such a tribute to his importance, readily promised to undertake what was required of him, and proposed that his private secretary, Huart, who possessed his entire confidence, should accompany Bassompierre back to France, on the pretext of attending to some business affairs of his master there, and act as a means of communication between the Margrave and the French Government.

Very satisfied with the result of his visit to the Margrave, Bassompierre returned to Nancy, where he found despatches from Henri IV awaiting him, in which he was instructed to sound the Duke of Lorraine in regard to the Clèves affair. He had no difficulty in obtaining from the Duke an assurance that he would preserve the strictest neutrality; but on the question of the proposed marriage between his elder daughter and the Dauphin, the poor prince appeared quite unable to come to a decision. At length, after keeping Bassompierre waiting for nearly three weeks, he sent him, through the President Bouvet, a very flattering message, in which he informed him that the remembrance of the great services which his family had rendered the House of Lorraine, and the esteem which he entertained for M. de Bassompierre personally, had decided him that he could not do better than ask his advice as to the answer he should make to the King.

Bassompierre replied that it was impossible for him to act as the counsellor of a sovereign to whom he was accredited; but, at the same time, he would be very willing to submit to his Highness the different answers which it would be possible for him to make to his master's proposition, and leave him to choose between them.

He then proceeded to draft a long and elaborate memoir, which occupies many pages of his *Journal*, wherein, notwithstanding that he had just expressly declined the honour of advising the Duke of Lorraine, he proceeded to give that prince some very sound counsel indeed. Space forbids us to attempt even a summary of this document, but, in the light of subsequent events, one portion of it is of real interest.

Combating the objection that the marriage of the Duke's elder daughter to the Dauphin might lead, in the event of the extinction of the male line of the House of Lorraine, to the duchy being incorporated with France, Bassompierre, as a loyal son of Lorraine, boldly declared his opinion that such an occurrence would be wholly to the advantage of his compatriots, whose national customs and institutions would be respected by France as she had respected those of Brittany, while, like the Bretons, able and ambitious Lorrainers would find in the service of France opportunities for advancement which they could never hope to meet with in their own little country. If, on the contrary, the Duke were to reject the French alliance and give his daughter to a prince of the House of Austria, which, in a like eventuality, would regard Lorraine merely as a new province to be exploited for the benefit of the Spanish or Imperial Exchequer, or to some German or Italian sovereign of the second rank, whose descendants, brought up in a distant country, would have nothing in common with the people of Lorraine and would be powerless to protect them from the aggression of their powerful neighbours, their lot would be very different.

Time has abundantly justified what Bassompierre wrote, and it is not a little unusual to find so much sagacity and good sense concealed beneath so frivolous an exterior.

In conclusion, Bassompierre pointed out that there were four answers which the Duke of Lorraine might make to the proposal which he had received from Henri IV: (1) An absolute refusal, which the writer, of course, strongly deprecated; (2) A refusal based on the ground that the parties were not yet of marriageable age, accompanied by a promise not to entertain a proposal for his daughter's hand from any other quarter, so long as the King of France continued in the same mind; (3) An acceptance, accompanied by a stipulation that the affair should be kept secret, until he had had time to gain the approval of his subjects and of his relatives, which he would undertake to do as soon as possible; (4) An unqualified acceptance.

This memoir was duly submitted to the duke, and, the following day, the President Bouvet came to see Bassompierre, and told him that his unfortunate master was in a pitiable state of uncertainty, now inclining to one decision and now to another. "I think," said he, "that what you have proposed to his Highness has given him the means to decide, but you have more embarrassed him than ever; and I believe that, if you had given him one counsel, he would have followed it, because he wishes to follow all four, not knowing which to choose." He was, however, of opinion that he would eventually choose the third, and anyway he had promised to let Bassompierre have his answer in two days' time.

Bouvet added that whatever answer Bassompierre carried back to the King it would be a verbal one, since the proposal had been made verbally; besides which the duke entertained the strongest objection to committing his reply to writing.

Bassompierre then said that he had received express orders from the King that, in the event of the Duke giving an absolute or qualified acceptance, he was to hand him a written offer, signed by him on behalf of his Majesty; that the King had also instructed him to bring back a reply signed by the Duke; and that he could take no other message. "The affair is of importance," he continued, "subject to disavowal; I am young and a new Minister, and, apart from that, a vassal of his Highness. I might easily be suspected of having added or taken away, suppressed or invented, something in the affair. For which reasons I desire that his letter and his seal should speak, and that I should be the bearer only."

Bouvet replied that he feared that it would be very difficult indeed to persuade the timorous prince to consent to what was required of him. To which

Bassompierre rejoined that, if the Duke persisted in his refusal to give him a written answer, the only alternative was for him to send Bouvet, or some other duly accredited agent, to Henri IV to acquaint him with his decision.

The next morning the Duke invited Bassompierre to play tennis with him that afternoon, and, on his arrival at the palace, led him into the gallery of the tennis-court and told him that he was "fully resolved to conform to the wishes of the King and accept the honour which he wished to do him"; stipulating, however, that he should be allowed time to dispose his subjects favourably to the idea of such an alliance and to overcome the objections of his relatives. And he requested Bassompierre to beg the King very humbly on his behalf to observe the most absolute secrecy in regard to the affair, until the time should come to reveal it.

Bassompierre had, however, all the difficulty in the world to get this decision committed to writing and signed by the Duke. The poor prince appeared convinced that, if this were done, some unauthorised use would be made of the document. He feared his subjects; he feared his relatives; above all, he feared the ill-will of the Courts of Vienna and Madrid; and he protested that he would prefer to die rather than the affair should become known. At last, however, he yielded, and at the beginning of September Bassompierre returned to France with his answer duly signed and sealed.

CHAPTER XII

Return of Bassompierre to the French Court—Frenzied passion of Henri IV for the young Princesse de Condé—His extravagant conduct—Condé flies with his wife to Flanders—Grief and indignation of the King, who summons his most trusted counsellors to deliberate upon the affair—Sage advice of Sully, which, however, is not followed—The Archduke Albert refuses to surrender the fugitives—Condé retires to Milan and places himself under the protection of Spain—Failure of an attempt to abduct the princess—Henri IV and his Ministers threaten war if the lady is not given up—The "Great Design"—Bassompierre appointed Colonel of the Light Cavalry and a Counsellor of State—His account of the last days and assassination of Henri IV.

ON Bassompierre's return to Court, Henri IV expressed himself highly satisfied with the results of his mission and "gave him very great proofs of his good-will." Scarcely, however, had he concluded his account of his diplomatic activities than the King "requested an audience of *him*, in order to tell him of his passion for *Madame la Princesse* and of the unhappy life that he was leading separated from her." "And assuredly," adds Bassompierre, "this love of his was a frenzied one, which could not be contained within the bounds of decorum."

We must here explain that this interesting little affair had not been developing at all in accordance with his Majesty's anticipations. Condé had accepted with becoming gratitude the handsome pension which the King had bestowed upon him and appeared far more interested in his wife's dowry than in her person; while the fair Charlotte, on her side, scarcely troubled to conceal her indifference to a husband who was shy, awkward, and close-fisted, and lacking in all those qualities calculated to appeal to the imagination of a young girl. Indeed, there can be no doubt that she preferred the company of the King, despite his grey hairs and his wrinkled visage, and she appears to have given the amorous monarch no little encouragement, though perhaps innocently enough.

But Condé, with all his faults, was an honourable man, and when he clearly understood the odious part which his royal "uncle" intended should be his; when he saw the King, usually so painfully neglectful of his person, powdered and scented and bedecked like the youngest gallant of his Court; when he learned that he was bombarding his wife with passionate sonnets, obligingly composed for him by Malherbe and other facile rhymesters; when he heard that the princess had stepped one night on to the balcony of her apartments and there unbound her hair and allowed it to fall about her shoulders to gratify a whim of her elderly admirer, who stood beneath "transported with admiration"; when, in short, he found that the King's infatuation was the talk of Court and town, he began, as his Majesty expressed it, "to play the devil." And, after several angry scenes, in which Henri IV entirely lost his temper, and all sense of dignity and decorum along with it, and Condé appears to have forgotten the respect which he owed to his sovereign in his resentment against the man who wished to dishonour him, the prince carried off his wife to the Château of Muret, in Picardy, not far from the Flemish frontier.

The lovelorn King followed his inamorata, and, dressed as one of his own huntsmen, and with a patch over his eye, stood by the roadside to see her pass; and, in the same disguise, penetrated into a house where she was dining, and when she appeared at a window, kissed one hand to her, while he pressed the other to his heart.

A few days later, Condé received a letter from the King, written in a strain half-coaxing, half-menacing, summoning him to Court, to be present at the approaching accouchement of the Queen. Etiquette required that the first Prince of the Blood should be in attendance on these auspicious occasions, and it was impossible for him to refuse. But he came alone.

Henri IV was furious, and his anger rendered him so insupportable to those about him, that Marie de' Medici herself begged Condé to send for his wife, promising to keep strict watch over her. Such was the King's wrath that he could not trust himself to interview his kinsman personally, but sent for his secretary, Virey, and bade him tell his master that, if he declined to bow to his will, or attempted any violence against his wife, he would give him cause to rue it. He added that, if he had been still only King of Navarre, he would have challenged the prince to a duel.

After receiving this message, Condé decided to feign submission, and accordingly begged his Majesty's permission to fetch his wife. This request, as we may suppose, was readily granted, and on November 25—the day on which the ill-starred Henrietta Maria was born—he set out for Picardy.

On the evening of the 29th, while Henri IV was playing cards with the Comte de Soissons—*Monsieur le Comte*, as he was styled—Bassompierre, Guise, d'Épernon, and Créquy in his private cabinet, word was brought him that a messenger had arrived from Picardy, with intelligence that *Monsieur le Prince* had early that morning left Muret in a coach with his wife, accompanied by his equerry the Baron de Rochefort, Virey, and two of the princess's ladies. Condé had given out that he was bound on a hunting-expedition; but the messenger—an archer of the Guard named Laperrière—had ascertained from his father, who was in the prince's service, that the party had taken the road to Flanders.

"I sat nearest to the King," writes Bassompierre, "and he whispered in my ear: 'Bassompierre, my friend, I am lost. That man is taking his wife into a wood. I know not if it is to kill her or to take her out of France. Take care of my money and continue the game, while I go to learn further particulars.' Then he went with d'Elbène[72] into the Queen's apartments.

"After the King had gone, *Monsieur le Comte* begged me to tell him what had happened. I replied that his nephew and niece had fled. MM. de Guise, d'Épernon and de Créquy asked me the same question, and I gave them the same answer. Upon this they all withdrew from the game, and I, taking the opportunity of returning to the King the money which he had left on the table, entered the room where he was.

"Never did I see a man so distressed or so frantic. The Marquis de Cœuvres, the Comte de Cramail, d'Elbène, and Loménie were with him, and to each suggestion that one of them made he forthwith assented: such as to send the Captain of the Watch after *Monsieur le Prince* with his archers; to send Balagny[73] to Bouchain to try and catch him; to send Vaubecourt [governor of the county of Beaulieu-en-Argonne], who was then in Paris, to the frontier of Verdun to prevent his passage in that direction; and other ridiculous things."

Meanwhile, the distracted monarch had sent to summon his most trusted counsellors, as though for an affair of State of the first importance; and, as each one arrived, he hurried up to him to inform him of what had occurred and to ask his advice.

"The Chancellor[74] was the first to arrive, and the King, having acquainted him with the matter, demanded of him what ought to be done. He answered gravely that this prince was taking the wrong road; that it was to be regretted that he had not been better counselled; and that he ought to have moderated his impetuosity. 'That is not what I am asking you, *Monsieur le Chancelier*,' cried the King angrily. 'What I desire is your advice.' The Chancellor then said that severe proclamations ought to be issued against him and against all who should follow him or render him aid, whether by money or counsels.

"As he said this, M. de Villeroy entered, and the King impatiently demanded his advice. He shrugged his shoulders and appeared to be very astonished at the news; and then said that letters ought to be written to all the King's Ambassadors at foreign Courts to acquaint them with *Monsieur le Prince's* departure without permission of the King and contrary to his orders, and to instruct them to take such steps with the princes to whom they were accredited as would cause them to refuse him an asylum in their dominions, or to send him back to his Majesty."

The Président Jeannin had arrived at the same time as Villeroy, and the King demanded his advice also. The President was for strong measures, and said without hesitation that his Majesty ought immediately to send one of the captains of his Guards after *Monsieur le Prince* to endeavour to bring him back. If that could not be effected, then an envoy ought to be despatched to the sovereign in whose dominions he had taken refuge to demand that he should be surrendered, and, in case that was refused, to threaten war. In his opinion, there could be little doubt that he had gone to Flanders, to demand an asylum of the

Archduke Albert, Sovereign of the Netherlands; but, since Condé was not personally acquainted with that prince, he did not suppose that the latter was privy to his flight, and, unless he were to receive express orders from Madrid to protect him, he would in all probability prefer to send him back, or, at any rate, order him to leave Flanders, rather than risk trouble with France.

"The King," continues Bassompierre, "approved of this expedient, but he did not wish to decide until he had heard what M. de Sully had to say about the matter. The latter entered some time after the others, in a rough,

HENRI IV., KING OF FRANCE.

abrupt manner. The King went up to him and said: 'M. de Sully, *Monsieur le Prince* has fled and has taken his wife with him.' 'Sire,' answered he, 'I am not surprised; and, if you had followed the counsel I gave you a fortnight since, when he left to go to Muret, you would have put him in the Bastille, and I should have kept him safe for you.' 'Well,' said the King, 'the thing is done; it is useless to say more about it; but tell me what I ought to do now.' 'By God, Sire! I know not,' he replied; 'but let me go back to the Arsenal, where I shall sup and sleep, and in the night I shall think of some good counsel, which I will bring you in the morning.' 'No,' said the King, 'I wish you to give it me at once.' 'I must think,' said he, and with that he turned to the window which looked into the courtyard, and for a little time drummed upon it with his fingers. Then he came back to the King, who said: 'Well, have you thought of something?' 'Yes, Sire,' said he. 'And what ought I to do?' 'Nothing, Sire.' 'What! Nothing?' cried the King. 'Yes, nothing,' said M. de Sully. 'If you do nothing at all, and show that you do not care about him, people will despise him; no one will assist him, not even the friends and servants whom he has here; and in three months, urged by necessity,[75] and by the little account that one takes of him, you will get him back on whatever conditions you please. But if you show that you are uneasy and are anxious to have him back, they will regard him as a personage of importance; he will be assisted with money by those without the realm; and divers persons, thinking to do you a despite, will protect him, although they would have left him alone if you had not troubled about him.' "

The King, however, was in no mood to follow this sage counsel, and preferred the strong measures proposed by Jeannin. He accordingly launched the Captain of the Watch in pursuit of the fugitives, and, when that officer returned empty-handed, sent Praslin to Brussels, where, as was generally expected, Condé had taken refuge, to demand his surrender from the Archduke Albert. The Archduke felt that he could not without shame deliver up a prince who came to seek an asylum against an all-powerful monarch who was endeavouring to dishonour his wife. On the other hand, he did not wish to offend Henri IV and afford him a pretext, which he might be only too ready to seize, for breaking the peace. He therefore tendered his good offices and made every effort to bring about an accommodation. But the King insisted on Condé's unconditional submission and immediate return; while the prince demanded a place of surety on the frontier, with a convenient back-door, to enable him, at the first alarm, to leave the kingdom again.

The attitude assumed by Henri IV was so threatening, that Condé, judging it to be unsafe to remain in Flanders, confided his wife to the care of the Archduchess and took refuge at Milan, the governor of which, the Count de Fuentes, was a declared enemy of Henri IV and France. He had already appealed to Spain for protection; and Philip III instructed his Ambassador at the French Court, Don Inigo de Cardenas, to inform Henri IV that "he had taken the

Prince de Condé under his protection, with the object of acting as a mediator in the matter and contributing by all means in his power to the repose and happiness of the Very Christian King." The remainder of the despatch, however, shows that Philip was actuated by very different motives.

Condé's departure from Brussels did not leave the Archduke in a less difficult position. It was not the prince, but the princess, whose return Henri IV most eagerly desired. He endeavoured to have her carried off, but the attempt failed.[76] He obliged the Constable to demand that she should be sent back to the paternal roof. The Archduke replied that he could not do so, except by her husband's desire.

The King was the more exasperated by the resistance of the Archduke, as he had reason to believe that his ridiculous passion was returned. The princess, this child of sixteen, who had no affection for her husband and resented the inconvenience to which he had subjected her in order to save her honour, weary of her exile, far from her relatives and the Court of France, did not refuse the letters and presents of the King. Her entourage and Madame de Berny, the wife of the French Ambassador at Brussels, chanted continually the praises of her crowned adorer. She received verses in which Malherbe depicted in touching terms the grief of the great Alcandre. But Henri IV himself, in a letter to one of his agents, is not less pathetic:—

"I am writing to my beautiful angel: I am so worn out by these pangs that I am nothing but skin and bone. Everything disgusts me. I avoid company, and if, to observe the usage of society, I allow myself to be drawn into some assemblies, my wretchedness is complete."

The princess, in her turn, appealed to "his heart," and besought him, as "her knight," to effect her deliverance.

For his "pangs" Henri IV regarded the Archduke and the Spaniards as responsible. Already on December 9, 1609, he had caused the Pope to be informed that "if the Spaniards contemplated employing the person of *Monsieur le Prince* to stir up trouble in his realm, he had the means and the courage to resent it, and to avenge the injuries and the offences which they might be able to do him." The conduct of the Archduke was irreproachable; he had merely safeguarded his own dignity, and it was certainly not his fault that Condé was not reconciled to the King. But Philip III and his Government, although they had neither foreseen nor aided the prince's flight, were now asking themselves what advantage they might derive from it. In the event of war with France, the first Prince of the Blood would be a valuable ally, and it is not improbable that a most imprudent manifesto which Condé issued at Milan, wherein, after detailing his grievances against Henri IV, he claimed to be the rightful heir to the throne of France, on the ground that the King's first marriage had not been truly annulled, was inspired by Spain, with the idea of still further widening the breach between him and his sovereign.

Henri IV and his Ministers, finding persuasion of no avail with the Court of Brussels, had recourse to threats, representing that, unless the fair Charlotte were surrendered, war would follow. "Peace and war depend on whether the princess is or is not given up," said Jeannin to Pecquius, the Archduke's Ambassador in Paris; and the King himself reminded him that Troy fell because Priam would not surrender Helen.

The gravity of the situation was enhanced by the warlike preparations which were going on all over France for the execution of the "Great Design": the scheme of liberating Europe from the domination of the House of Austria and of giving France her rightful place in the world which Henri IV had cherished ever since his accession to the throne. It was, however, believed by many that these formidable preparations had no other object that the forcible recovery of the Princesse de Condé, and Malherbe wrote:—

"Deux beaux yeaux sont l'empire
Pour que je soupire."

The question of how far the course of events was influenced by Henri IV's infatuation for the Princesse de Condé has been much discussed. The probability is that the affair did little more than determine the King to hasten by a few weeks the war so long resolved upon, and that this was due rather to his irritation against the Spaniards for their support of Condé than to the refusal of the Court of Brussels to surrender the princess. Henri had not scrupled to use the large forces assembled for quite a different purpose as a bugbear to frighten the Archduke. But when the latter refused to purchase security by a compliance inconsistent with his honour, it was not on Brussels that the French armies prepared to march. On the contrary, a few days before his death, the King in the most friendly terms requested the Archduke's permission to lead his troops across his territory to the assistance of his German allies, a permission granted by the Archduke, notwithstanding the opposition of the Spanish party in his Council.

By the end of April France was ready to strike. Châlons, Mezières and Metz were the chief rendezvous. The King hoped to have 30,000 men on foot, to join them on May 15, and to march at their head into the duchies. A second army under Lesdiguières was to enter Piedmont, where it would effect a junction with the forces of the Duke of Savoy, and then proceed to invade the Milanese. A third army was to observe the Pyrenees. Maurice of Nassau, with 30,000 Dutch, was to join Henri IV in Clèves.

Never had Bassompierre stood higher in the royal favour than on the eve of the outbreak of war. Henri, anxious to make amends to him for the loss of Charlotte de Montmorency and her dowry, and to recompense him for the zeal and ability which he had shown in his mission to Lorraine and Germany in the previous year, overwhelmed him with benefits. He appointed him, quite unsolicited, Colonel of the Light Cavalry, made him a Counsellor of State, gave him 50 guards, and a pension of 4,000 crowns, and again proposed to marry him to the heiress of Beaupréau and revive in her favour the duchy of that name. "But," says Bassompierre ingenuously, "I was then in the high follies of my youth, in love in so many quarters, and well received in most, that I had not the leisure to think of my advancement."

But the sun which shone upon him with such warmth and splendour was now about to be clouded for ever. The tragic end of the first Bourbon King has been so often told that we have no intention of narrating it; but there are circumstances recorded by Bassompierre which are not to be found in the memoirs and correspondence of his contemporaries, and which afford a curious insight into the state of Henri IV's mind just before his assassination:—

"We now entered that unhappy month of May, fatal to France, by the loss sustained therein of our good King.

"I shall relate many things touching the presentiment which the King had before his death, and which gave warning of that event. A little while before, he said to me: 'I know not how it is, Bassompierre, but I cannot persuade myself that I am going into Germany; neither does my heart tell me that you are going into Italy.' Several times he said to me, and to others also: 'I believe that I shall die soon.' And on the first day of May he returned from the Tuileries by way of the grand gallery, leaning upon M.

de Guise on one side, and upon me on the other (for he always leaned on someone), and, on leaving us to enter the Queen's cabinet, said: 'Don't go away; I am going to tell my wife to dress, that she may not keep me waiting for dinner.' For he usually dined with her. While we waited, leaning on the iron balustrade overlooking the courtyard of the Louvre, the maypole which had been planted in the middle of the courtyard fell down, without being disturbed by the wind or for any apparent cause, and tumbled in the direction of the little staircase leading to the King's chamber. Upon which I said to M. de Guise: 'I would have given a great deal rather than this should have happened. It is a very bad omen. May God preserve the King, who is the May of the Louvre!' 'How can you be so foolish as to think seriously of such a thing?' he replied. 'In Italy and Germany,' I rejoined, 'they would take much more account of such an omen than we do here. May God preserve the King and all belonging to him!'

"The King, who had but stepped into the Queen's cabinet and out again, here came up very softly to listen to us, for he imagined that we spoke of some woman; and, hearing all that I said, broke in upon our talk, saying: 'You are fools to amuse yourselves with such prognostications. For the last thirty years all the astrologers and charlatans who pretend to be wise have predicted to me every year that I was fated to die; and in that year wherein I shall actually die, all the omens which have occurred in the course of it will be remarked and thought a great deal of, while nothing will be said of those which happened in preceding years.'

"The Queen had a peculiar and ardent desire to be crowned before the King's departure for Germany. The King did not wish it, both by reason of the expense and because he did not like these grand festivals. Yet, since he was the kindest husband in the world, he consented and delayed his departure until she should make her entry into Paris.[77] He commanded me to stay also, which I did because of his desire, and also because the Princesse de Conti had asked me to be her cavalier at the ceremony of the *Sacre* and the entry.[78]

"The Court went on May 12 to stay at Saint-Denis, to be in readiness for the morrow, the day of the Queen's *Sacre*, which was celebrated with the greatest possible magnificence. The King, on this occasion, was extraordinarily gay.[79] In the evening everyone returned to Paris.

"The following morning, the 14th of the said month, M. de Guise passed by my lodging and took me to go and meet the King, who had gone to hear Mass at the Feuillants. On the way we were told that he was returning by the Tuileries, upon which we went to intercept him and found him talking to M. de Villeroy. He left him, and taking M. de Guise and myself, one on either side of him, said: 'I come from the Feuillants, where I saw the chapel which Bassompierre is having built there, and on the door he has had placed this inscription: *Quid retribuam. Domino pro omnibus que retribuit mihi?* And I said that, since he was German, he should have put: *Calicem salutaris accipiam.*' M. de Guise laughed heartily and said to him: 'You are, to my mind, one of the most agreeable men in the world, and our destiny created us for one another. For, had you been a man of middling station, I would have had you in my service, cost what it might; but, since God has made you a great king, it could not be otherwise than that I must belong to you.' The King embraced him, and me also, and said: 'You don't know me now; but I shall die one of these days; and, when you have lost me, you will know my worth and the difference there is between me and other men.' Upon this I said to him: '*Mon Dieu*, Sire, why do you never cease afflicting us by saying that you will soon die? These are not good words to utter; you will live, if it please God, long and happy years. There is no felicity in the world equal to yours; you are but in the flower of your age, in perfect strength and health of body, full of honours beyond any other mortal, in the tranquil enjoyment of the most flourishing country in the world; loved and adored by your subjects; possessed of property, of money, of beautiful residences, a beautiful wife, beautiful mistresses and beautiful children, who are growing up. What more could you have or desire to have?' Then he sighed and said: 'My friend, all this I must leave.' "

Before parting from the King, Bassompierre informed him that he had received a complaint from the captains of the Light Cavalry, of which he had recently been appointed Colonel, that their companies were insufficiently armed and that they were unable to obtain the weapons which they required, and begged his Majesty to give orders that these should be supplied to them. Henri IV told him to come to him that afternoon at the Arsenal, where he proposed to go to visit Sully, who was ill, and he would direct the Minister to let him have the arms he wanted. And, upon Bassompierre observing that he would very willingly give Sully at the same time the money which they were worth, to enable him to replace them, he laughingly replied by quoting two verses from a well-known song, which ran:

> "Que je n'offre à personne,
> Mais à vous je les donne."

Bassompierre thanked his Majesty, kissed his hand and withdrew, little imagining that he was never to see him alive again.

"After dinner," he says, "I went to visit Descures[80] in the Place-Royale, to inquire about the routes which the different companies [of the Light Horse] were to follow; and then I proceeded to the Arsenal, to await the King, as he had told me to do. But alas! it was in vain, for, shortly afterwards, came people crying out that the King had been wounded, and that he was being carried back to the Louvre. I ran like a madman, seized the first horse I could find, and rode full gallop towards the Louvre. Opposite the Hôtel de Longueville I met M. de Blérencourt,[81] who was returning from the Louvre, and he whispered to me: 'He is dead!' I ran up to the barriers which the French Guards and the Swiss had occupied, with lowered pikes, and *Monsieur le Grand* and I passed under the barriers and ran to the King's cabinet, where we saw him stretched on his bed, and M. de Vic,[82]

Counsellor of State, seated on the same bed. He had put his cross of the Order to the King's lips, and was bidding him think of God. Melon, his chief physician, was in the *ruelle*, and some surgeons, who wanted to dress his wounds; but he was already gone.... Then the chief physician cried: 'Ah! it is all over; he has gone!' *Monsieur le Grand*, on arriving, went down on his knees in the *ruelle* of the bed, and took one of the King's hands and kissed it. As for myself, I had thrown myself at his feet, which I embraced, weeping bitterly...."

CHAPTER XIII

Incidents at the Court and in Paris after the assassination of Henri IV—Meeting between Bassompierre and Sully—Marie de' Medici declared Regent—Her difficult position—Return of Condé—Greed and arrogance of the grandees—Quarrel between the Comte de Soissons and the Duc de Guise—Grievance of *Monsieur le Comte* against Bassompierre—He persuades Madame d'Entragues to endeavour to compel Bassompierre to marry her daughter, Marie—Proceedings instituted against that gentleman—Announcement of the "Spanish marriages"—Magnificent fêtes in the Place-Royale—Intrigues at the Court—The Princes and Concini in power—Assassination of the Baron de Luz by the Chevalier de Guise—Marie de' Medici and the Princes—Conversation of the Regent with Bassompierre—Bassompierre reconciles the Guises with the Queen-Mother—The Chevalier de Guise kills the son of the Baron de Luz in a duel—The Princes, on the advice of Concini, return from Court.

ON that fatal day, when the knife of Ravaillac changed the destinies of France and of Europe, Louis XIII, the successor of the murdered King, was not yet nine years old. The fear of troubles within the realm and of complications without exacted the immediate institution of a regency, and Villeroy and the Chancellor, Brulart de Sillery, exhorted Marie de' Medici, who was lying upon her bed prostrated with grief, to act "as man and as King."

The great nobles, out of pity or the desire to assert their own importance, were zealous in the Queen's cause; and some who had scarcely been on bowing terms with each other for years were seen to embrace and vow to die together sword in hand if the necessity should arise.

D'Épernon, Colonel-General of the French infantry, caused the approaches to the Louvre and the Pont-Neuf to be occupied by the French Guards; Guise, with part of a force of some 300 horse which he and Bassompierre had mustered, proceeded to the Hôtel de Ville to obtain from the Corporation a formal recognition of the new King and Regent; while Bassompierre, with the remainder, paraded the streets "to appease tumults and seditions." Sully alone showed himself undecided, feeble and timorous. At the news of the King's assassination, ill though he was, he had mounted his horse and set out for the Louvre, accompanied by some forty of his guards and attendants. Near the Place Saint-Jean he met Bassompierre and his cavalcade, the sight of whom appears to have filled him with misgivings.

"He began," writes Bassompierre, "to say to us in lachrymose tones: 'Gentlemen, if the service which you have vowed to the King, whom, to our great misfortune, we have just lost, is also imprinted in your souls, as it ought to be in those of all good Frenchmen, swear now at once to preserve the same fidelity to the King his son and successor, and that you will employ your blood and your life to avenge his death.'

" 'Monsieur,' I replied, 'it is we who are making others take this oath, and we have no need of anyone to exhort us to do a thing to which we are already so committed.'

"I know not whether my answer surprised him, or whether he repented of having come so far from his fortress; but he turned back forthwith, and went to shut himself up in the Bastille, sending at the same time to seize all the bread that could be found in the markets and the bakers' shops. He sent orders also to M. de Rohan, his son-in-law, to face about with 6,000 Swiss who were in Champagne, and of whom he was Colonel General, and to march straight on Paris.... MM. de Praslin and de Créquy went to invite him to present himself before the King, like all the other grandees; but he did not come until the morrow, when M. de Guise brought him with difficulty, after which he countermanded his orders to his son-in-law and the Swiss, who had already advanced a day's march towards Paris."

Of the Princes of the Blood who might have been able to aspire to the regency, one, Condé, was a voluntary exile in the dominions of the King of Spain; the other, the Comte de Soissons, had left Paris in high dudgeon before the coronation of the Queen, because Henri IV had refused to permit *Madame la Comtesse* to wear on her ceremonial mantle a row of *fleurs de lys* more than the wife of his legitimated son the Duc de Vendôme. As for the Prince de Conti, he was deaf, afflicted with an impediment in his speech, and almost imbecile. Outside the Princes of the Blood, and in the absence of the States-General, there was only one power recognised by all—the Parlement of Paris. And to this body Marie de' Medici at once addressed herself.

In her name, the Procurator-General demanded that "now and without adjourning, the Parliament should provide, as it had been accustomed to do, for the regency and the government of the realm." The Parlement was too convinced of its right and too flattered by the part it was asked to play to hesitate. But, as a matter of form, it was proceeding to deliberate upon the matter, when d'Épernon, in his doublet, with his drawn sword in his hand, swaggered into the chamber, and, having begged the assembly to excuse his discourtesy, invited it to hasten. As he left, Guise entered in the same costume, took his seat and protested his devotion to the Crown. The First President, Achille de Harlay, solemnly ordered the duke's words to be recorded; and the Court unanimously declared the Queen Mother Regent, "to have the administration of the affairs of the realm during the minority of the said lord her son, together with all power and authority." It was quick work: Henri IV had not been dead two hours.

It was much, without doubt, to have settled so expeditiously the future government of France. But what a task for a woman, for a foreigner, for one, too, who bore a name little calculated to reassure the bulk of the nation, which remembered only too well the troubles in which the rule of another Medici had involved it, to be called upon to exercise supreme power in circumstances so difficult! Without, a war on the point of breaking out; within, princes affecting an entire independence and even negotiating with the foreigner; a turbulent nobility whom even the strong hand of Henri IV had not always been able to keep in check; the Protestant party entrenched in the West and South of France, with its own organisation, its privileges, its places of surety; finally, the governors of the different provinces, possessed of the most extensive powers and strong enough to renounce practically all obedience to the Crown. Marie de' Medici has often been reproached with weakness, and weak in many ways she certainly was; but it would have required the energy and the resolution of an Elizabeth or a Catherine the Great to have steered the ship of State uninjured through the shoals and quicksands which beset its course.

The Regent retained the Ministers of the late King, Villeroy, Jeannin, Sillery, and Sully, and, to calm the apprehensions of the Protestants, lost no time in confirming the Edict of Nantes. But the war so long meditated against the House of Austria was promptly abandoned, though a small army under Le Châtre and Rohan was sent to co-operate with Maurice of Nassau in recovering Juliers, which was handed over to the Electors of Brandenburg and Neuburg, on their undertaking not to interfere with the exercise of the Catholic religion in that duchy.

It was a wise decision, since there were embarrassments enough within half-a-mile of the Louvre. The Princes of the Blood had returned; Soissons, three days after the death of Henri IV; Condé, in the middle of July. The former complained that the regency had been settled in his absence, and demanded the post of Lieutenant-General of the Kingdom. To appease him, Marie de' Medici gave him the post of governor of Normandy and a *gratification* of 200,000 crowns. Condé, to the Regent's great relief, was apparently well-disposed towards the new government, and, to confirm him in his peaceable intentions, she purchased for 400,000 crowns the Hôtel de Gondi, in the Faubourg Saint-Germain, and presented it to him, together with furniture to the value of 40,000 crowns; confirmed him in all his offices and appointments; increased his pension to 200,000 crowns, and gave him a large sum to pay his debts. The Regent hoped, by setting a price upon them, to keep within bounds all the ambitions of the grandees; it was her system of government. She paid Guise's debts, and authorised him to marry the immensely wealthy widow of the Duc de Montpensier, a union to which, for political reasons, Henri IV would never have consented; she promised to pay the debts of the Duc de Nevers; she accorded to all the governors the right of appointing their successors.

"The grandees did not weary of receiving, and said to one another: 'The time of kings has passed, and that of great nobles and princes has come; we must take every advantage of it.' " Their arrogance and ostentation knew no bounds. They seldom left their houses unless accompanied by numerous and brilliant escorts. Fifteen hundred cavaliers went to meet Condé on the day of his arrival in Paris; the Duc de Guise had a suite of five or six hundred horse. The young King remained almost alone in the Louvre, and Marie de' Medici was obliged to reconstitute the two hundred gentlemen halberdiers, disbanded by Henri IV, from motives of economy.

Happily for the Crown, the grandees were divided, and such parties as did exist were merely associations of a few covetous nobles, animated by no common motive except that of filling their pockets. The Guises, flattered and lavishly paid, boasted of their loyalty to the Regent. Bouillon was at enmity with Sully, like himself a chief of the Protestants. The Prince de Conti had for some years been on bad terms with his brother, the Comte de Soissons, and at the beginning of 1611 their antipathy to one another found vent in a violent quarrel, in which Guise, whose sister, it will be remembered, Conti had married, found himself involved, and which threatened for a moment to develop into a sort of civil war.

"It happened," writes Bassompierre, "that, three days after these nuptials [the marriage of Guise to the Duchesse de Montpensier], the Prince de Conti quarrelled with the Comte de Soissons, his brother, because their coaches had collided in passing one another, and their coachmen had fought. M. de Guise, whom the Queen had desired, that same evening, to go to M. de Conti to compose this quarrel, set out the following morning from the Hôtel de Montpensier, where he had passed the night, to go to the Abbey of Saint-Germain, where the Prince de Conti was lodging, and was accompanied by twenty-five or thirty horse. He happened to pass the Hôtel de Soissons, which was on his way, and this gave offence to *Monsieur le Comte*, who summoned his friends and told them that M. de Guise had come to defy him. Thereupon M. de Guise's friends flocked to the Hôtel de Guise in such numbers that there were more than a thousand gentlemen assembled there. *Monsieur le Comte* sent to beg *Monsieur le Prince* to come to him, and together they proceeded to the Louvre to demand of the Queen that she should call M. de Guise to account for his insolence. Nevertheless, *Monsieur le Prince* was playing in this affair the part of the friendly arbitrator, and said that he should take neither side, and only desired to reconcile the parties and to prevent disorder.

"This tumult lasted all that day and the following one, upon which the Queen, apprehending graver disturbances, gave directions that the chains should be made ready to be put up at the first order, and that, in every quarter, the citizens should be prepared to take up arms on the instant that the command to do so was sent them.

"However, all the day following was employed in seeking means to accommodate the affair, each of the Princes having a captain of the Gardes du Corps near his person to protect him. In the evening, *Monsieur le Prince* sent to ask M. de Guise to send him one of his confidential friends; and M. de Guise, having taken counsel with the princes and nobles who supported him, as to whom they should choose to act as envoy, finally, on their advice, asked me to go."

Bassompierre then goes on to relate at great length his interview with Condé, to whom he pointed out that Guise could have had no intention of "defying" *Monsieur le Comte*, since, if such had been his object, he would have sallied forth with a much more imposing retinue than a mere score or so of attendants, and would have passed before the front entrance of the Hôtel de Soissons, whereas he had only passed the corner of the house. The prince appears to have been greatly impressed by this argument, and, after Bassompierre had been backwards and forwards several times between Condé's house and the Hôtel de Guise, the momentous affair was satisfactorily settled.

But it did not end here, so far as he himself was concerned. For "*Monsieur le Comte* was mortally offended with those who had assisted M. de Guise in his quarrel, and particularly with me, who had formerly professed to be his servant; and, to revenge himself upon me, he determined that I should see Antragues no more."

The prince accordingly sought an interview with Madame d'Entragues, whom he reproached with allowing her family to be dishonoured by the notorious intimacy between Bassompierre and her younger daughter, adding that, as he was distantly related to the d'Entragues, he felt that his own honour was concerned in the matter.

Now, it had happened that, in the previous August, Marie d'Entragues had given birth to a son, of whom Bassompierre did not deny the paternity; indeed, on the lady informing him that she proposed to present him with a pledge of her affection, he had, following the famous example of Henri IV with her elder sister, given his inamorata a letter containing a promise of marriage in the event of her bearing him a son. But this letter was written merely for the purpose of appeasing the wrath of Madame d'Entragues, who was threatening to turn her erring daughter out of the house. For Bassompierre had not the least intention of regularising his connection with this too-celebrated beauty, of whom, if he were the most favoured, he was far from being the only successful admirer; indeed, to do so would mean the loss of a considerable fortune, since his mother had threatened to disinherit him if he married the lady.[83] He had, therefore, at the same time, demanded and obtained from Marie d'Entragues a letter which purported to be an answer to his own, in which she expressly disclaimed any intention of taking advantage of his offer. This, in the opinion of "three famous advocates" whom he had taken the precaution to consult, effectually discharged him from his obligation.

Well, Bassompierre's letter was in the possession of Madame d'Entragues, who, however, of course, knew nothing of the one which her daughter had given that gentleman; and when the Comte de Soissons reproached her with her indifference to Mlle. Marie's indiscretions, she informed him that she was not so careless a mother as he appeared to imagine, and could easily prove it. The prince pressed her to do so, upon which she triumphantly showed him the promise of marriage.

"*Monsieur le Comte*," says Bassompierre, "very pleased to have found an opportunity of injuring me, assured her of his protection and begged her to follow his counsel in this affair, in which he promised to secure for her a favourable result. This foolish woman, to satisfy the malignity of *Monsieur le Comte*, placed herself entirely in his hands, and he counselled her to press me to execute this promise, and, in case of my refusal, to cause me to be summoned before the diocesan court."

Madame d'Entragues did not fail to follow this advice and, on meeting with a flat refusal from Bassompierre, promptly instituted proceedings against him.

"I soon recognised the hand which had cast this stone at me, and *Monsieur le Comte* boasted publicly that he was in a position to ruin me in fortune or honour. I assembled a council of my advocates to learn how I was to comport myself in this situation.

They were unanimously of opinion that, in strict justice, I had nothing to fear, but that *Monsieur le Comte* was a redoubtable enemy, and advised me to drag the affair out until a favourable time arrived."

Bassompierre endeavoured to persuade the Regent to intervene in his behalf, but, though Marie de' Medici, with whom he was a favourite, since he was one of the few nobles whose loyalty to the Crown admitted of no question, was very sympathetic and promised him every assistance in her power, her position was far too precarious just then to admit of her offending a Prince of the Blood. All he could do, therefore, was to act upon the advice of the legal luminaries whom he had consulted; and, on various pretexts, he succeeded in deferring his appearance before the diocesan court for some months, at the end of which he appealed to the jurisdiction of the Archbishop of Sens, who was the metropolitan of the Bishop of Paris. This insured him a further respite, and, before the case came on for trial, he appealed to the Parlement of Paris, and was beginning to plume himself on his astuteness, when the Comte de Soissons interposed and got the affair transferred to the Parlement of Rouen, to the great consternation of Bassompierre, who knew that Soissons would not scruple to use all his influence as Governor of Normandy to prejudice that body against him.

The annoyance and expense which this affair was occasioning him, and for which, it must be admitted, he is hardly entitled to much sympathy, did not prevent Bassompierre from continuing his life of pleasure, and he took a prominent part in the splendid fêtes in honour of the double betrothal of Louis XIII to Anne of Austria, and of the Infant Philip, afterwards Philip IV of Spain, to Élisabeth of France, eldest daughter of Henri IV. For Marie de' Medici had completely reversed the foreign policy of her husband, and Spanish influence was once more in the ascendant at the Court of France.

These fêtes, originally fixed to begin on March 25, 1612, the day on which the formal announcement of the approaching marriage was made at the Louvre, in the presence of the Spanish Ambassador and the officers of the Crown of France, had been postponed until April 5, owing to the death of the Queen's brother, Vincenzo I, Duke of Mantua. Their principal feature was a carousal in the Place-Royale on a scale of unprecedented magnificence, in which Bassompierre appeared as one of the challengers.

"At three o'clock in the afternoon, the Queens, princesses and ladies took their places on the stands which had been prepared for them, besides which there were all round the Place-Royale, rising from the pavement to the level of the first floor of the houses, other stands holding 200,000 people. Then the cannon placed on the bastion fired a salvo, after which the thousand Musketeers who lined the barriers fired another, a very beautiful one. This finished, M. de Praslin, marshal of the camp of the challengers, emerged from the Palace of Felicity, from which came the sound of all kinds of musical instruments. He was splendidly mounted and attired, and was followed by twelve lackeys habited in black velvet bordered with gold lace. He came, on our behalf, to demand from the Constable (who occupied a private stand with the Maréchal de Bouillon, de la Châtre, de Brissac, and de Souvré) the camp which he had promised us. The Constable and the marshal descended from their stand and advanced to that of the King and Queen; and the Constable said: 'Madame, the challengers demand the camp which I have promised them by your Majesty's order.' The Queen answered: 'Monsieur, grant it them.' Upon which the Constable said to M. de Praslin: 'Take it; the King and the Queen accord it you.' Then he returned to us, and the great door of the palace, which was opposite that of the Minims, was flung open, and we entered the camp, preceded by all our retinue, war-chariots, giants,[84] and other things so beautiful that it is impossible to describe them in writing; and I shall only say that nearly five hundred persons and two hundred horses took part in our entry alone, all habited and caparisoned in crimson velvet and white cloth-of-silver, and our costumes were so richly embroidered that nothing could exceed them in magnificence. Our entry cost the five challengers 50,000 écus.[85] The troupe of the Prince de Conti entered after ours, followed by that of M. de Vendôme, who danced a very beautiful ballet on horseback.[86]Then came M. de Montmorency, who entered alone, and the Comte d'Ayen[87] and the Baron d'Ucelles,[88] under the names of Amadis and Galaor.

"We [the challengers] kept the lists against all these opponents, and when the night drew near, the fête was concluded by a new salvo of cannon, followed by that of the thousand Musketeers; and, when darkness fell, there was the most beautiful display of fireworks over the Château of Felicity that was ever seen in France.

"On the morrow, at two o'clock in the afternoon, we returned to the camp in the same order as on the first day, together with the troupe of M. de Longueville,[89] who made his entry alone,[90] of the Nymphs,[91] of the Knights of Felicity, that of d'Effiat and Arnaut,[92] and, the last, that of the twelve Roman emperors,[93] all of whom ran against us, and the fête was terminated by the same salvoes and another display of fireworks."

On the following day, "because all the innumerable people of Paris had not been able to witness this fête," the various troupes passed in procession through the town, that of the challengers, resplendent in their crimson velvet and cloth-of-silver, bringing up the rear.

The fête concluded with a grand tilting-match in the Place-Royale, the prize being a ring of great value given by *Madame Royale*, the future Queen of Spain, which was won by the Marquis de Rouillac, a nephew of d'Épernon.

At night there was another display of fireworks, a salvo fired by two hundred cannon, a bonfire at the Hôtel de Ville, and an illumination of Paris with "lanterns made of coloured paper, in such great profusion in every window that the whole town seemed on fire."

In November the old Connétable de Montmorency took leave of the Regent and the young King and retired from Court to spend his last days in retirement on his estates of Languedoc. "We escorted him to Moret," writes Bassompierre, "where he feasted us, and afterwards bade farewell to his chief friends, with so many tears that we thought that he would die in that place. He was a good and noble lord, who loved me as though I were his own son; I am under a great obligation to honour his memory."

The fêtes in honour of the betrothal of the young King and his eldest sister were but a brief interlude in the sordid struggle for place and power between the ambitious and greedy princes and nobles which had begun before Henri IV was in his grave. Marie de' Medici distributed honours and emoluments with a lavish hand, increased the pensions of the grandees and made serious inroads into the millions accumulated in the coffers of the Bastille by the prudent Sully, who in January, 1611, had resigned his post of Comptroller of the Finances, on finding that he was no longer listened to, and that he could not maintain his position "without offending the Princes." But the appetites she strove to satisfy were insatiable, and the more she gave, the more she was expected to give.

After the death of the Comte de Soissons, the most restless of the Bourbons, at the beginning of November, 1612, the Regent forsook Guise and d'Épernon, who had until then enjoyed a large measure of her favour, and, at the instigation of Concini, that singular Italian adventurer who governed her through his wife Leonora Galigaï, the Queen's *dame d'atours* and confidante, and for whom she had purchased the marquisate of Ancre, allied herself with Condé and his friends Bouillon, Nevers, and Mayenne.[1]

"At this time," says Bassompierre, "the aspect of the Court entirely changed; for a close alliance was formed by *Monsieur le Prince*, MM. de Nevers, Mayenne,[94] Bouillon, and the Marquis d'Ancre; and the Queen threw herself entirely on that side. The Ministers were discredited, and no longer had any power, and everything was done according to the desire of these five persons... MM. de Guise, d'Épernon, de Joinville, and the Grand Equerry were very much out of favour."

In December, Guise and d'Épernon sent for Bellegarde, who was in his government of Burgundy, to come to Court, "in order to strengthen their tottering party"; but on his way thither he was met by a messenger from Marie de' Medici, with orders forbidding him to come to Paris, and he was obliged to return to his government.

The chief agent in Concini's intrigues was the old Baron de Luz, who had formerly been an adherent of the Guises, but had been persuaded by the favourite to enter the service of the Queen, or rather his own. The Guises avenged themselves for what they were pleased to call his treason in characteristic fashion. About midday on January 5, 1613, the Chevalier de Guise, the youngest of the brothers, stopped Luz as he was driving in his coach along the Rue Saint-Honoré, challenged him to fight him there and then, and, without giving the old man time to draw his sword, ran him through the body and killed him.

This affair created an immense sensation.

"The Queen was extremely exasperated," writes Bassompierre. "I went, just at this time, to the Louvre, and found her in tears, and that she had sent for the Princes and Ministers to hold a council on the affair. She said to me as soon as I entered: 'You see, Bassompierre, how I am treated, and what a brave action it was to kill an old man without defence and without warning. But these are the tricks of the family. It is a repetition of the Saint-Paul affair.'[95] There was a great murmur against this action, and everyone was scandalised to learn that a great crowd of the nobility had assembled at the Hôtel de Guise, and that M. de Guise was coming accompanied by a large retinue to speak to the Queen. Upon this, the Queen was advised to send M. de Châteauvieux to see the said Sieur de Guise and forbid him to approach the Queen until she sent for him, and to command, in her Majesty's name, all those who had gone to his hôtel to disperse."

Châteauvieux returned and reported that Guise had advised his adherents to obey the Queen's command, but that three or four of them, including the Comte de la Rochefoucauld, Master of the Wardrobe to the King, had shown marked reluctance to do so. It was thereupon resolved that La Rochefoucauld should be exiled to his estates, and that the Parlement should be directed to hold an inquiry into the affair and bring the Chevalier de Guise to trial.

The Parlement, however, seemed in no hurry to do what was required of it, for the Guises still retained much of their traditional popularity with all classes of the Parisians, and before many days had passed, an event occurred which obliged the Queen to abandon all idea of punishing the assassin.

For some little time Marie de' Medici had been chafing beneath the domination of the Princes, who set altogether too high a price upon their loyalty. Condé, indeed, appeared to consider that, now that his brother Soissons was dead, he was entitled to receive double wages; and one fine morning Nevers, Mayenne, and Concini waited upon the Queen and demanded, on his behalf, the government of Château-Trompette, the citadel of Bordeaux, pointing out that, since *Monsieur le Prince* was Governor of Guienne, it was only fitting that the citadel of the chief town in his government should be entrusted to him also. Now, Marie had heard the late King say that if, in the time of Henri III, this fortress had been in his hands, he would have made himself Duke of Guienne, and she knew that its governor had always been one in whose loyalty to the Crown the most implicit confidence could be placed. She determined to resist and to be reconciled with the Guises and the Ministers.

Dissembling her indignation, she informed Nevers and his friends that she would think the matter over, upon which they pressed her for a speedy answer, saying that *Monsieur le Prince* was impatient to know her decision. This she promised, and then, changing the subject, informed them that she had just discovered a love-affair in which Bassompierre was engaged and which she knew he was very anxious should not be discovered. What ought she to do? "You should tell him about it, Madame," answered Nevers. Upon which she turned to Bassompierre, and, beckoning him to follow her, moved to one of the windows.

Here, standing with her back to the room, so that none might see her face, she told him that the matter upon which she desired to speak to him was very different from the one she had mentioned. She then asked him if Guise had spoken to him about the exile of his friend La Rochefoucauld. Bassompierre answered that the duke had done so, and begged him to make intercession with the Queen for his recall, and that he had added that, if he were not successful, he must persuade Condé to use his influence, and make La Rochefoucauld's recall the price of his reconciliation with that prince and his friends. The Queen was silent for a moment, while "four or five tears welled up in her eyes." Then, recovering herself, she said: "These wicked men have made me leave those princes [the Guises] and despise them, and have made me also abandon and neglect the Ministers; and then, seeing me deprived of support, they wish to usurp my authority and ruin me. See how they have come to demand insolently for *Monsieur le Prince* the Château-Trompette, and they will not remain content with that. But, if I am able, I will surely prevent them obtaining it."

"Madame," answered Bassompierre, "do not distress yourself; when you will, I am sure that these princes and Ministers will be at your disposal; at least, we must find some way to bring them back."

The Regent then told him to come to her when she had finished dinner, and that, meanwhile, she would think of some way to effect this.

At the hour when her Majesty usually rose from table Bassompierre returned, and followed her into her cabinet, pretending that he had some favour to ask of her.

"As I entered, she said to me, 'I have eaten nothing but fish, to such a degree is my stomach weakened and turned. If this continues long, I believe that I shall lose my reason. In one word, Bassompierre, you must endeavour to bring M. de Guise back to me. Offer him a hundred thousand crowns in cash, which I will arrange to give him.'

'Madame,' I replied, 'I will serve you well and faithfully.' 'Offer him,' said she, 'the post of lieutenant-governor of Provence for his brother, the Chevalier.[96] Offer his sister the reversion of the Abbey of Saint-Germain,[97] and assure him that La Rochefoucauld shall be recalled. In short, provided that I can withdraw him from this cabal and that I am assured of his support, I give you *carte blanche*.' "

Bassompierre assured her that, as she had empowered him to make the Guises such a generous bid for their support, he had no fear that he should return to her "without having completed the purchase." And, in point of fact, on the following day he returned triumphant, pluming himself not a little on having succeeded without the necessity of promising the post of lieutenant-governor of Provence to the Chevalier de Guise, "having endeavoured," said he to Marie de' Medici, "to act like those prudent valets who bring back at the bottom of the purse a part of the money which their masters give them to settle their bills."

The Queen, however, was so pleased at the success of his negotiations that she, nevertheless, determined to offer the post in question to the chevalier, in order that the reconciliation between her and his family might be the more complete, and directed Bassompierre to inform the Princesse de Conti of her gracious intentions.

A few days after these humiliating concessions to the rapacity of the House of Guise, the Chevalier killed the son of the Baron de Luz in a duel at Charenton, though it is only fair to the former to observe that the other had called him out, and that the combat had been conducted in strict accordance with the rules governing these "affairs of honour."

On this occasion, Bassompierre, experienced courtier though he was, is unable to conceal his astonishment:—

"And here I saw a strange instance of the changes of the Court; that when the Chevalier de Guise killed the father, the Queen commanded the Parlement to take cognizance of it, to institute proceedings against him and to try him; but when, in less than a week afterwards, he killed the son, so soon as he returned from the combat, the Queen sent to visit and to inquire how his wounds were."

Guise being thus reconciled with the Queen, no difficulty was experienced in persuading d'Épernon to follow his example, after which Bassompierre addressed himself to the Ministers, who, tired of being mere cyphers, were only too ready to forgive and forget; and, in an interview between Marie de' Medici and Jeannin at the Luxembourg, an understanding was arrived at.

The Princes and Concini were outwitted. In any case, the latter pretended to be. Hearing the Queen give directions that seats were to be reserved for d'Épernon, and his friend Zamet also, at a play which was to be performed in her apartments, he remarked to Bassompierre in that strange mixture of Italian and bad French which he affected in moments of excitement: *"Par Dio, Mousu, je me ride moy della chose deste monde. La roine a soin d'un siège pour Zamet, et n'en a point pour M. du Maine [Mayenne]; fiez-vous à l'amore dei principi."*

He advised Condé and his friends to accept the situation and withdraw from Court, predicting that the Regent would soon grow weary of the exigencies of the Guises, and promising to watch over their common interests. And this the Princes decided to do.

CHAPTER XIV

The affair of Montferrato—Intrigues of Concini with Charles Emmanuel of Savoy—Arrest of Concini's agent Maignan—Bassompierre warns the Italian favourite of his danger and advises him to throw himself on the clemency of the Queen-Mother—Concini follows his advice, and is pardoned and shielded by Marie de' Medici, while his agent is executed—Bassompierre goes to Rouen, where the d'Entragues' action against him is to be heard—The Regent recommends his cause to the judges—The d'Entragues object to the constitution of the court, and the case is adjourned—Duplicity of Concini—He intrigues to ruin Bassompierre with the Queen-Mother—Semi-disgrace of Bassompierre—He is reconciled with Marie de' Medici—He is appointed Colonel-General of the Swiss—The Princes surprise Mézières—Peace of Saint-Menehould—Bassompierre accompanies Louis XIII and the Queen-Mother to the West.

IN the spring trouble arose with Charles Emmanuel of Savoy, who was disputing the claim of Ferdinando di Gonzaga to the throne of Mantua, and had invaded Montferrato. The French Government, judging it dangerous to allow the Duke of Savoy, an uncertain friend and a possible enemy, to get possession of Casale, one of the strongest places in Italy, announced its intention of supporting Ferdinando, and Concini, on the pretext that it was desirable that France should present a united front in the event of hostilities breaking out, persuaded Marie de' Medici to summon the Princes to Court. Spain, however, in order to prevent French intervention in Italy, hastened to send orders to the Governor of the Milanese to compel Charles Emmanuel to abandon his prey, and that prince, recognising the impossibility of resistance, evacuated Montferrato.

It was believed, for a moment, that the affair of Montferrato would bring about the ruin of the Concini. The Duke of Savoy, to assure the neutrality of France, had succeeded in corrupting the Italian favourites of the Queen and several other prominent persons, and had kept up an active correspondence with Concini, the agent employed by the latter being a priest named Maignan. An intercepted letter caused the arrest of this man, who, in the admissions that were extorted from him, comprised Concini, his creature the advocate Dolet, and the Marquis de Cœuvres.

On the day Maignan was arrested, Bassompierre, who was with the Court at Fontainebleau, happened to sup with Zamet, where he met Loménie, the Secretary of State. It had been Loménie's duty to be present at the first examination of the prisoner, and he told Bassompierre of the serious admissions that the man had made and the names he had mentioned. He added that he was to be examined further on the following morning, when doubtless still more interesting revelations would be forthcoming.

Now, Bassompierre was on intimate terms with Concini, for, though he would appear to have despised him heartily, the Italian's influence with the Queen made him a valuable friend, besides which he was in the habit of winning large sums from him at play. He accordingly decided to warn him of the danger which threatened him, and went that same night to his house, but was told that he was in bed and could not be disturbed. He had therefore to wait until the following day, when he stopped him as he was about to enter the chapel to hear the Whit-Sunday sermon, invited him to take a turn in the cloisters, and, so soon as they were alone, inquired bluntly: "Who is Maignay?"

"At these words, utterly astounded, he said to me: '*Pourquoi, Mousou, de Masnay? Que sol dir Magnat? Che cosa e Maignat?*' 'You are deceiving me,' I rejoined. 'You know him better than I do, and you pretend to know nothing about him.' '*Per Dio, Mousou!*' he exclaimed, 'I do not know Magnat; I do not understand what you mean; I do not know who he is.' 'Monsieur, Monsieur,' said I, 'I speak to you as your servant and friend, not as a judge or a commissioner. Maignan was arrested yesterday and examined forthwith, again in the evening, and this morning for the third time. He was arrested in the act of posting a packet of letters, which speaks of many things and mentions persons by their names. If you are aware of it already, I have only lost time in telling you; but, if you are not, I think that, as your servant, I gain much by warning you of it, in order that you may extricate M. Dolet from this affair, in which people will endeavour to involve him.' He said to me, very confused: 'I, Mousou, I do not think that M. Dolet knows who Magnat is. It is no concern of mine.' 'Monsieur,' I replied, 'I shall only take in this affair the part which you wish to give me in order to serve you; that is my sole object and intention.' He thanked me and left me abruptly."

That afternoon the Queen went for a drive in the park, and Bassompierre accompanied her, occupying a seat in the Grand Equerry's coach. As they were driving by the side of the canal, one of Concini's gentlemen came galloping up and informed Bassompierre that his master wished to see him immediately, and he sprang from his horse and offered it him. "Ah! he wants to win my money," remarked Bassompierre, as he prepared to mount; and when the

Queen inquired where he was going, he replied that he was going to play cards with the Marquis d'Ancre. He rode back to the palace, and found Concini awaiting him in the Cour Ovale.

"He led me," he writes, "into the Queen's gallery, shut the door upon us and walked to the end of it without speaking a word. At length, drawing himself up, he said: 'M. *Bassompier*, my good friend, I am undone; my enemies have gained the ascendancy over the Queen's mind, in order to ruin me.' Thereupon he began to utter strange blasphemies and wept bitterly. I allowed him to rave a little, and then said to him: 'Monsieur, it is no time to swear and to weep when affairs press; you must open your heart and reveal the wound to the friend to whom you desire to entrust its cure. I imagine that you sent for me to tell me of the evil, not to bewail it.' 'The Ministers have reduced me to extremities,' he replied; 'they desire to ruin me and M. Dolet likewise.' "

Bassompierre told him that he had many remedies against the enmity of the Ministers, of which the most efficacious were the good graces of the Queen, which he would undoubtedly possess when he returned to his duty and abandoned all practices which were not agreeable to her Majesty. He had also, he continued, his innocence to plead for him, and, if that were not as complete as might be desired, it would be advisable to interview, and come to some arrangement with, the commissioners who had the examination of Maignan in hand (for he did not doubt that that was his present difficulty), and "to have recourse to the kindness and compassion of the Queen, who would receive him, he felt assured, with open arms, provided he spoke to her with sincerity of heart and an entire resignation to her will."

Concini followed his advice and proceeded to throw himself upon the clemency of the Queen, "in whom he found all kinds of gentleness and kindness." Marie de' Medici, indeed, was unable to dispense with either the husband or the wife. "The one," observes Henri Martin, "dominated her by habit and by the superiority of an active and restless mind over a mind indolent and dull; the other probably by a warmer feeling."[98] She accepted all their excuses; the two commissioners by whom Maignan was tried suppressed everything which might compromise Concini and his accomplices;[99] and while the unfortunate agent was condemned to death and broken on the wheel, the man who had employed him—this precious rascal who had sought to betray the country upon which he had so long been battening—was raised to new honours. The Queen only exacted from him that he should be reconciled with the Ministers and definitely abandon the party of the Princes. And, as the price of his obedience, she gave him, in the following November, the bâton of a marshal of France![100]

Towards the end of May, Bassompierre went to Rouen to make arrangements for the conduct of his case in the action which the d'Entragues were bringing against him, and which, on various pretexts, he had succeeded in delaying until now. He found, to his disgust, however, that the plaintiff had stolen a march upon him, for, though he applied in turn to all the chief advocates of the Parlement of Rouen, not one of them would undertake the case, the reason being that they had all been consulted by the other side, which, of course, rendered it impossible for them to hold a brief for the defence.

He returned to Paris and complained bitterly to Marie de' Medici of the sharp practice of which the d'Entragues had been guilty. Upon which she said: "*Mon Dieu!* Bassompierre, the Procurator of the Estates of Nantes, who is so eloquent, is eligible to plead your cause, for he was formerly an advocate of Rouen. He is here now." And she sent for him and ordered him to undertake the case, which he did very ably.

At the beginning of June, Bassompierre returned to Rouen, "accompanied or followed by over 200 gentlemen," and accompanied, too, by the good wishes of the Queen, who did not confine her good offices to providing him with an advocate. She wrote to the Maréchal de Fervacques, the Governor of Rouen, "to assist him in all that he might demand of him"; she ordered her own company of light horse, which was in garrison at Évreux, to come to meet him and escort him to Rouen; she sent one of her gentlemen with letters recommending his cause to all the presidents and counsellors of the Parlement; and every other day she despatched a courier to ascertain how the case was proceeding.

All Normandy appears to have flocked to Rouen to attend this *cause célèbre*, and seldom had the old city been so gay.

"Numbers of ladies who were there, many strangers who came, and the band of nobles whom I had brought, made all the time I spent at Rouen, where

I remained a month, pass like the Carnival, with continual banquets, balls and assemblies."

There can be little doubt that, in this breach of promise, popular sympathy was with the faithless gallant rather than the injured lady. But Bassompierre's friends were denied the pleasure of applauding his victory at the Palais de Justice, for, after the case had been in progress for some time, the d'Entragues, seeing that the day was likely to go against them, succeeded in obtaining an adjournment for six months, to enable the King's Council to decide whether the Court was impartially constituted; their contention being that some of the judges were related to the defendant on his mother's side.

Not long after Bassompierre's return to Court, the post of lieutenant-governor of Poitou became vacant, and, as he was anxious to secure this office for his brother-in-law Saint-Luc, he solicited Concini's good offices with the Queen, thinking, not unnaturally, that, after the service he had lately rendered him, the Italian would be only too ready to oblige him. Concini assured both Bassompierre and his brother-in-law that he would do everything in his power for them, and appeared delighted at the opportunity of discharging the obligation under which the former had placed him. Nevertheless, the post was given to Condé's favourite, the Baron de Rochefort, at Concini's earnest entreaty, the Queen told Bassompierre, as she herself preferred Saint-Luc.

So much for the favourite's sense of gratitude! But this was not all:

"The Marquis d'Ancre told me the same day that he was in despair that the Queen had given that place to Rochefort, and he begged me to assure M. de Saint-Luc that he had done all he could in his favour, but that the authority of *Monsieur le Prince* had prevailed. I, who knew what the Queen had told me, replied that, when he wanted me to impose upon some indifferent third person, I was very much at his service; but that, when it was a question of deceiving my own brother-in-law, I begged him to employ someone else, since we were too nearly related."

After this, Saint-Luc, as was only to be expected, was somewhat cold in his manner towards Concini, whereupon that worthy, persuaded that this was due to his brother-in-law's influence, determined to be avenged and, says Bassompierre, "assisted by his wife, began to instill into the Queen's mind the belief that I boasted of the kindness which she showed me, and that people were talking about it; and they told her that I was estranging her servants from her, and that I was turning everyone against her."

This intrigue was only too successful, and on Bassompierre's return to Fontainebleau from a visit to Paris, whither he had been sent by the Queen to settle a quarrel between the Duc de Montbazon and the Maréchal de Brissac, he perceived a change in her Majesty's manner towards him, which seemed rather less cordial than usual. This continued for some days and was succeeded by an "entire coldness."[101]

Bassompierre remained in this state of semi-disgrace for about a month, when, his patience exhausted, he "resolved to quit the Court of France and the service of the King and Queen, although several beautiful ladies performed the impossible to turn him from this design." He accordingly asked Sauveterre, the usher of the Queen's cabinet, to obtain for him an audience of her Majesty, in order that he might request her permission to retire from the Court and France, which Sauveterre did. But, no sooner was he in the royal presence than, to his astonishment and relief, the Queen, addressing him with all her old cordiality, said: "Bassompierre, I am going to-morrow to Paris. [She was going to visit her younger son, the

Duc d'Orléans—*Monsieur*, as he was called—who was lying ill at the Louvre.] I have ordered everyone to remain here; but, as for you, if you wish to come, I give you permission. But do not go by the same road, so that they may not say that I have made an exception to the general rule."

Next day, Bassompierre went to Paris, accompanied by Créquy and Saint-Luc, and awaited the Queen's arrival at the Louvre, where he assisted her to alight from her coach and escorted her to *Monsieur's* apartments. "The others then retired," says he, "and I remained until she was in her cabinet, when I had full leisure to speak to her, and left her with the assurance that she did not believe any of the things which they had tried to persuade her to believe against me, concerning which I gave her a complete explanation."

Early in 1614, Condé and the other Princes who, in the preceding year, had been allied with Concini, indignant at the latter's reconciliation with the Ministers and jealous of his increasing favour, retired from Court and assumed so threatening an attitude that Marie de' Medici decided to raise an army without delay, and applied to the Swiss Cantons for a levy of 6,000 men, who were intended to form the nucleus of this force. Now, the Colonel-General of the Swiss in the French service, who would, of course, take command of the new levy, was the Duc de Rohan, a nobleman of whose loyalty the Regent was exceedingly suspicious, and with good reason, since, when hostilities broke out, he entered into an alliance with the Princes. She therefore resolved to purchase this post from him and to appoint in his place someone in whom she had absolute confidence.

At a meeting of the Council called to decide the question of Rohan's successor, Villeroy suggested that the post should be given to the Duc de Longueville, by which means, he assured the Queen, she would certainly draw him away from the party of the Princes, which he seemed more than half-inclined to join. Her Majesty, however, very sensibly preferred to bestow it on someone who would not regard his appointment as in the nature of a bribe to do his duty, and proposed that Bassompierre should be the new Colonel-General, "both on account of the German tongue, which he had in common with the Swiss, and because he was their neighbour." Upon this, Villeroy pointed out that, by the ancient conventions of the Kings of France with the Swiss Cantons, it was expressly provided that the Colonel-General should be a prince of the Blood

Royal of France or, at any rate, a prince of some other royal house.[102] The Queen then proposed the Chevalier de Guise, who was a prince of the House of Lorraine; but to this Villeroy objected, on the ground that the Guises had already been overwhelmed with benefits and that to add to them would be bound to create a great deal of jealousy. And the Council rose without any decision having been arrived at.

"As she returned to her cabinet," writes Bassompierre, "she said to me: 'Bassompierre, if you had been a prince, I would have given you to-day a fine appointment.' 'Madame,' I replied, 'if I am not a prince, it is not because I should not have been very glad to be one. Nevertheless, I can assure you that there are princes who are greater fools than myself.' 'I should have been very pleased if you had been one,' said she, 'because that would have saved me from seeking for a suitable person for the post I speak of.' 'Madame, may I ask what it is?' 'To appoint a Colonel-General of the Swiss,' said she. 'And why, Madame, can I not be Colonel-General, if it is your wish?' On which she told me that the Swiss had a convention with the King according to which no one but a prince could be their Colonel-General."

Bassompierre saluted her Majesty and withdrew, anathematizing the wretched convention which stood between him and one of the highest offices under the Crown, and wondering whether by any possibility the obstacle could be overcome. Of that there seemed but little chance, as time pressed, and perhaps by the morrow the post would have been filled. Fortune favoured him, however, for, as he was on his way to dinner, he happened to meet Colonel Gaspard Gallaty, a veteran Swiss officer in the service of France,[103] with whom he was on very friendly terms. To him he related what the Queen had just told him, when Gallaty said that he believed he possessed sufficient influence with his countrymen to persuade them to accept him as their Colonel-General, notwithstanding the convention. And he offered to set out at once for Switzerland to obtain their consent, and begged Bassompierre to return to the Queen and tell her that, if she wished to give him the post, the Swiss would consent.

"She [the Queen] said to me, 'I give you a fortnight; nay, I will give you three weeks, for this; and if you can obtain the consent of the Swiss, I will give you the post. Then I spoke to Gallaty, who asked me to obtain permission for him to go to his own country, saying that he would set out in two days' time. And this he did, and, within the time that he had promised me he sent me a letter from the Cantons, who were assembled at Soleure, to authorise the levy which the King was demanding from them, by which they informed the King that, if it pleased him to honour me with this charge, they would accept me as willingly as any prince whom he might give them."

By the Queen's orders, Bassompierre then communicated with Rohan, who was in Poitou, and, as he feared that it might be some little time before the Treasury saw its way to pay the large sum demanded by that nobleman for the surrender of his post, he himself offered to advance it; and on March 12, 1614, he took the oath as Colonel-General of the Swiss.

Two days later, news arrived that the Princes had surprised Mézières, from which place Condé despatched a lengthy memorial to the Queen, setting forth the grievances of himself and his party, protesting against the Spanish marriage and demanding the convocation of the States-General. The seizure of Mézières was followed by that of Sainte-Menehould, but the arrival of the Swiss, in two regiments, each 3,000 strong, of whom Bassompierre at once went to take the command, greatly perturbed the rebels, and there can be no doubt that at the cost of a little bloodshed the Regent could easily have crushed the insurrection. Instead of doing so, she preferred to treat, and the result of the negotiations which ensued was the Peace of Sainte-Menehould (May 15, 1614), which stipulated that the States-General should be convoked; that Condé should hold Amboise, as a place of surety, until the meeting of the States, and receive a sum of 450,000 livres; that Mayenne, who was already Governor of the Île-de-France, should have the reversion of the government of Paris, together with 300,000 livres; Longueville 100,000 livres, and Bouillon "the doubling of his gendarmes." It was a direct incentive to the Princes to take up arms again on the first convenient opportunity.

As the Duc de Vendôme, who had retired into his government of Brittany, showed himself discontented with the peace and had, not only refused to dismantle the fortifications of Lamballe and Quimper, as he was required to do by the treaty, but had even seized upon Vannes, Marie de' Medici, on the advice of Villeroy, decided to show the young King to his people, and to "go in person to pacify the western provinces." Bassompierre accompanied her, with one of the two regiments of Swiss, the other having been disbanded on the signing of peace, and was employed in superintending the razing of the fortifications which Vendôme had erected. The appearance of the young King aroused great enthusiasm in the West, and Vendôme soon decided to make his submission.

Louis XIII returned to Paris, and on October 2 proceeded in great state to the Parlement to declare his majority. He thanked his mother "for having taken so many pains on his behalf, and begged her to continue to govern and command as heretofore." "I desire and I order," he added, "that you be obeyed in everything and everywhere, and that you be after me the chief of my Council."

CHAPTER XV

Bassompierre, during his absence in Lorraine, condemned by the Archbishop of Aix to espouse Mlle. d'Entragues, on pain of excommunication—The archbishop's decision quashed by the Parlement of Paris—Financial and amatory embarrassments of Bassompierre—Death of his mother—The action which the d'Entragues have brought against him finally decided in his favour—Condé withdraws from Court and issues a manifesto against the Government—Civil war begins—Marriage of Louis XIII and Anne of Austria—Peace of Loudun—Fall of the old Ministers of Henri IV—Concini and the shoemaker—Condé becomes all-powerful—He obliges Concini to retire to Normandy—Arrogance of Condé and his partisans, who are suspected of conspiracy to change the form of government—The Queen-Mother sends for Bassompierre at three o'clock in the morning and informs him that she has decided upon the arrest of the Princes—Preparations for this *coup d'état*—Arrest of Condé—Concini's house sacked by the mob—The Comte d'Auvergne and the Council of War—Bassompierre conducts Condé from the Louvre to the Bastille.

IN January, 1615, Bassompierre set out for Lorraine, to visit his mother, who was lying dangerously ill at Nancy. "The joy of seeing me," says he, "restored her to some degree of health," and, after remaining with her a fortnight, he went to visit some of his friends in Germany. About Easter he returned to Nancy, and was about to set out for France when he received a most astonishing piece of intelligence.

It appears that the d'Entragues, aware that their plea that the court at Rouen was improperly constituted was certain to be overruled by the King's Council and the case sent back to Rouen for trial, in which event their chance of obtaining a verdict would be a very remote one, had decided to appeal to Rome, and proceeded to petition the Pope to direct that the affair should be adjudicated upon by ecclesiastical commissioners appointed by his Holiness. The petition was granted, though it would appear to have been very unusual for the Vatican to do so, unless it had first been ascertained whether the other party were willing for the case to be submitted to a Papal tribunal; and one of the commissioners appointed was the Bishop of Dax. But, by some error, due no doubt to the similarity of names, the Papal authority to try the case was sent, not to this prelate, but to the Archbishop of Aix. Now, the Archbishop of Aix, if we are to believe Bassompierre, was "a needy rogue, and generally regarded as mad"; and when the Bishop of Beauvais, at whose suggestion the appeal to Rome had been made, and whom the writer accuses of being in love with Marie d'Entragues, offered him a bribe of

1,200 crowns to defeat the ends of justice, he promptly accepted it. Thereupon, without condescending to consult his fellow-commissioners he sent a citation to Bassompierre's house, summoning him to appear before him; and, after waiting three days, without troubling to ascertain whether that gentleman had ever received the citation, and without hearing any evidence, pronounced, on his own authority, the promise of marriage—which he had not even seen, as it was, with the other documents connected with the case, at Rome—good and valid, and condemned Bassompierre to execute it within fifteen days after Easter, on pain of excommunication.

On learning of these extraordinary proceedings, Bassompierre returned to Paris in all haste, and appealed to the Parlement; and that body, always very jealous of Papal interference with matters which it considered within its own jurisdiction, promptly quashed the archbishop's decision. He then went to the Queen-Mother, who, "indignant, like everyone else, at the infamy of this man," issued an order for the prelate's arrest, which Bassompierre set out to execute, at the head of 200 stalwart Swiss. The archbishop, however, had prudently gone into hiding, where he remained until the Nuncio and the other bishops, fearing a scandal, succeeded in pacifying the infuriated Bassompierre, "the Nuncio giving him his word that within three months at latest his Holiness would quash, as the Parlement had already done, all the proceedings of this fool. And this he did."

This new development of the d'Entragues affair was only one of many difficulties which beset Bassompierre on his return to Paris:—

"I found myself on my return in very great perplexity; not only in consequence of this affair, but also on account of six hundred thousand livres which I owed in Paris, without any means of paying them; and my creditors, who, on seeing me set out to visit my mother, who was dangerously ill, entertained some hope that, with the property I should inherit from her, I should be able to satisfy them, now that I was returned and my mother recovered, lost all hope of settling their affairs with me, and were consequently very mutinous. There was a quarrel in a certain house between a husband and wife on my account, which gave me pain; and, worst of all, there was a girl for whom I daily feared a discovery attended with a great scandal and evil consequences for me."

However, his fortunate star prevailed over these complicated effects of his extravagant and amorous propensities:—

"It happened that, within a few days, I heard of the quashing of the proceedings of this precious Archbishop of Aix, and of the death of my mother, which brought me fifty thousand crowns in money and saleable property to the value of a hundred thousand, so that I paid seven hundred thousand livres of debts, which placed me greatly at my ease; the quarrel between the husband and wife was made up (August); the girl was happily brought to bed without anyone knowing of it (August 5); and I went to Rouen, where I gained my case against Antragues finally and completely. So that at the same, or within a little, time I was delivered from all these divers and distressing inconveniences."

Towards the end of March, Condé, who for weeks past had been secretly fomenting opposition to the Court, left Paris, followed, at intervals, by his chief adherents, and issued a manifesto protesting against the Ultramontane tendencies of the Government and the Spanish marriage. Marie de' Medici, who intended shortly to set out for the Spanish frontier to make the exchange of the princesses and conclude the marriage of Louis XIII and Anne of Austria, and naturally feared to leave Condé behind her, sent him a letter from the King commanding the prince to accompany him. But Condé excused himself from following his Majesty until he had remedied the evils of the State, of which he designed the Maréchal d'Ancre as the principal author.

The Queen-Mother, in consequence, was obliged to raise two armies: one to escort the King and herself to Bordeaux, the other to watch the princes. The latter force was placed under the command of the Maréchal de Bois-Dauphin, with Praslin as his chief of staff; and to this Bassompierre and the Swiss were attached.

The King and his mother left Paris on August 17, Bassompierre and the Swiss accompanying them so far as Bernis, not far from Sceaux, where they received orders to return and join Bois-Dauphin's army. Before doing so, however, Bassompierre went to Rouen, where on September 4 the Parlement pronounced judgment in his favour; and this unedifying affair, which had dragged on for nearly four years and must have involved both sides in enormous expense, finally terminated. He then returned in triumph to Paris, whence he proceeded to

Meaux, where Bois-Dauphin had established his headquarters.

Bassompierre gives a long and detailed account of the operations which ensued, through which, however, we do not propose to follow him, since they are of little interest, consisting mainly of unimportant skirmishes and the reduction of such places as had declared for the Princes or had been seized by them. In what fighting took place he appears to have displayed both courage and activity; while he endeavoured, though without success, to impart some of his own energy to the old Maréchal de Bois-Dauphin, who, in his youth, had been one of the most dashing officers in the armies of the League, but with age had grown slow and cautious. Happily for the marshal, Condé was equally incapable; otherwise, he would no doubt have taken advantage of his opponent's inaction to march upon Paris.

Meanwhile, the Court had reached Bordeaux in safety, from which town the greater part of the Royal army was despatched to the frontier to fetch the Infanta Anne of Austria, whom Philip III, undisturbed on his side by war's alarms, had brought from Madrid. The exchange of the princesses took place at Andaye, on the Bidassoa, after which Anne of Austria, escorted by the Royal troops, set out for Bordeaux, where her marriage with Louis XIII was celebrated on November 28.

Her object accomplished, Marie de' Medici became anxious for peace at any price, while Condé and his friends, now deprived of their chief pretext for rebellion and aware that the Queen would be prepared to pay them handsomely to return to their allegiance, had no desire to prolong the war. A suspension of arms having been agreed upon, a congress met at Loudun to negotiate peace, which was signed on May 3, 1616.

Its terms were another triumph for the party of the Princes, and particularly for their leader, who, in exchange for his government of Guienne, received that of Berry and of the citadel and town of Bourges, the right of signing all the decrees of the Council, and 1,500,000 livres, to compensate him for the inconvenience and expense to which he had been put in being obliged to take up arms against his sovereign. He was certainly finding rebellion a most profitable occupation. The other grandees, his accomplices, received altogether 6,000,000 livres.

The Peace of Loudun brought about the downfall of the Ministers of Henri IV. In both peace and war they had shown only weakness, which is scarcely surprising, considering that the Chancellor, the youngest of the three, was seventy-two. He was obliged to surrender the Seals to Du Vair, First President of the Parlement of Toulouse; while Villeroy and Jeannin were also dismissed, and replaced by Mangot, First President of the Parlement of Bordeaux, and the Queen-Mother's intendant Barbin, an intelligent and energetic man, who was devoted to Concini and Marie de' Medici.

As for Concini, he was more in favour at Court than ever; nevertheless, his position was not altogether an enviable one, since, though he was temporarily reconciled with Condé, Mayenne and Bouillon were breathing fire and slaughter against him and were quite capable of putting their threats into execution should a favourable occasion present itself; while he had rendered himself odious to the Parisians by an act of intolerable insolence.

It happened that, one night during the war, Concini had wished to leave Paris by the Porte de Bussy, in order to go to Saint-Germain. But, as he had neglected to provide himself with the necessary passport—such trifles being, of course, beneath the notice of so great a man—the officer of the citizen militia in charge of the gate, who, when not girded with a sword, followed the peaceful occupation of a shoemaker, had refused to let him out. The shoemaker was only doing his duty, but Concini was furious, and, so soon as peace was signed, determined to be revenged, and accordingly sent two of his lackeys to chastise the impertinent fellow who had dared to put such an affront upon a marshal of France. The sequel was a tragedy, for the shoemaker shouted for help with all the strength of his lungs; the people came running from all directions to his assistance, seized the unfortunate lackeys, and, after keeping them locked up for some days, hanged them in front of the shoemaker's shop, vowing that they would serve their master in the same way when they could lay their hands on him.

All things considered, it is not surprising that the marshal should have decided that the air of Paris was just then unsuited to his health and remained at his country seat at Lesigny, though even there he appears to have been far from safe from his enemies, since Bassompierre tells us that "MM. de Mayenne and de Bouillon made an attempt to blow him up with a petard, but did not succeed."

However, on July 20 Condé returned to Paris, to be received with enthusiasm by the people, though surely no one was ever less deserving of popular acclamations than this vain, greedy, and meddlesome young man, who had not scrupled to plunge his country into the miseries of civil war to serve his own selfish ends! Unwilling to offend the prince by failing to pay him his respects, Concini thereupon decided to go to Paris, even at the risk of his life, and wrote to Bassompierre, who had apparently quite forgiven him for the shabby way he had behaved two years before, asking him to meet him at the Porte Saint-Antoine at three o'clock on the following afternoon, with as many friends as he could muster.

At the appointed hour Bassompierre proceeded to the Porte Saint-Antoine, accompanied by thirty horse, passing on the way the Hôtel de Mayenne, which stood at the corner of the Rue Saint-Antoine and the Rue du Petit-Musc. Presently, Concini appeared, riding in his gilded coach, which was surrounded by forty mounted retainers, all, of course, armed to the teeth. The marshal alighted, and mounted a horse which Bassompierre had brought for him, and the two cavalcades joined forces and proceeded through the streets to the Louvre. Here they waited while Concini entered to salute the Queen, and then made their way to the Hôtel de Condé, in the Faubourg Saint-Germain. By this time the marshal's escort, swollen by the accession of friends of his own and Bassompierre's, amounted to over one hundred horse; but it seemed as though even this force might be insufficient to protect him, as the first person whom they saw on entering the courtyard of the Hôtel de Condé was Concini's enemy the shoemaker. His presence in that aristocratic mansion was no doubt accounted for by the fact that it was part of *Monsieur le Prince's* policy to court the leaders of the populace, as the Guises had done so effectively in days gone by.

No sooner did the shoemaker catch sight of Concini, than he hurried away, shouting out that he was going to raise the people of his quarter against the Italian. The latter, greatly alarmed, paid his respects to Condé as briefly as etiquette would permit, and then he and his escort turned their horses' heads towards the river. On this occasion, Bassompierre and his followers rode some two hundred paces ahead of Concini, as it had been decided that if, as was fully expected, they found the Pont-Neuf occupied by an armed mob too numerous to allow of them cutting their way through, the vanguard should hold the enemy in check, while the marshal, under the protection of the rest, retreated to the shelter of the Hôtel de Condé. To their relief, however, the bridge was unoccupied—apparently the shoemaker had not had sufficient time to mobilise his quarter—and they reached the Porte Saint-Antoine in safety, where Concini reentered his coach and returned to Lesigny.

After Condé's return to Paris, the management of affairs fell almost entirely into his hands, and his hôtel was besieged at all hours by petitioners and sycophants. "Almost all the grandees," says Bassompierre, "were of his party and his cabal, and even MM. de Guise[104] joined him, under pretext of dissatisfaction with the Maréchal d'Ancre and his wife."

At the beginning of August, Concini returned to his

CONCINO CONCINI, MARÉCHAL D'ANCRE.
From an engraving by Aubert.

house in the Faubourg Saint-Germain, emboldened apparently by a promise of his protection which Condé had given him. A few days later, having some business with the prince, he had the hardihood to go to the Hôtel de Condé, attended by a suite of thirty gentlemen, at a time when Condé was giving a sumptuous fête in honour of Lord Hay, the British Ambassador Extraordinary, to which all the princes and great nobles had been invited. The company were at table when he arrived, but he went into the banquet-hall, in which he found Bouillon, Mayenne and other sworn enemies of his, spoke with Condé for some time, and then took his departure, "all these gentlemen glaring at him and he at them."

Next morning, the prince sent for Concini and told him that he had had great difficulty on the previous day in restraining his friends from falling upon him and killing him as he was leaving his hôtel, and that they all threatened to abandon him if he did not withdraw his protection from the marshal. In consequence, he was unable to protect him any longer, and he counselled him strongly to retire to Normandy, of which province he had recently been appointed lieutenant-general, in exchange for the surrender of a similar office in Picardy. Concini followed the prince's advice—or rather his orders—went to the Louvre to take leave of the King and the Queen-Mother, and left Paris the next day (August 15). "It is impossible to say," adds Bassompierre, "how much his departure discredited the Queen-Mother, when it was seen that a servant of hers could not live in safety in Paris, save so long as *Monsieur le Prince* pleased; while it augmented the reputation and authority of *Monsieur le Prince*."

Chief of the grandees and also chief of the King's counsellors, Condé might perhaps have been content to live on good terms with the Queen-Mother and to use with moderation the large share of power which she had abandoned to him. "But his partisans were unable to suffer their reunion." Longueville surprised Péronne; Bouillon, the "demon of rebellion," the turbulent Mayenne, the restless Vendôme, urged him to seize the supreme power, on pain of abandoning him. He is said to have avowed to Barbin that "it was plain that nothing more remained for him but to remove the King from his throne and put himself in his place." If he had really entertained any such intention, he would hardly have made a confidant of one of the most devoted of the Queen-Mother's adherents; but, any way, the Court believed that he was secretly stirring up the people and the clergy and tampering with the officers of the Guards and the captains of the citizen militia, and was plotting to change the form of government. On the advice probably of the new Ministers Barbin and Mangot, and of Concini's wife, Marie de' Medici resolved to forestall Condé by arresting him, together with Bouillon, Mayenne, and Vendôme. Fearing that the officers of the Guards might refuse to lay hands on the first Prince of the Blood, she decided to dispense with their services and to entrust the task to the Marquis de Thémines, a brave old Gascon noble who had served with distinction in the Wars of Religion, assisted by d'Elbène, a captain of light cavalry.

"On Thursday, the first day of September, at three o'clock in the morning," says Bassompierre, "I was awakened by a gentleman-servant of the Queen named La Motte, who came to tell me, on her behalf, to come to the Louvre, disguised and alone, which I did. On entering the Louvre, I found one of the Gardes du Corps of the King named La Barre, who happened to be on guard that night. La Barre was Quartermaster of the Swiss, and I told him to come with me into the Queen's ante-chamber and wait at the door while I entered her chamber, as I did not doubt that it was some matter relating to the Swiss which was the cause of my being sent for.

"I found the Queen in deshabille, with MM. Mangot and Barbin on either side of her, while M. de Fossé[105] was standing a little way behind them. As I entered, she said to me: 'You do not know why I have sent for you so early, Bassompierre.' 'Madame,' I answered, 'I do not know the reason.' 'I will tell you anon,' said she, and then began to walk about, and so continued for near half-an-hour; while I spoke to M. de Fossé, whom I was very astonished to see there, as the Queen had dismissed him for having accompanied the Commandeur de Sillery when he was exiled from the Court.[106]

"At length, the Queen entered her cabinet, bidding us follow her, and said to me: 'I intend to make prisoners of *Monsieur le Prince* and MM. de Vendôme, Mayenne, and Bouillon. I desire that the Swiss be here at eleven o'clock this morning, that is to say, about the Tuileries, for, if I am forced by the people to leave Paris, I shall retire with them to Mantes. I have my jewels packed up and 40,000 crowns in gold—they are here—and I shall take my children with me, if I am forced to go, though I pray that God may forbid it, and I do not think it will be necessary. But I am fully resolved to submit to any peril and inconvenience that I may encounter rather than lose my authority and suffer that of the King to perish. I desire also that, when the time arrives, you will go, with your Swiss, to the gate [of the Louvre], to resist an attack, if one should be made, and to die there for the service of the King, as I promise myself that you will be ready to do.' 'Madame,' I replied, 'I shall not deceive the good opinion that you entertain of me, as you will know to-day, if such should be the case. Meantime, Madame, be pleased to permit me to go and summon the Swiss from their quarters.' 'No,' said she, 'you shall not go out.' 'It is strange of you, Madame,' said I, 'to distrust a man to whom you are confiding the person of the King, your own, and those of your children. However, I have at this door a man whom I can trust, and I will send him to the quarters of the Swiss. Rely on me, Madame, and rest assured that the fête will not be spoiled by me.' She permitted me to go out, and I sent La Barre to fetch the Swiss. I asked her what she intended to do with the French Guards, when she said that she feared that M. de Créquy[107] had been won over by *Monsieur le Prince*. 'Not against the King, Madame,' said I, 'for I know that for the King he would die a thousand deaths, if that were possible.' Upon that she said: 'I must send for him, and neither of you must go out until *Monsieur le Prince* has entered.' She sent also for M. de Saint-Géran[108]; while La Curée[109] came with the King when he descended to the Queen-Mother's apartments at nine o'clock. The Queen spoke to these gentlemen, and when I asked her by whom *Monsieur le Prince* was to be arrested, she answered: 'I have provided for that.'

"*Monsieur le Prince* came at eight o'clock to attend the Council, and the Queen-Mother, looking at him as everyone came to hand him petitions, said:

'There is the King of France, but his royalty will be like that of the Twelfth Night King; it will not last long.'

"Upon that, she despatched Créquy and myself to the gate of the Louvre to place the Guards under arms, and meantime she sent to summon *Monsieur le Prince* to her presence. Afterwards she sent to tell us that if *Monsieur le Prince* came to the gate, we should arrest him. We sent back word that this was so important an order that we ought to have it from her own lips, and that she should have given it us while we were in her chamber; but that, if it pleased her to send a lieutenant of the Guards du Corps to arrest him, we would render him every assistance, and, meantime, I would give orders that no one was to pass out of the gate. And I placed thirty Swiss halberdiers there, while Créquy gave a like order to the French Guards.

"A moment later, there came a *valet de chambre* of the Queen to tell us that *Monsieur le Prince* had been arrested."[110]

So soon as the arrest of Condé had been effected, Saint-Géran and La Curée, with detachments of the Gensdarmes and Light Cavalry of the Guard, were sent to apprehend Bouillon, Mayenne, and Vendôme; but all three princes had prudently taken to flight.

Much to the relief of Marie de' Medici, the bulk of the populace remained unmoved, though the Dowager-Princesse de Condé drove about the streets, crying out: "To arms, good people! The Maréchal d'Ancre has caused *Monsieur le Prince* to be assassinated!" A crowd, however, collected before Concini's house in the Faubourg-Saint-Germain, broke in the door and sacked it from basement to attic, after which they were proceeding to demolish it, when the French Guards arrived and dispersed them.

"A little while after the arrest of *Monsieur le Prince*," says Bassompierre, "some rioters, or some members of the said prince's household, began to throw stones against the windows of the Maréchal d'Ancre's house. Then, others joining them with the hope of plunder, took the pieces of timber from beyond the Luxembourg, which was then being built, to break open the door of the said house. Eight or ten men and women who were within escaped, terror-stricken, by a back door; and a number of masons from the Luxembourg having joined the mob, they entered and pillaged this rich house, in which they found furniture worth more than 200,000 crowns. So soon as the Queen-Mother heard of it, she ordered M. de Liancourt, Governor of Paris, to go and put a stop to the tumult. He went with the archers of the Watch, but, perceiving that it was no place for him, returned; and the people continued to pillage all day, and were not interfered with.... The next day the King commanded M. de Créquy to take the companies of the French Guards just relieved from duty and drive away the people, who were continuing, not to plunder—for that was already accomplished—but to demolish the Maréchal d'Ancre's house. This M. de Créquy did, and placed soldiers there to guard it."

The same day that Condé was arrested, the King, at his mother's request, created Thémines a marshal of France. His appointment, Bassompierre tells us, aroused great indignation amongst a number of gentlemen who considered that their own military services gave them a better claim to that dignity, and they complained loudly, the loudest of all being M. de Montigny, formerly Governor of Paris, who, while travelling to the capital that morning, had met Vendôme flying for his life, and had obligingly lent him his own post-horses, which were fresh, as the prince's were exhausted. To pacify Montigny, the King created him a marshal likewise. Then Saint-Géran, "perceiving that it was only necessary to complain to get what one wanted," extorted from his

Majesty a written promise that he too should be made a marshal, while Créquy obtained a brevet of duke and peer. The Queen-Mother said to Bassompierre that evening: "Bassompierre, you have not asked for anything like the others." "Madame," was the diplomatic answer, "an occasion on which we have only performed our simple duty is not one on which to ask for recompense. But I hope that when, by great services, I shall have merited them, the King will bestow upon me honours and emoluments without my asking him."

On September 5, Marie de' Medici instituted a Council of War, to which she summoned the Maréchal de Brissac, Praslin, Saint-Luc, Saint-Géran, and Bassompierre, and also the recently dismissed Ministers Villeroy and Jeannin, to discuss the means of raising an army to combat the fugitive princes, who had established themselves at Soissons, where their adherents were gathering round them. This Council, however, had only held one or two meetings, under the presidency of the Maréchal de Brissac, when a most embarrassing incident caused its sittings to be suspended.

It will be remembered that, in 1605, the Comte d'Auvergne, Charles IX's son by Marie Touchet, now

Madame d'Entragues, had been condemned to death for high treason, a sentence subsequently commuted by Henri IV to perpetual imprisonment in the Bastille. This commutation, however, had not been a formal one, so that the death-sentence remained nominally suspended over the captive's head. At the end of the previous June, the Queen-Mother had set Auvergne at liberty, with the object of opposing him to the cabal of the Princes; and when, a few weeks later, the news arrived that Longueville had seized Péronne, she sent him, at the head of two companies of the French Guards and a detachment of cavalry, to invest the place. But, by some extraordinary oversight, she had omitted to furnish Auvergne with the usual letters of *abolition*, and, in the absence of his sovereign's formal pardon for his offences, he occupied a position somewhat analogous to that of a convict on ticket-of-leave.

A day or two after the Council of War had been appointed, Auvergne returned from Péronne, and asked Barbin whether he were expected to attend its sessions. Barbin gave him to understand that he was; and at the next meeting of the Council the prince entered the room and coolly took his seat at the head of the table. Brissac was so overcome with astonishment and indignation that he was quite unable to utter any protest; but Bassompierre, boiling with rage at the sight of a man who had twice conspired against the life of his beloved master, and was still technically a traitor under sentence of death, presuming to attend, much less to preside, over their counsels, rose at once and moved to one of the windows, beckoning Saint-Géran and Créquy to follow him. His friends shared his indignation, and, having consulted together, they called Brissac and told him that it would be "a reproach and a shame to him" if he suffered the Comte d'Auvergne to take his place. The marshal thereupon declared that, provided that they and La Curée would support him—for these four with their troops were masters of the Louvre—he would kill the count with his own hand, if he returned for the afternoon session and again took his place at the head of the council-board. The others applauded this decision, but, happily, Praslin joined them, and, on learning of what was intended, pointed out that the wisest course would be to request the Queen-Mother to order the Comte d'Auvergne not to attend the Council or to suspend its sessions, whereby they would escape the "inconvenience" which might arise were a marshal of France to kill a Prince of the Blood at the council-board.

It was decided to follow his advice, and to delegate to him the duty of informing the Queen-Mother that they would not permit the count to preside over the Council or even attend it. Marie de' Medici, we are told, took their remonstrances in very good part, and, since she did not care to offend Auvergne by excluding him from the Council, decided that that body should not meet again.

On September 25, Guise and his brother Joinville, who had followed the other princes to Soissons, with the apparent intention of throwing in their lot with them, returned to Paris and came to the Louvre to pay their respects to the Queen-Mother and assure her of their unalterable fidelity. Her Majesty received them very graciously; nevertheless, she appears to have entertained a strong suspicion that they had other motives in returning to the capital. For that evening, when the courtiers were retiring from her apartments, she desired Bassompierre to remain, as she wished to speak to him, and said: "Bassompierre, I have resolved to transfer *Monsieur le Prince* from here, and intend to entrust his removal to you. Here is the Maréchal de Thémines, who arrested him, and who has guarded him in the Louvre with difficulty. But it is to be feared that, if I keep him here any longer, some attempt may be made to rescue him, which could easily be done.... Besides, if he remains here, the King and I are prevented from leaving, should we desire to go to Saint-Germain or some other place, since, in that event, he would no longer be in security. In consequence, I have resolved to place him in the Bastille, and desire that you should take charge of his removal."

"She then told me," says Bassompierre, "that it was the King's intention that I should not wait for *li honori, li bieni, li carichi*. These were her words."

Bassompierre replied that the honour of her Majesty's confidence was in itself sufficient recompense for the slight service which she was demanding of him, and that he would readily undertake to conduct the prince safely to the Bastille. About this she need have no fear, since, even if Condé's adherents were to get wind of what was intended, long before they had had time to gather in sufficient numbers to attempt a rescue, he would have the prisoner under lock and key again.

He then inquired if the Queen-Mother had any orders to give as to the manner of the prince's removal, and, on being told that she left all the arrangements entirely to his discretion, proceeded to form the escort, which was composed of 200 of the French Guards and 100 Swiss, chosen from those who were posted before and behind the Louvre—for the palace was guarded night and day, like a beleaguered fortress upon which an assault might at any moment be delivered—another body of 50 Swiss, whom he summoned from their quarters in the Faubourg Saint-Honoré, a few of his own and the Queen's gentlemen, on horseback, a dozen men of the Gardes du Corps, and six of the Swiss of the Guard (the *Cent-Suisses*). The French Guards were posted opposite the gate of the Louvre; the rest were drawn up in the courtyard, where a coach was in waiting to convey the prisoner and Thémines, who was to ride with him, to the Bastille.

His preparations completed, Bassompierre, accompanied by Thémines, ascended to the room where Condé was confined, and awakened the prince, "who was in great apprehension," being evidently under the impression that they had come to conduct him to execution. Thémines having reassured him on this score, he went with the marshal down to the courtyard and entered the coach; Bassompierre mounted his horse, and the cortège moved off. Bassompierre, with the mounted gentlemen and fifty of the Swiss, led the way; then came the coach, guarded on either side by the Gardes du Corps and the Swiss of the Guard, with their partizans and halberds; while the French Guards and the rest of the Swiss brought up the rear. Thus they wended their way through the dark, silent streets towards the Faubourg Saint-Antoine, no one being encountered on their march save a few belated pedestrians, and, in less than an hour after they left the Louvre, the gates of the Bastille had closed upon the first Prince of the Blood.

Before setting out for the Bastille, Bassompierre had judged it advisable to send a messenger to assure the Duc de Guise, whose hôtel lay on their way[111] and who, he thought, might take alarm if he learned that soldiers were approaching, that nothing was intended against him. The messenger was only just in time, for Guise, warned by a friend living near the Louvre that troops were assembling at the palace, and persuaded that his arrest was their objective, had promptly decided on flight; and he and some of his attendants were already dressed and preparing to get to horse.

CHAPTER XVI

Serious illness of the young King, who, however, recovers—Bassompierre and Mlle. d'Urfé—Gay winter in Paris—Richelieu enters the Ministry as Secretary of State for War—His foreign policy—His energetic measures to put down the rebellion of the Princes—Return of Concini—His arrogance and presumption—Singular conversation between Bassompierre and Concini, after the death of the latter's daughter—Policy pursued by Marie de' Medici and Concini towards Louis XIII—Humiliating position of the young King—His favourite, Charles d'Albert, Seigneur de Luynes—Bassompierre warns the Queen-Mother that the King may be persuaded to revolt against her authority.

AT the end of October, Louis XIII fell ill, and on All-Hallows' Eve "had a convulsion, which it was apprehended would develop into apoplexy." His physicians were of opinion that if he had a second attack it would probably prove fatal; and Marie de' Medici, on learning of this, sent for Bassompierre and kept him at the Louvre all night, so as to be in readiness to summon the Swiss to her support, in the event of the King's death. However, the young monarch passed a good night, and by the morning all danger was over.

On the following day, Bassompierre set out for Burgundy, at the head of 300 cavalry, to meet and take command of a new levy of two regiments of Swiss, raised to assist the Government in dealing with the rebellious Princes. He left Paris with no little reluctance, since he had just embarked in a new love-affair with Mlle. d'Urfé, who is described by Tallemant des Réaux as the flower of the Queen's maids-of-honour; and it was naturally most provoking to have to go campaigning at such a moment. However, love had to give place to duty.

Bassompierre's orders were to hold the Swiss and his little force of cavalry at the disposal of Bellegarde, Governor of Burgundy, who had been sent into the Bresse to the assistance of Charles Emmanuel's heir, the Prince of Piedmont, who was defending Savoy against an army commanded by his kinsman, the Duc de Nemours. This army had originally been raised by Nemours to co-operate with the forces of Charles Emmanuel in the war which had broken out between him and Spain; but the duke had been persuaded, by the specious promises of the Governor of Milan, to turn it against his relatives. However, on reaching Provins, Bassompierre learned that, through the intervention of Bellegarde, a treaty had been signed between the Prince of Piedmont and Nemours, and that the latter had disbanded his army.

At Saint-Jean de Losne, near Beaune, he met the Swiss, and, having administered to them the usual oath of fidelity, led them to Châtillon-sur-Seine, where he received orders to send one regiment into the Nivernais and the other into Champagne, to be distributed amongst different garrisons in those provinces.

At the beginning of December, he returned to Paris, eager to sun himself once more in the smiles of Mlle. d'Urfé; and his disgust may therefore be imagined when, scarcely had he arrived, than he received a visit from his kinsman, the wealthy Duc de Cröy,[112] who informed him that the same lady's charms had made so deep an impression upon him that he proposed to lay, not only his heart, but his ancient title and all his possessions at her feet. And, all unconscious that his relative had a prior claim to Mlle. d'Urfé's affections, he begged him to make, on his behalf, a formal proposal for her hand to her parents.

Dissimulating his mortification, Bassompierre accepted this commission; but, as he is not ashamed to confess, with the intention of preventing the marriage, if by any means that could be effected. However, "his efforts were in vain, for the duke surmounted all the difficulties that he put in his way," and at the beginning of 1617 Mlle. d'Urfé became Duchesse de Cröy.

Bassompierre did not, as we may suppose, waste much time in regrets for the loss of his inamorata, since, notwithstanding that a civil war was in progress and that almost every day brought such cheerful intelligence as that one gentleman's château had been sacked or another's unfortunate tenants rendered homeless, the winter of 1617 in Paris was a very gay one, and what with dancing, gambling and love-making, his days and nights must have been pretty well occupied:—

"I won that year at the game of trictrac, from M. de Guise, M. de Joinville and the Maréchal d'Ancre, 100,000 crowns. I was not out of favour at the Court, nor with the ladies, and had a number of beautiful mistresses."

To turn, however, from trivial to important matters.

At the end of 1616 Bassompierre writes in his journal:

"During my journey to Burgundy, the Seals had been taken away from M. du Vair and given to

Mangot, and Mangot's charge of Secretary of State to M. de Lusson."

Now, the "M. de Lusson" of whom Bassompierre speaks was none other than Armand Jean du Plessis de Richelieu, Bishop of Luçon, afterwards Cardinal de Richelieu, who on November 30, 1616, had entered the Ministry as Secretary of State for War.

Scarcely had this great man touched public affairs than it was recognised that a firmer and surer hand was guiding the helm; a new spirit seemed to be infused into the Government. The tone of Henri IV suddenly reappeared in French diplomacy, and the ambassadors at Courts opposed to the pretensions of the House of Austria, justly alarmed by the Spanish marriages, were instructed to inform the sovereigns to whom they were accredited that these marriages were by no means to be regarded as portending any intention on the part of the Very Christian King to embrace the interests of Spain or the Holy See, to the detriment of the old alliances of France or to the principle of religious toleration in his realm.

And, at the same time as he reassured the old allies of France, Richelieu took energetic measures to put down rebellion at home. He appealed to public opinion by the issue of pamphlets and proclamations, in which he effectively combated the arguments advanced by the Princes to justify their revolt, and pointed out that these same men who complained of the disorder of the finances had themselves bled the State to the tune of over fourteen million livres—he gave a schedule showing the sums paid to each of them—not counting the emoluments of the charges bestowed upon them and the pensions and *gratifications* accorded to their friends and servants.

Nor did he confine himself to words. This time, the Government, inspired by him, showed none of its accustomed pusillanimity. A royal declaration was launched against Nevers, who, now that Condé was in prison, had assumed the leadership of his party; a second against Mayenne, Vendôme, and Bouillon; three armies were raised to take the field against them, which one by one reduced their strongholds to submission; the estates of many of their supporters were sequestrated; soldiers who had taken up arms to join them were, if captured, hanged without mercy; and, finally, a decree, duly registered by the Parlement, notwithstanding that it struck at at least one of that body, provided for the confiscation of the property of all the rebels.

It was the misfortune of Richelieu and his colleagues that they passed for the creatures of a foreign favourite detested by everyone. At the beginning of December, 1616, Concini, who had remained in Normandy since the scene at the Hôtel de Condé which had led to his compulsory withdrawal from the capital, returned to Paris, more arrogant and more presumptuous than ever, and burning to avenge the humiliations he had suffered. To strike terror into the partisans of the Princes, he caused gibbets to be erected in different parts of the town; he "caused everyone to be watched and spied upon, even in the houses, to see who entered or left Paris," and "imprisoned those who gave him the smallest umbrage, without any form of trial." Already in possession of the citadel of Caen, he occupied the Pont-de-l'Arche, the strongest fortress in Normandy; proposed to rebuild the fort of Sainte-Catherine, above Rouen, which had been destroyed during the Wars of Religion; acquired by purchase the governments of Meulan, Pontoise, and Corbeil; offered Bassompierre 600,000 livres for his post of Colonel-General of the Swiss, and was credited with the intention of getting himself named Constable of France. It was evident that he contemplated making himself a sort of king in Normandy, and that, when the Princes were crushed, there would be no limits to his ambition. He had, however, at the beginning of 1617, a moment of alarm and despondency. The death of his only daughter, Marie Concini, to whom he was tenderly attached and for whom he had dreamed of some alliance which would unite his fortunes to those of one of the great families of France, struck him with a superstitious fear, as the precursor of the ruin of himself and his wife.

"The marshal's daughter fell ill and died," writes Bassompierre, "at which both he and his wife were cruelly afflicted. I shall relate a conversation which passed between him and myself on the day of her death, by which one may see that he had a prevision of what afterwards happened to him.

"I went to visit him on the morning of that day, and again after dinner, at that little house on the Quai du Louvre to which he and his wife had retired. But he had given orders that I was to be requested to defer our interview until some other time, and afterwards he sent to ask me to come to see him at his house in the evening. Finding him in sore distress, I endeavoured sometimes to console, sometimes to divert, him; but his grief augmented the more I spoke to him, and he answered nothing to all I said, save: 'Signor, I am

undone! Signor, I am ruined! Signor, I am miserable!'
At last, I bade him consider the character of a marshal
of France, which he represented, and which did not
permit of him indulging in lamentations, pardonable in
his wife, but unworthy of him. And I went on to say
that assuredly he had lost a very amiable daughter and
one who would have been very useful to advance his
fortunes, but that he had four nieces to take his
daughter's place, who might afford him as much
consolation, if he brought them to live with him, and
much support to his fortunes, by means of alliances
with four of the great families of France, of which he
would have the choice. And I said several other things
which God inspired me to tell him. At length, after
weeping for some time, he said to me:—

" 'Ah, Monsieur! I do truly regret my daughter,
and shall regret her so long as I live. Yet am I a man
who could patiently endure such an affliction; but the
ruin of myself, my wife, my son,[113] and my family
which I see approaching before my eyes and which,
owing to the obstinacy of my wife, is inevitable,
makes me lament and lose all patience. I reveal this to
you as to a true friend, from whom I have all my life
received assistance and friendship, and to whom, I
confess, I have not rendered the like, or acted as I

should and might have done. But, *basta!* I will make amends, please God! Know, Monsieur, that ever since I mingled with the world I have learned to know it, and to see, not only the elevation of fortunes but their decline and fall; and that a man attains to a certain point of felicity, after which he descends or falls headlong, according to the height which he has reached. If you did not know the meanness of my origin, I should endeavour to disguise it from you; but you saw me in Florence, debauched, dissolute; sometimes in prison, sometimes banished, and always plunged in a disorderly and evil course of life. I was born a gentleman and of good parentage; but when I came to France, I had not a sou and owed 8,000 crowns. My marriage and the favour of the Queen gave me great influence during the lifetime of the late King, and brought me much wealth, advancement, charges and honours during the regency of the Queen; and I laboured to second and push on Fortune as much as any man could have done, so long as I perceived that she was favourable. But when I recognised that she was ceasing to favour me, and that she was giving me warnings of her departure and her flight, I resolved to make an honourable retreat and to enjoy in peace, with my wife, the great riches which the liberality of the Queen had bestowed upon us or our own industry had acquired. For which reason, for some months past, I have importuned my wife in vain, and at every blow I receive from Fortune I renew my entreaties. When I saw that a powerful party had arisen in France which had taken me for the pretext for its revolt, and had proclaimed me one of the five tyrants whom it was seeking to destroy;[114] when M. Dolet, who was my creature,[115] my counsellor, my trusted friend, and, I may say, my servant, died; when an infamous shoemaker of Paris put an affront upon me—upon me, a marshal of France!—when I was forced to quit my establishments in Picardy and my citadel of Amiens, and to leave Ancre as a prey to M. de Longueville, my enemy; when I was compelled to retire, or rather to fly, into Normandy, I represented to my wife that amongst the great obligations we owed to God, that of warning us to retreat was not the least. We have seen since then our house sacked, with the loss of more than 200,000 crowns; and we have seen two of our people hanged before our faces for having given, as we ordered them, a beating to that scoundrel of a shoemaker. What had we to wait for but the death of my daughter to warn us that our ruin is at hand, but that there is yet the chance to escape, if we resolve promptly to seek a retreat. For this I have provided by offering the Pope 600,000 crowns for the usufruct during our lives of the duchy of Ferrara, where we might have passed the remainder of our days in peace and have still left two millions in gold to our children. And this I will make apparent to you. We have real property to the value of at least a million livres in France: in the marquisate of Ancre, Lesigny, my house in the Faubourg (Saint-Germain) and this one. I have redeemed our estate at Florence, which was mortgaged, and my share in it is worth 100,000 crowns. I have a million livres besides, even after the pillage of our house, in furniture, jewels, plate and money. My wife and I have also appointments which will sell for a million livres at a fair valuation, in those of Normandy, First Gentleman of the Chamber, Intendant of the Queen's Household, and *dame d'atours*, retaining my office of marshal of France. I have 600,000 crowns invested with Fedeau,[116] and more than 100,000 pistoles in other concerns. Might we not, Monsieur, be content with this? Have we anything further to wish for, if we do not desire to offend God, Who is warning us by such evident signs of our entire ruin? I have been all the afternoon with my wife imploring her to retire; I have been on my knees before her, seeking to persuade her the more effectively. But she is more determined than ever to remain, and reproaches me with wishing to abandon the Queen, who has given us, or enabled us to acquire, so many honours and so much wealth. Monsieur, I see myself so irremediably ruined that, if I were not, as everyone knows, under such great obligations to my wife, I would leave her and go where neither the nobles nor the people of France would come to seek me. Judge, Monsieur, whether I have not reason for my distress, and whether, apart from the loss of my daughter, the approach of this second disaster ought not to torment me doubly.'

"I said what I could to console him and divert him from these thoughts," concludes Bassompierre, "and withdrew. I wish to show from this discourse how men, especially those whom Fortune has elevated, have inspirations and forebodings of disaster, without possessing the resolution to prevent or escape it."

Concini's despondency passed as quickly as it had come, and scarcely was his daughter in her grave, than he was once more flaunting his wealth and his power in the faces of Court and town. No Prince of the Blood had ever gone abroad attended by a more numerous or more gorgeous retinue; his pride was so great that he scarcely deigned to notice the existence of any but the great nobles; while, as for the Ministers, he regarded them as his servants, and not finding them sufficiently docile, planned to replace them by creatures of his own. Marie de' Medici herself began to grow weary of the presumption of the husband and the ill-humour of the wife, who appears to have been a martyr to neuralgia, and often treated her mistress in a manner against which even the Queen-Mother's sluggish nature rebelled. At length, she suggested the advisability of the precious pair returning to Florence with the spoil which they had amassed; but Concini wished to tempt Fortune to the end.

Fortune, however, might have smiled on him for some time longer, if only he had possessed sufficient foresight to assure himself of the affection of the young King. Unhappily for him, he had done just the contrary. On his advice, the Queen-Mother had pursued towards Louis XIII much the same policy which Catherine de' Medici had adopted in the case of Charles IX, and carefully kept at a distance from her son all those whom she considered might attempt to inspire him with a thought of ambition. But, less astute than Catherine, Marie had seen no reason to distrust a Provençal gentleman, Charles Albert, Seigneur de Luynes, twenty-three years older than the King, who excelled in the training of hawks and falcons. Falconry was a sport in which Louis XIII delighted above all others, and he soon became so much attached to Luynes that his *gouverneur* Souvré grew jealous and forbade the latter to enter the King's chamber. Héroard, Louis XIII's first physician, relates in his curious *Journal* that the lad was overcome by grief and indignation on learning of this; begged his mother to dismiss Souvré, and "from excess of anger, had five days of fever." From "Master of the birds of the Cabinet" the young King made his favourite chief of his gentlemen-in-ordinary, and in 1615 gave him the government of Amboise.

Notwithstanding that her son had now, according to the laws of France, attained his majority, Marie de' Medici excluded him from Councils and all discussion of State affairs, and forbade the Ministers and Counsellors of State even to speak to him, on the ground that his Majesty's health was too delicate for him to be troubled with the cares of his realm. As he grew older, the Queen-Mother and Concini watched him more closely, and, fearing lest he might escape from them, no longer allowed him to visit Saint-Germain or Fontainebleau, on the pretext that, in the disturbed condition of the country, it was unsafe for the King to leave Paris. For some months past, therefore, the unfortunate youth, who was passionately fond of hunting, had been deprived of his favourite amusement, and had found himself reduced to a walk in the Tuileries, where he might often be seen watching the gardeners at their work and sometimes helping them.

Often the Maréchal d'Ancre, escorted by two or three hundred gentlemen, passed through the courtyard of the Louvre, on his way to or from the Queen-Mother's apartments, before the eyes of his sovereign, who was generally accompanied only by Luynes and a few valets; and the young monarch, who was not without a sense of his kingly dignity, was shocked that a subject should venture to parade his ill-gotten wealth in this fashion in his own palace. For, thanks to Luynes, he was by this time perfectly well-informed as to the source of Concini's riches. He himself was habitually kept short of money, and, on one occasion, was unable to obtain a sum of 2,000 crowns from the Treasury, the Queen-Mother having given orders that it was to be refused him. And, to complete his humiliation, Concini offered to advance him the money. The parvenu boasted of having raised at his own expense a force of 6,000 Liégeois for service against the Princes, and wrote to the King begging him not to trouble about the expense which he had incurred for his Majesty's service—as though his vast fortune was not entirely composed of the money of him he was pretending to oblige.[117]

It seems strange that Marie de' Medici and Concini, so careful to keep away from the King everyone whom they considered might encourage him to assert his independence of his mother's tutelage, should have for so long entertained no suspicion of Luynes. At length, however, their eyes began to be opened, and one day towards the end of January, 1617, Luynes sent one of his servants to Bassompierre to inform him that the Queen-Mother purposed to exile him (Luynes) from the Court, on the ground that "he wished to carry off the King and take him out of Paris," and to ask for his good offices to disabuse her Majesty's mind. These were unnecessary, as it proved to be merely a rumour; but "Luynes made the King believe that it was the Maréchal d'Ancre who had spread this report, to see how the King would take it; whereby the King became more and more incensed against the Maréchal d'Ancre, and high words passed between Luynes and the said marshal."

"The same evening," continues Bassompierre, "as the Queen was speaking to me about this matter, I said to her: 'Madame, it seems to me that you do not think enough of yourself, and that, one of these days, they will take away the King from under your wing. They are inciting him against your creatures first, and afterwards they will incite him against you. Your authority is only precarious, which will cease from the moment that the King no longer desires it, and they will harden him little by little until he does not desire it any more. And it is easy to persuade young people to emancipate themselves. If the King were to go, one of these days, to Saint-Germain, and were to order M. d'Épernon and myself to come there to him, and then told us that we were no longer to recognise your authority, we are your very obliged servants, but we should be unable to do any other thing than to come and bid you farewell, and to beg you very humbly to excuse us, if, during your administration of the State, we had not served you as well as we ought to have done. Judge, Madame," I continued, "whether the other officers would be able to act otherwise, and whether you would not be left with empty hands after such an administration."

CHAPTER XVII

Bassompierre joins the Royal army in Champagne as Grand Master of the Artillery by commission—Surrender of Château-Porcien—Bassompierre is wounded before Rethel—He sets out for Paris in order to negotiate the sale of his office of Colonel-General of the Swiss to Concini—He visits the Royal army which is besieging Soissons—A foolhardy act—Singular conduct of the garrison—The Président Chevret arrives in the Royal camp with the news that Concini has been assassinated—Details of this affair—Bassompierre continues his journey to Paris—His adventure with the Liégeois cavalry of Concini.

ABOUT the middle of March, Bassompierre was sent as Grand Master of the Artillery by commission to join the army of Champagne, commanded by the Duc de Guise, who had as his second in command the Maréchal de Thémines, while Praslin was also serving under him. He found the army laying siege to Château-Porcien, situated on the right bank of the Aisne, two leagues from Rethel. Nevers, who was Governor of Champagne and Brie and Duc de Rethelois, occupied, in virtue of this double title, several places in that part of the country, and their reduction was the chief object of the campaign.

Guise bombarded the citadel of Château-Porcien for some days with little effect; but when he turned his guns on the town, it speedily surrendered; and

Bassompierre, with four companies of the French Guards and as many of the Swiss, marched in and took possession. In the course of the day the commandant of the citadel sent to ask for a parley, and was conducted by Bassompierre to Guise's quarters, where, after a lively discussion as to whether or not the garrison were to be permitted to march out with the honours of war, terms were arranged, and next morning the citadel capitulated.

After Guise, with a part of his cavalry, had made an unsuccessful attempt to surprise an infantry regiment of the enemy quartered in a village near Laon, and the Château of Wassigny had been taken, Thémines was despatched to Rocroi to dismantle and bring up six of the guns from that fortress; and on April 8 the army advanced to Rethel and laid siege to it.

Here Bassompierre's troubles began; and artillery officers who served during the late war in that part of France under similar climatic conditions will appreciate the difficulties with which he had to contend.

"Rain fell continuously," he says, "and, as the soil in the Rethelois is clay, we encountered a thousand difficulties, chiefly in moving our cannon, which sunk in it over the axle-trees. At last we made ready a battery of eight pieces below the town, but when I came on Friday morning, the 14th of April, to see if Lesines[118] had kept his promise to have the eight pieces in position by daybreak, I found that there were only two. A third was at thirty paces from the battery, sunk so deeply in the ground that they had been unable to move it; while a fourth was a hundred paces distant. This last had been abandoned by the officers because, in bringing it up, a driver and some of the horses had been killed, upon which the other drivers had unyoked their horses and fled."

However, Bassompierre had his redoubtable mountaineers to fall back on.

"Then," he continues, "I took fifty Swiss, to whom I promised fifty crowns, to bring those two pieces into position for me; and they harnessed themselves to them in place of the horses, having first dug a trench beneath the wheels of each piece and lined it with stout planks, so as to prevent it from sinking deeper in the mud. We drew the first into position without being fired upon from the town; but, as we were occupying ourselves with the more distant one, and had drawn it close to the battery, and I was lending them a hand, the enemy fired a salvo at us, by which two Swiss were killed and three wounded, and I myself hit by a musket-ball in the right side of the abdomen. I thought that I was wounded to the death, and the Maréchal de Thémines, who was in the battery, thought so too. However, God willed that the quantity of clothes which the ball encountered (for it pierced five folds of my cloak and two folds of my furred *hongroline*, my sword-belt, and my coat-skirt) caused it to stop on the peritoneum without penetrating it, so that when the wound was probed the ball was found in the thick flesh of the belly, where they made an incision, and out it fell. I only kept my bed for one day, although my wound was a month in healing, by reason of the cloth which was within."

The following day, Praslin, who had replaced Bassompierre in command of the artillery, was also wounded by a musket-ball in the thigh, while directing the fire of the battery. But the ball did not injure the bone, and he was cured as quickly as his friend.

Rethel surrendered a few days later, and Guise, after placing a garrison there, resolved to lay siege to Mézières, where Nevers himself commanded. But, before doing this, he decided to send for additional siege-guns, and, as it would be at least ten days before they could arrive, Bassompierre asked for leave to go to Paris, in order to negotiate the sale of his office of Colonel-General of the Swiss to Concini. The marshal, as we have mentioned, had offered him 600,000 crowns for the post; but Bassompierre had asked for another 50,000, which the other was not at the time inclined to give. However, he was evidently so anxious to secure it that it was very probable that he would be willing to reconsider his offer.

The same evening he received very gracious letters from the King and Queen-Mother, who appear to have been under the impression that he was far more severely wounded than was the case, and another from the Maréchal d'Ancre, "who wrote me," says he, "that, if I were trying to get myself killed, he would like to be my heir; and that, if I were well enough to come to Paris to conclude the matter of the Swiss, he would give me, instead of the 50,000 francs in dispute, 10,000 crowns' worth of jewels at a goldsmith's valuation."

On April 21 he left Rethel, accompanied by the Marquis de Thémines, eldest son of the marshal, the Comte de Fiesque, Zamet, and more than fifty officers, who had also obtained leave, which appears to have been granted with amazing liberality in those days. But, instead of making straight for Paris, they decided to take a busman's holiday by breaking their journey at Soissons, to see what progress the Comte d'Auvergne—now formally rehabilitated and therefore once more fit for the society of gentlemen—was making with the siege of that town, in which Mayenne commanded for the princes. On the 23rd they arrived in the Royal camp, where they were met by the Duc de Rohan, La Rochefoucauld, Saint-Géran and Saint-Luc, who conducted them to the general's quarters.

To their astonishment, they learned that, though Auvergne had been blockading Soissons for more than ten days, the trenches had not yet been opened; indeed, it appeared to be an open question whether he was to be regarded as the besieger or the besieged, since they found him engaged in giving instructions for the erection of formidable earthworks to defend his troops against the perpetual sorties of the garrison, who gave him no rest. Only the previous night, Mayenne, who possessed all the dashing courage of his House, had sallied out, bringing with him two field-pieces, attacked and practically destroyed the regiment of Bussy-Lameth,[119] made its colonel prisoner and carried off its colours, which were now mockingly displayed on the bastions of the town.

However, notwithstanding this unfortunate incident, Auvergne seemed brimful of confidence, and assured them that within a fortnight he would be master of Soissons.

The next day, after making the round of the camp, under the guidance of an officer, who pointed out to him the parts of the town which it was proposed to bombard, Bassompierre agreed with La Rochefoucauld, who, like himself, was a visitor to Auvergne's army, to show their hosts what fine fellows they were, and to do what at this epoch, when rashness so often passed for valour, appears to have been regarded as a proof of the highest courage.

"As we were of a different army," says he, "and wished to let them see that we had no fear of musket-shots, we went out to draw the enemy's fire upon us. They, however, allowed us to approach without firing, and, since we did not wish to return without seeing them shoot, we walked right up to the edge of the moat. Still they did not fire. When we noticed their silence, we broke ours and shouted insults at them, which they returned, but never fired a shot. At length, after talking together for rather a long time, just as if we belonged to the same side, we retired; and they let us depart without once firing at us."

The explanation of this singular conduct on the part of the besieged was not long in coming. That evening, Bassompierre, with Auvergne and Rohan, were supping with the Président Chevret, of the Chambre des Comptes, who had come to visit the army in connection with some legal business, when one of the president's clerks arrived in all haste from Paris and whispered something to his master, who appeared very astonished. Then Chevret turned and spoke in a low voice to Auvergne, who sat next him, and Bassompierre remarked that the prince seemed no less astonished than the president. He begged them to let him know what news they had received, upon which they told him that, at eleven o'clock that morning, the Maréchal d'Ancre had been killed by the Marquis de Vitry, one of the captains of the Guards, and that it had been done by the King's orders! Then Bassompierre remembered that when, a few hours before, he and La Rochefoucauld were standing on the edge of the moat of Soissons, one of the garrison had shouted to them: "Your master is dead, and ours has killed him!"—words to which he had attached no importance at the time—and marvelled that the enemy should have received so much earlier information of the event than the Royal army.

But let us see what had been happening in Paris since Bassompierre's departure for the army in the middle of March, which had culminated in the tragedy of that morning.

We have related, in the last chapter, how Marie de' Medici and Concini had begun to grow suspicious of the influence that Louis XIII's favourite, Luynes, had acquired over the mind of the young King, and how a rumour had spread that he was about to be banished from the Court. No action, however, had been taken against him; nevertheless, Luynes felt quite certain that his disgrace was only a question of time, and he resolved to anticipate his enemies. Clever and crafty, greedy and ambitious, and entirely without scruple, this Provençal was a dangerous man, and, while seeking by a show of subservience to the Queen-Mother and the marshal to disarm the suspicions they had formed of him and so secure a respite to enable him to execute his projects, he worked unceasingly to embitter the young King's mind against them. He succeeded so well that at length Louis was fully persuaded that his crown and even his life were in peril, and that his mother and

Concini contemplated setting his younger brother on the throne, in order to have a new minority to exploit.

Having persuaded the King of his danger, Luynes spoke of the various means of escaping it, and these were debated in midnight councils between the King of France, his favourite, Déageant, Barbin's chief clerk, who had been gained over by Luynes,[120] an obscure priest, three gentlemen, a soldier, a gardener from the Tuileries, and some valets. The composition of this strange council, as Henri Martin observes, was indeed a biting satire on the education which Marie de' Medici had given her son and the isolation in which she had left him. The King proposed to make his escape from Paris and to retire to Amboise, of which place Luynes was governor, or to join the army of the Princes. But Luynes, who desired to render the mother and the son irreconcilable, rejected these expedients in favour of one more easy and more sure: that of getting rid of Concini by surprise. And this was decided upon.

The Marquis de Montpouillan, one of the sons of the Maréchal de la Force, and a playmate of Louis XIII in his boyhood, was admitted to their confidence; and Montpouillan, a young man of a bold and violent disposition, offered to poniard Concini in the King's cabinet, if his Majesty would but get him there. The marshal came; but, at the last moment, Luynes's courage failed him, and he would not allow the design to be executed.

The conspirators then addressed themselves to the Marquis de Vitry, one of the captains of the Guards, who entered on his term of service at the beginning of April. He was a son of that Vitry who had arrested Biron at Fontainebleau fifteen years earlier, and one of the few men at the Court who had refused to bow before the power of the favourite. Assured that Vitry would be prepared to execute any orders that he might receive, Louis XIII sent for him and directed him to arrest the Maréchal d'Ancre as he was entering the Louvre to visit the Queen-Mother, which he did every morning when he was in Paris. The bâton of a marshal of France was to be his reward, if he succeeded. "But, if he defends himself?" said Vitry. "Then," cried Montpouillan, "the King intends you to kill him!" "Sire, do you command me?" asked the officer, turning to the King. "Yes, I command you to do it," was the reply.

About ten o'clock on April 24, Concini entered the Louvre by the great gate on the side of Saint-Germain l'Auxerrois, accompanied by some fifty gentlemen. The moment he passed the gate, a signal was given and it was closed; and Vitry, followed by several of his men with pistols hidden beneath their cloaks, advanced to meet him. He joined the marshal between the drawbridge and the bridge which led to the inner court of the palace, and laying his hand on his right arm, said: "The King commands me to seize your person." "*À moi!*" cried Concini; but scarcely had he spoken, than several pistol-shots rang out, and he fell dead on the parapet of the bridge. "It is by order of the King," cried Vitry, and the murdered favourite's followers, who had laid their hands on their swords, dispersed without attempting to avenge him.

Louis XIII and Luynes were waiting anxiously in the King's *cabinet des armes*, prepared to fly if the blow miscarried, for which purpose a coach was in readiness near the Tuileries. The cries of "*Vive le Roi!*" told them that it had succeeded, and a moment later d'Ornano, the colonel of the Corsicans, son of the marshal of that name, came knocking at the door of the cabinet. "Sire," cried he, "now you are King! The Maréchal d'Ancre is dead!" Louis XIII hurried to the window, and d'Ornano, seizing his young sovereign round the body, lifted him up to show him to the cheering crowd of gentlemen and soldiers of the Guard who had gathered in the courtyard below. *"Merci! Merci à vous!"* cried Louis, and then repeated the words of d'Ornano: "Now I am King!"

The King gave orders that the Parlement and the municipal authorities should be informed of what had occurred, and announced his intention of recalling "the old servants of his father." Villeroy, Jeannin, and the oldest of the Counsellors of State at once hurried to the Louvre, and couriers were despatched to summon the Sillerys and the ex-Keeper of the Seals, Du Vair, who had been banished from Paris.

Meantime, tidings of the tragedy had been carried to the Queen-Mother. Marie understood at once that it was the end of her power. *"Povretta de mi!"* she exclaimed. "I have reigned for seven years; I have nothing more to expect but a crown in heaven!" One of her attendants remarked that they did not know how to break the terrible news to the Maréchale d'Ancre, who was in her own apartments. But at such a moment the Queen had no thought for anyone but herself. "I have many other things to think about," she exclaimed impatiently. "Do not speak to me any more about those people." And she refused to see her hapless favourite, who, a few minutes later, was arrested and conducted to the Bastille. Marie then sent one of her gentlemen to her son to request an interview. It was curtly refused, and shortly afterwards her guards were removed from the ante-chamber and replaced by soldiers of the Gardes du Corps, every exit from her apartments, save one, blocked up, and she found herself a prisoner.

Marie's Ministers fell with her. Mangot, the Keeper of the Seals, was at the Louvre; Luynes took the Seals from his hands and bade him begone. Barbin was arrested and sent to join the widow of Concini in the Bastille. Richelieu attempted to make head against the storm and repaired to the King's apartments, where he found his Majesty receiving the felicitations of a crowd of courtiers with the air of one who had just gained a great battle. The King received him graciously enough, and told him that he knew him to be a stranger to the evil designs of the Maréchal d'Ancre and that "it was his intention to treat him well"; while Luynes advised him to go to the Council, which was assembling. He went and found Villeroy, Jeannin and Du Vair seated at the council-table. Villeroy, with a triumphant air, demanded in what quality M. de Luçon presented himself there; the others "continued to expedite affairs without occupying themselves with him." "And so," he writes, "after having been in that place long enough to say that I had entered there, I softly withdrew."

While this revolution of the palace was proceeding, Paris resounded with acclamations, and when evening fell, bonfires blazed at all the crossways. The people went almost frantic with joy at their deliverance from the arrogant foreign favourite whom they had come to regard as a public enemy. The Parlement, which hastened to declare that "the King was not bound to justify his action," the municipality, all the public bodies of the town, sent deputations to felicitate his Majesty, and everyone applauded his *coup de main* as if he had committed the finest action in the world. "They gave him the name of 'Just,' for having caused a man to be killed without trial!" observes Henri Martin.

This explosion of public joy was followed by atrocious scenes. The following morning some noblemen's lackeys, followed by a rabble drawn from the dregs of the populace, entered the Church of Saint-Germain l'Auxerrois, where the body of Concini, "naked, in a wretched sheet," had been secretly buried the previous night, disinterred it, dragged it through the streets with obscene cries, in which the name of the Queen-Mother was mingled with that of the murdered marshal, and finished by tearing it to pieces and burning the remains before the statue of Henri IV on the Pont-Neuf.

At three o'clock in the morning of the 25th, the Comte de Tavannes, grandson of the celebrated marshal of that name, arrived in Auvergne's camp with orders from the King to suspend hostilities against Soissons; and, a few hours later, Bassompierre and his party set out for Paris. Scarcely had they crossed the Aisne, than they encountered a regiment of Liégeois cavalry, part of the force which had been raised by Concini for service against the Princes. The Liégeois, who had just learned of the marshal's assassination, called upon them to halt, and their officers held a sort of informal council of war. Bassompierre suspected that it was their intention to take him and his friends along with them as hostages for their safe return to their own country; and when presently an officer detached himself from the rest and came towards them, he assumed the air of a hunted fugitive and, before the other had time to open his mouth, inquired anxiously whether, if his party joined them, they would undertake not to surrender them if called upon to do so. The officer, thinking from this that they must be some of the Maréchal d'Ancre's personal following, who were perhaps pursued, told him bluntly the Liégeois had quite enough to do to provide for their own safety, and that everyone must look to himself. Upon which he turned on his heel and rejoined his comrades, and the whole regiment mounted their horses and rode away. Bassompierre and his friends waited until they were out of sight, and then resumed their journey to Paris.

CHAPTER XVIII

Bassompierre arrives in Paris—Marie de' Medici is exiled to Blois—
Bassompierre's account of the parting between Louis XIII and his
mother—The rebellious princes return to Court and are pardoned,
but Condé remains in the Bastille—His wife solicits and receives
permission to join him there—Arrest of the Governor and
Lieutenant of the Bastille, on a charge of conniving at a secret
correspondence between Barbin and the Queen-Mother—
Bassompierre is placed temporarily in charge of the fortress—The
Prince and Princesse de Condé are transferred to the Château of
Vincennes—Bassompierre goes to Rouen to attend the assembly
of the Notables—A rapid journey.

ON the following day—April 26—Bassompierre
reached Paris and lost no time in waiting upon Louis
XIII, who received him very graciously and
"commanded him to love M. de Luynes, who was a
good servant." He inquired if he might be permitted to
pay his respects to the Queen-Mother, who since the
24th had been kept a close prisoner in her apartments.
The King replied that he would consider the matter,
which meant that the request did not meet with his
approval. Bassompierre, however, was anxious not to
appear to fail in respect to a princess who had been so
good a friend to him, and whose disgrace, besides,
might very well prove to be but a temporary one. And
so, in default of being able to convey them himself, he

sent his compliments to her Majesty every evening, through the medium of her dressmaker, the only person, with the exception of her servants, who was permitted to enter her apartments.

Meanwhile, negotiations were in progress for the Queen-Mother's retirement from Paris and the Court, upon which Luynes had persuaded the King to insist. It was Richelieu who negotiated the conditions on Marie's behalf. That astute personage, recognising that the victorious party was not inclined to pardon him, had attached himself to Marie de' Medici, who had appointed him chief of her counsellors, hoping ere long to succeed in reconciling her with Luynes and Louis XIII, or with Louis XIII against Luynes, and, in either event, to recover the position he had lost. He obtained, after considerable difficulty, permission for her to reside no further off than Blois, for which she set out on May 3.

Bassompierre has left us an interesting account of the parting between Louis XIII and his mother, of which he was an eye-witness:

"All the morning people seemed to be doing nothing but load carts with the Queen's baggage. The King, meantime, was at the Council, where the things which the Queen was to say to the King on parting from him, and the answers which the King was to make, were decided upon and committed to writing. It was also agreed that nothing further should be said on either side, and that when the Queen was dressed for her journey, the princesses should see her, while the men were to take leave of her after the King had done so. Neither the Maréchal de Vitry[121] nor his brother, Du Hallier[122] were to be amongst them.

"Then the King descended to the Queen's apartments; where the Queen was awaiting him in the passage leading from her chamber, so as to enter it at the same moment as he did. The three Luynes[123] walked before the King, who held the eldest by the hand. M. de Joinville and I followed the King and entered after him. The Queen kept a good countenance until she saw the King approaching. Then she began to weep bitterly and put her handkerchief to her eyes and her fan before her face; and, when they met, she led him to the window which overlooks the garden, and removing her handkerchief and her fan, spoke as follows: 'Monsieur, I am sorry that I have not governed your State during my regency and my administration more to your satisfaction than I have done. Nevertheless, I assure you that it was neither from lack of care nor endeavour; and I beg you to regard me always as your very obedient servant and mother.' 'Madame,' replied the King, 'I thank you very humbly for the care and pains you have taken in the administration of my kingdom, with which I am content, and hold myself obliged to you; and I beg you to believe that I shall always be your very humble son.'

"Upon this the King expected that she would stoop to kiss him and take leave of him, as had been arranged. But she said to him: 'Monsieur, I am going to crave a parting favour of you, which I wish you to promise that you will not refuse me. It is that you will restore to me my intendant Barbin.' The King, who was not expecting this demand, looked at her without making any reply. She said to him again: 'Monsieur, do not refuse me this request that I am now making you.' But he continued to look at her without answering. She added: 'Perhaps it is the last I shall ever make you.' And then, seeing that he answered nothing, she said: '*Orsu!*' and then stooped and kissed him. The King made a reverence and then turned his back. Upon that M. de Luynes advanced to take leave of the Queen, and spoke to her some words which I could not hear, nor yet those in which she answered him. But after he had kissed the hem of her gown, she added that she had made a request to the King to restore Barbin to her, and that he would be doing her an agreeable service and a singular pleasure in prevailing upon the King to grant her request, which was not so important that he ought to refuse it. As M. de Luynes was about to reply, the King cried five or six times: 'Luynes, Luynes, Luynes!' And upon that M. de Luynes, making the Queen understand that he was obliged to go after the King, followed him. Then the Queen leaned against the wall between the two windows and wept bitterly. M. de Chevreuse [Joinville] and I kissed the hem of her gown, weeping likewise; but either she was unable to see us by reason of her tears, or she did not wish to speak to or look at us. This caused me to wait to take leave of her a second time, which I did as she was returning to her chamber. But she did not see me, or wish to see me, any more than on the first occasion.

"Upon that the King placed himself on the balcony before the chamber of the Queen, his wife, to see the departure of the Queen, and, after she had left the Louvre, he hastened into his gallery to see her again as she passed over the Pont-Neuf. Then he entered his coach and went to the Bois de Vincennes."

On May 5, the rebellious princes Vendôme, Mayenne and Bouillon, who, on learning of Concini's death, had hastened to lay down their arms, open the gates of their fortresses and disband their soldiers, as though they had been fighting only against the favourite, came to Vincennes, accompanied by a number of their principal followers, to salute the King and assure him of their allegiance. Although Louis XIII must have known very well that no reliance whatever could be placed in their professions of loyalty, and that, unless he made it worth their while to keep the peace, they would rise again on the first plausible pretext, they were received as though they had taken up arms for, and not against, the royal authority. On May 12 a declaration of the King reinstated them in all their property, honours, and offices, and excused them having taken up arms, "although unlawfully," on the ground that they had done so in order to defend themselves against the tyranny of the Maréchal d'Ancre.

Logic would have demanded that the reconciliation should have gone further, and that Condé, whose arrest had been the pretext for the revolt, should have been released from the Bastille and reinstated as chief of the Council. Nothing of the kind happened, however. Louis XIII entertained a strong antipathy to his turbulent kinsman, which need occasion no surprise; Luynes feared that he might attempt to dispute his ascendancy over the young King; while the other princes, who were bound to their chief neither by affection nor even by party-loyalty, did not press for his liberation. And so he remained a prisoner.

The King stayed at Vincennes for some days and then returned to Paris; but, shortly afterwards, removed to Saint-Germain. After having been so long confined to the capital and a sedentary life, he was revelling in his new-found liberty, and the opportunity it afforded him of indulging in his favourite sports of hawking and hunting.

While the Court was at Saint-Germain, the Princess de Condé arrived there to ask the King's permission to share her husband's captivity. Although, for some time before Condé's arrest, the relations between him and his wife had been very cool, the princess, on learning of the misfortune that had befallen him, had shown real magnanimity. Without a moment's delay, she set out for Paris—she was at Valery at the time—sent the prince messages assuring him of her sympathy and devotion, and begged the

Queen-Mother to allow her to join him. Her request, however, was refused, and she received orders to leave Paris at once and return to Valery.

Now, however, she did not plead in vain, and Louis XIII not only granted her request, but gave her permission to take with her "one demoiselle and her little dwarf, who had begged his Majesty to consent to his not abandoning his mistress." The same day (May 26) the princess entered the Bastille, "where she was received by *Monsieur le Prince* with every demonstration of affection, nor did he leave her in repose until she had said that she forgave him."[124]

In the following October, the authorities of the Bastille were discovered to be conniving at a secret correspondence which Barbin was carrying on with the Queen-Mother, and first Bournonville, the Lieutenant of the fortress, and brother of the Governor, the Baron de Persan, and subsequently Persan himself, were arrested.[125] Bassompierre was then sent with sixty Swiss to take charge of the Bastille, but he did not have the Prince and Princesse de Condé under his supervision, as, about a month previously, they had been transferred to the Château of Vincennes, where Condé was allowed a great deal more liberty than had been permitted him in Paris.

Bassompierre only remained at the Bastille about ten days, at the end of which he received orders to hand over the command to the new favourite's youngest brother, Brantes.

In December Bassompierre went to Normandy to attend the assembly of the Notables which Louis XIII was holding at Rouen. While he was there, news arrived that the Princesse de Condé had given birth to a still-born child and was in a critical condition; and the King being desirous of sending some important personages to make inquiries on her behalf, or, in the event of the princess being dead, to offer his condolences to Condé, Bassompierre and the Duc de Guise offered to go. They set out in a coach, a kind of conveyance which did not usually lend itself to rapid travelling; but, by arranging for an unusual number of relays, reached Paris the same day, and made the return journey with similar expedition. Bassompierre assures us that never before had a journey by coach been made in so short a time at that season of the year.

The princess recovered, "though she was more than forty-eight hours without movement or feeling," and "never was a person in greater extremity without dying."[126]

CHAPTER XIX

Luynes succeeds to the power and wealth of Concini—Trial and execution of Concini's widow, Leonora Galigaï—Luynes begins to direct affairs of State—His marriage to Marie de Rohan—Conduct of the Duc d'Epernon—His quarrel with Du Vair, the Keeper of the Seals—His disgrace—He begins to intrigue with the Queen-Mother—Escape of the latter from Blois—Treaty of Angoulême—The Court at Tours—Arnauld d'Andilly's account of Bassompierre's lavish hospitality—Favours bestowed by the King on Bassompierre—Meeting between Louis XIII and the Queen-Mother—Liberation of Condé—Bassompierre entertains the King at Monceaux—He is admitted to the Ordre du Saint-Esprit.

THE heir of the power of Concini was Luynes. He was, as we have mentioned, a gentleman of Provence—a very unimportant gentleman the Court had thought him before he had contrived to insinuate himself into the good graces of the young King. His father, an officer of fortune, the fruit, if we are to believe Richelieu, of a *liaison* between one d'Albert, a canon of Marseilles, and a chambermaid, was the owner of the Château of Luynes, near Aix, the vineyard of Brantes, and the islet of Cadenet in the middle of the Rhone, *seigneuries*, says Bassompierre, which a hare could jump over, but which, in default of revenues, furnished titles for his three sons. Charles

Albert, the eldest, had begun life as page to the Comte du Lude, and was afterwards placed by Henri IV with the Dauphin. Both he and his younger brothers, Brantes and Cadenet, were exceedingly good-looking men, skilled in all bodily exercises, well-educated and possessed of ingratiating manners; but there were no limits to their ambition or their greed, and they did not intend to allow any little scruples to stand in the way of their advancement.

Despite the adage:

"Devrait-on hériter de ceux qu'on assassine,"

Luynes inherited, not only the power of Concini, but also the greater part of his charges and possessions: lieutenancy-general of Normandy, government of the Pont-de-l'Arche, domain of Ancre (the name of which was changed to Albert), his post of First Gentleman of the Chamber, his hôtel in Paris, his estate of Lesigny, and so forth. When people saw the confiscated property of the Concini pass straight from the royal demesne into the greedy hands of the new favourite, they began to ask themselves whether the country was after all likely to gain much by the change that had taken place.

But the confiscation of the property of the Florentine couple, though it might suffice, for the moment, the cupidity of Luynes, did not suffice his policy. He desired to widen the gulf which he had opened between Louis XIII and his mother,[127] by dragging the name of the latter through the mire of a criminal court; and, at his instigation, the Maréchale d'Ancre was brought to trial as a sorceress who had bewitched the Queen-Mother by her arts,[128] and on July 8, 1617, condemned to be burned alive in the Place de Grève for the crime of *lèse-majesté* human and divine.

It was with great difficulty, however, that Luynes succeeded in obtaining this verdict. The Advocate-General, Lebret, at first refused to demand the death penalty, and it was only on Luynes giving him his word that the prisoner would be pardoned after the decree that he consented to do so. But the only clemency that the unfortunate woman was able to obtain was that her head should be cut off before her body was committed to the flames. She died with great courage and resignation.

The death of Villeroy, in November, 1617, enfeebled the group of old counsellors who had been recalled to office after the assassination of Concini; and Luynes, whose favour with the King was constantly increasing, began to direct the State, although he was totally ignorant of public affairs. His Government benefited for some time by the unpopularity of the Maréchal d'Ancre; the grandees remained tranquil, and Luynes, by his marriage with the beautiful Marie de Rohan, daughter of the Duc de Montbazon, destined one day to become so celebrated under the name of the Duchesse de Chevreuse, assured himself of the support of the House of Rohan.

Alone amongst the great nobles, d'Épernon did not hurry himself to come and compliment the King on his assumption of the government of his realm and to salute the man to whom he had delegated the royal authority. As Colonel-General of the French Infantry, d'Épernon was a power in the land, and when at last, towards the end of March, 1618, he condescended to visit the Court, the colonels of all the regiments stationed in and around Paris and in Picardy and Champagne went so far as Étampes to meet him and escort him to the capital. Haughty and choleric and excessively touchy on the question of his rights, this former *mignon* of Henri III was not long in mortally offending the King, already incensed against him by his long delay in presenting himself at Court, which

Luynes had not failed to represent as a gross want of the respect due to his sovereign.

Finding that Du Vair, to whom the Seals had been restored after the dismissal of Mangot, was in the habit of taking his seat at the Council above all the nobles, even when the Chancellor was present, although the Keeper of the Seals was not an officer of the Crown, his gorge rose at once, and he went to the King to protest against so intolerable an affront to his own dignity and that of his order. Du Vair happened to be with the King, and, says Bassompierre, "as M. d'Épernon was a little violent, he attacked the Keeper of the Seals, who answered him more sharply than he should have done." Three days later, Louis XIII summoned the duke and Du Vair to his cabinet, and, in the presence of Bassompierre and several other courtiers, ordered them to be reconciled. By way of answer, d'Épernon shrugged his shoulders, upon which the young monarch, who was seated, rose in great indignation, and severely reprimanded him. Then, observing that he had affairs of importance to attend to, he abruptly quitted the room.

D'Épernon retired, followed by Bassompierre, but, to their astonishment, they found all the doors of the ante-chamber closed and locked. It looked "as though the King intended to have the duke arrested, and had given orders for the doors to be secured, in order to allow time for an officer of the Guards to be summoned." However, it occurred to Bassompierre that perhaps the door leading to the King's private staircase, which was opposite that of his chamber, might not be locked, and, finding it unfastened, he fetched d'Épernon, and they descended the stairs and made their way to the Salle Haute, where the old noble's attendants were awaiting him.

As d'Épernon was leaving the Louvre, he asked his friend "to send him warning if anything had been resolved against him." Bassompierre accordingly spoke to Luynes on the subject, and was informed that, as M. d'Épernon intended going to his government of Metz, he would be well advised to hasten his departure, since there were persons who might incite the King against him. Bassompierre, of course, understood very well who it was who was likely to incite the King.

On being assured that his Majesty was prepared to treat him as though nothing had happened when he went to ask permission to retire to Metz, d'Épernon proceeded to the Louvre, where the King received him "with a very good countenance," and granted his request. Louis XIII was under the impression that the duke intended to leave Paris the following day; but, five days later, while the King was at Vanves, a village in the environs of the capital, he learned that d'Épernon was still there and that a great number of people were visiting him. His Majesty angrily told Bassompierre that if, when he returned to Paris on the morrow, he found M. d'Épernon there, it would be the worse for him; and Luynes advised Bassompierre to go and tell him that "he would not remain much longer, if he were wise." This he did, and d'Épernon requested him to inform the King that he would leave Paris before noon on the morrow. He took his departure within the time specified, but, instead of proceeding to Metz, he only went so far as Fontenay-en-Brie, near Coulommiers, where he had a country-seat. Louis XIII was furious, and proposed to send a detachment of the Guards to arrest him; but the Chancellor, Sillery, who was a friend of d'Épernon, sent a messenger in all haste to the duke to warn him of what was intended, and d'Épernon, recognising that he had presumed too far on the young monarch's forbearance, lost no time in resuming his journey to Metz.

Although d'Épernon had only himself to blame for his disgrace, he was none the less bitterly incensed against the King and his favourite; and, to avenge his outraged dignity, forthwith proceeded to establish a secret correspondence with the Queen-Mother, whom he urged to protest by force of arms against the treatment she was receiving, and promised to support by every means in his power.

Marie required little prompting: she had already resolved to make her escape. Thanks to the enmity of Luynes, she found herself little better than a prisoner in the Château of Blois; all correspondence with persons at the Court was forbidden her; Richelieu, who had aroused the suspicions of the favourite, had been banished to Avignon, and other members of her entourage had also been removed. Nevertheless, she dissimulated her resentment, and in April, 1619, consented, at the instance of a Jesuit, Père Arnoux, whom Luynes sent to her, to sign a declaration, in which she swore "before God and His angels," to submit in all things to the wishes of the King, and to warn him immediately of "all communications and overtures contrary to his service."

Luynes, however, continued to offend her. At the end of 1618, an embassy from Savoy came to Paris to demand the hand of her younger daughter, Christine, for the Prince of Piedmont, eldest son of Charles Emmanuel. Marie was not consulted, the King confining himself to informing her of the betrothal; and on February 10, 1619, the marriage was celebrated without her being invited. It was the last straw; she resolved to fly at the first favourable opportunity. D'Épernon, anticipating her intention, had left Metz, towards the end of January, without permission of the King, and gone to await her in the Angoumois; and, in the night of February 21-22, Marie made her escape to Blois and went to Angoulême, whence she wrote to her son, demanding the redress of her grievances.

Luynes was at first greatly alarmed, fearing that the Princes, already beginning to show signs of irritation at the increasing power of the favourite, might join the Queen-Mother; but they remained quiet. In these circumstances, he might easily have crushed d'Épernon; but he wished to avoid war, and accordingly sent the Cardinal de la Rochefoucauld and Père Bérulle, the famous preacher of the Oratoire, to propose peace to Marie, and recalled Richelieu from Avignon "to pacify her mind." In this task the prelate succeeded, and on April 30, 1619, he signed with the

Cardinal de la Rochefoucauld a treaty at Angoulême which authorised the Queen-Mother to dispose of the offices of her Household and to reside where she pleased, and gave her, in exchange for the government of Normandy, that of Anjou, with the Château of Angers, the Ponts-de-Cé and Chinon. D'Épernon, against whom the usual royal declaration had been launched, recovered his charges and appointments, and Richelieu was given to understand that he might hope for a cardinal's hat at no very distant date.

However, Louis XIII, who had been on the point of setting out with the Court for the Loire when the news that peace had been signed reached him, determined to carry out his intention, Luynes no doubt thinking that, in view of the possibility of further trouble with the Queen-Mother, a visit of the young King to that part of his realm might be productive of good results. After a short stay at different towns, including Amboise, from which letters announcing the peace were sent to the Parlement of Paris for registration, at the end of May the Court arrived at Tours, where, says Bassompierre, "we remained three months and passed our time very pleasantly."

Arnauld d'Andilly, in his *Mémoires*, has left us an interesting picture of life at Tours and, more particularly, of the lavish hospitality dispensed by Bassompierre:—

"While at Tours, I happened to be lodged near M. de Bassompierre, who kept a table which you might say was worthy of one of the greatest nobles of the Court, since it was always full. He did me the honour to invite me to come every day and pressed me in such fashion that, not being acquainted with any of these grandees so intimately that I believed myself competent to say that there was no one in France of my condition who lived so habitually or on such familiar terms with them, I was unable to refuse a civility so obliging. Those whom I met there were, apart from their rank, persons of a merit so great, that some had filled already, and others have filled since, the most important offices of State, and commanded armies. Thus, there was much to learn from their conversation, and nothing was more agreeable than the pleasant familiarity with which they lived together. Ceremony, the constraint of which is insupportable to those who are nourished in the air of the great world, was unknown there. Each one seated himself where he pleased. Those who came the latest never failed to find a place at the table, although the others may already have been there a long while. However great was the good cheer provided, no one ever spoke about eating. People came without saying good-day, and went away without saying adieu. And the conversation ranged over all kinds of topics, and was, not only agreeable, but instructive."

On leaving Tours, the Court paid short visits to Le Lude, in the Maine, where the King was the guest of the Comte du Lude, whose page Luynes had once been, La Flèche, and Durtal, where he was entertained by the Comte de Schomberg. His Majesty was exceedingly gracious to Bassompierre about this time. On the death of the old Swiss colonel Galatty he offered him the choice of that veteran's appointments; gave him the Abbey of Honnecourt, in the diocese of Cambrai, for one of his ecclesiastical friends, who appears to have contented himself with drawing the revenues of the benefice and did not even take the trouble to get instituted until twenty-five years later; and bestowed other favours upon him.

At the beginning of September, the Court returned to Tours, the King having decided that it would be advisable to placate his mother, who was complaining that the terms of the treaty signed at Angoulême had not been properly executed, by a personal interview. On September 4 Marie de' Medici arrived at

Couzières, a country-house belonging to Luynes's father-in-law, the Duc de Montbazon, where she was received by the favourite, who was accompanied by all the princes and great nobles. On the following day she arrived at Tours, being met at some little distance from the town by Anne of Austria and all the princesses.

Marie remained with the King until the 19th, and then left for Chinon *en route* for Angers, while the Court proceeded to Amboise.

Bassompierre does not give us any information about Louis XIII's attitude to his mother during these two weeks, but, if we are to believe Richelieu, he showed towards her "an incredible tenderness." Anyway, Luynes appears to have become very uneasy, fearing lest the meeting at Tours might lead to a more or less complete reconciliation between mother and son; and one of his first acts when the Court returned to Paris was to persuade the King to set Condé at liberty and restore him to all his offices and dignities (October 20, 1619). He judged—and rightly, as it proved—that the harsh treatment to which the first Prince of the Blood had been subjected during the early months of his imprisonment in the Bastille would have so embittered him against the Queen-

Mother, that he could be trusted to use all his influence to prevent the *rapprochement* which the favourite had so much cause to dread. And, to nullify the effects of the "incredible tenderness" of which Richelieu speaks, he caused to be inserted in the declaration of Condé's innocence, which was registered by the Parlement on November 26, words which could not fail to be most offensive to Marie de' Medici: "Being informed," said the King, "of the reasons by which his detention has been excused, I have found that there was no cause, save the machinations and evil designs of his enemies, who desired to join the ruin of my State to that of my cousin."

In November, the King spent a fortnight at Monceaux, and Bassompierre, who was captain of the château, entertained him most magnificently. At the close of the year there was a large promotion to the Ordre du Saint-Esprit, five prelates and fifty-nine nobles being admitted. Bassompierre was amongst the latter, his name figuring twenty-fourth on the list of the new knights.

The promotions to the Ordre du Saint-Esprit furnished Marie de' Medici with yet another grievance, and she complained bitterly that they comprised all her chief enemies, to the exclusion of the friends whom she had recommended. Luynes seemed bent on exasperating her beyond endurance, and on making her little Court at Angers, where she had now established herself, a centre of disaffection.

CHAPTER XX

The grandees, irritated by the increasing power and favour of Luynes, decide to make common cause with the Queen-Mother against him—Departure of Mayenne from the Court—He is followed by Longueville, Nemours, Mayenne and Retz—Formidable character of the insurrection—Bassompierre receives orders to mobilise a Royal army in Champagne—He informs the King that the Comte de Soissons, his mother, the Grand Prieur de Vendôme and the Comte de Saint-Aignan intend to leave Paris to join the rebels—Alarm and indecision of Luynes—Advice of Bassompierre—It is finally decided to allow them to go—Success of Bassompierre in mobilising troops in Champagne despite great difficulties—The Duc de Bouillon sends a gentleman to him to endeavour to corrupt his loyalty—Reply of Bassompierre—The town and château of Dreux surrender to him—He joins the King near La Flèche with an army of 8,600 men—Combat of the Ponts-des-Cé—Peace of Angers.

LUYNES had contrived to exasperate many other important personages besides Marie de' Medici. The irritation of the grandees against him was increasing, in proportion as they beheld the King accumulating new favours on the head of his parvenu favourite. Luynes and his two brothers, Cadenet and Brantès, "devoured everything." Between them they had acquired eighteen of the most important governments in the kingdom, and had all three blossomed into dukes, the eldest brother having been created Duc de

Luynes, the second Duc de Chaulnes, while the youngest had married the heiress of the duchy of Piney-Luxembourg, and had secured the revival of that title in his favour. Cadenet had also been provided with the hand of a wealthy heiress of an illustrious house, and had become, not only a duke and peer, but a marshal of France. As for Luynes, he appeared to consider the bâton of marshal unworthy of his grandeur, and awaited a favourable opportunity of girding on the sword of Constable. Nor, while the three brothers were thus enriched and aggrandized, were their poor relations forgotten; they arrived "by battalions" from Provence and had their share of the spoils.

By family alliances Luynes had assured himself of the support of Condé, Lesdiguières and of all the Guises, with the exception of the cardinal, and he governed both the King and the State. The Ministers were only consulted as a matter of form. The engagements to the Queen-Mother were not kept; and, as the finances were in a state of indescribable confusion, the pensions of the grandees, with the exception of those who had the good fortune to be related by marriage to the favourite or his brothers, remained unpaid.

Before the winter was over the patience of the grandees was exhausted, and they decided to make common cause with the Queen-Mother against this new Concini. "In the middle of Lent," writes Bassompierre, "M. de Mayenne quitted the Court without taking leave of the King."[129]

Mayenne's unceremonious departure sounded the first note of warning. Others were not long in coming. At short intervals during the spring, Vendôme, Longueville, Nemours and Retz followed the example of the Lorraine prince, and when it became known that Vendôme, after going to his country-seat in Normandy, had proceeded to join the Queen-Mother at Angers, the Court could no longer doubt what was in the wind. The King and Luynes, much alarmed, pressed Marie to return to Court; but she did not wish to reappear there, "save with honour and safety," and did not consider the guarantees which were offered her sufficient. Richelieu counselled her to take the risk, but the grandees who surrounded the Queen-Mother opposed it, and civil war was decided upon.

In appearance, this insurrection was the most formidable that had been seen since the accession of Louis XIII. The malcontents believed themselves to be masters of France from Dieppe to Bayonne, and possessed, besides, in the East of France, the important position of Metz, of which d'Épernon was governor, which would permit them to introduce into the kingdom foreign mercenaries. Luynes was at first greatly perturbed; but Condé, eager to be avenged on the Queen-Mother, reassured him, and urged him to take vigorous measures to meet the danger. The plan of campaign they decided upon was well conceived. They, with the King, would march into Normandy with what troops could be spared from the defence of the capital, while Bassompierre, who had been appointed *maréchal de camp*—a rank corresponding to brigadier-general—of the troops in garrison in Champagne and on the frontier of Lorraine, went there to mobilise as large a force as possible. Then, when the safety of Normandy had been assured, they would turn southwards; Bassompierre would join them at some point north of the Loire, and their united forces would march on Angers.

On June 29 Bassompierre was entering the Louvre, to take leave of the King, before setting out for Champagne, when a note in a woman's handwriting was slipped into his hand, informing him that the Comte de Soissons[130] and his mother proposed to leave Paris that night to join the Queen-

Mother at Angers, and that the Grand Prieur de Vendôme, the duke's younger brother, and the Comte de Saint-Aignan were going with them. Shortly afterwards, he happened to meet the Chevalier d'Épinay, Commander of Malta, who was a friend of the Grand Prior, and questioned him on the matter, when the chevalier said that he had been correctly informed, and added that he himself was to be of the party.

Bassompierre found the King in his cabinet with Luynes, and informed them of what was intended. They both appeared very much disturbed at his news, and the King, who was going that afternoon to the Château of Madrid, in the Bois de Boulogne, said that he should remain in Paris, and announced his intention of sending for the Comte de Soissons and having him arrested. Luynes and Bassompierre, however, pointed out that "to arrest so great a personage without certain proofs did not seem to them to be expedient, and that the affair merited to be weighed and debated before any resolution was arrived at." And Luynes advised the King not to postpone his journey, "for fear of frightening the game," and said that he himself would remain in Paris and keep Bassompierre there that day, and that, so soon as they had come to a decision, they would acquaint his Majesty with it. He also asked that the Light Cavalry of the Guard, which his youngest brother now commanded, should be placed at his disposal, in order that he might effect the arrest of the prince and his friends, if that course were deemed advisable.

Louis XIII accordingly set off for Madrid, and Bassompierre, Luynes, his two brothers, and several of their friends met in solemn conclave at the favourite's hôtel in the Rue Saint-Thomas du Louvre to weigh and debate this important matter. Luynes seemed in great perplexity, nor did his relatives and friends appear able to help him to come to any definite decision. At length, he turned to Bassompierre, who had hitherto remained silent, and begged him to give them the benefit of his counsel.

Bassompierre modestly disclaimed any desire to express an opinion upon affairs of State, particularly upon a matter so intricate and delicate as the one under discussion. However, said he, as M. de Luynes had done him the honour to seek his counsel, he would give it for what it was worth.

He then said that, in this affair, he must speak like a

CHARLES D'ALBERT, DUC DE LUYNES, CONSTABLE OF FRANCE.

From a contemporary print.

shopkeeper, and say that there were only two alternatives: to take him or to leave him. If they decided to let *Monsieur le Comte* depart in peace, they might either say nothing to him at all, or inform him that his design was known, but that it was a matter of indifference to the King whether he executed it or not. If, on the contrary, they decided to arrest him, there were several ways in which it might be effected: they might advise the King to summon him to Madrid, warn him that he was informed of his design, and that, in the circumstances, he felt obliged "to assure himself of his person"; or they might send the Light Cavalry to invest his hôtel and arrest him there; or as he was leaving his house, or at the gates of the town; or, finally, at Villapreux (three leagues from Versailles), the rendezvous where Saint-Aignan and d'Épinay were to join him.

"It is now for you, Monsieur," he concluded solemnly "to deliberate upon and decide whether it be advisable to arrest him or let him go; and, should you judge it necessary to arrest him, to make choice also of one of the ways which I have proposed to you, and to execute it promptly and surely."

"Upon that," observes Bassompierre, "M. de Luynes was in greater uncertainty than ever"—we can well believe it—"and I was astonished to see the little aid and comfort which he received from the other gentlemen present, who showed themselves as irresolute as he was."

They continued their deliberations all the afternoon, and when evening came they were as far off a decision as ever. Then Bassompierre, whose patience was exhausted, said to Luynes: "Monsieur, you are wasting time in resolving what course ought to be pursued. It grows late; the King must be growing anxious at not hearing anything from you. Come to some decision."

"It is very easy for you to talk," answered the favourite petulantly; "but if you held the handle of the frying-pan, as I do, you would be in a like difficulty."

Bassompierre then suggested that perhaps, in the circumstances, it might be as well to take the Ministers into his confidence. Now, as we have mentioned already, M. de Luynes never condescended to consult these unfortunate old gentlemen—"the dotards" as they were irreverently called—except as a matter of form. Nevertheless, such was his perplexity on this occasion, that he caught at the proposal as a drowning man catches at a straw, and despatched a messenger in all haste to summon the Ministers to assemble at the Chancellor's house. Thither the conference adjourned, and, after a good deal of further discussion, it was resolved to let Soissons and his mother take their departure and to say nothing to them about it. This decision was arrived at on the advice of Jeannin, who pointed out that such vain and meddlesome persons as these two were more likely to cause dissensions in the Queen-Mother's party than to strengthen it; that, when hostilities began, it would be better to have them outside Paris than hatching mischief within its walls; and, further, that it would be easy at any time to draw *Monsieur le Comte* away from his confederates by pecuniary inducements, in which event he would very probably be followed by the other princes, since these exalted personages were like a flock of sheep: when one took the leap, the others followed him.

And so, at eleven o'clock that night, the Soissons and their friends left Paris by the Porte Saint-Jacques, and went off to join the Queen-Mother at Angers, no man hindering them; and on the following morning Bassompierre set out for Champagne.

Bassompierre passed the first night of his journey at Château-Thierry, where he received most alarming intelligence, to the effect that a gentleman of the name of Loppes, who was in the service of the Duc de Vendôme, was waiting with a troop of light horse between that town and Châlons, with the intention of making him a prisoner and carrying him off to Sedan. However, the rumour proved to be a false one, and he arrived safely at Châlons without seeing anything of M. de Loppes or his troop. Nevertheless, having ascertained that that gentleman was at his country-house some few miles from Châlons, he considered it advisable to pay him a visit, lest haply he should only have postponed the sinister designs attributed to him to some more convenient season.

A promise, in the King's name, of the command of the troop in which he was now only a lieutenant sufficed to draw the most fervid expressions of loyalty from M. de Loppes; and he volunteered to escort Bassompierre with thirty of his men to Vitry, where two companies of the regiment of Champagne were in garrison.

On the following morning, Bassompierre reviewed the garrison, which he found pretty well up to strength, and sounded the officers, who appeared loyal enough, though the lieutenant-colonel was under suspicion. However, as he was away on furlough, and not likely to return for some time, there was nothing to be feared from him.

From Vitry Bassompierre proceeded to Verdun, where he arrived on July 6. Here there was a different tale to tell.

There were two regiments in garrison at Verdun: that of Picardy and that of the Comte de Vaubecourt.[131] The latter had its full complement of all grades, but the Regiment of Picardy could not muster a third of its strength; and he was informed that part of the absentees had gone off to serve as volunteers in Germany, where the Thirty Years' War was just beginning; while the rest had been seduced from their duty by the Marquis de la Valette, d'Épernon's second son, and had thrown themselves into Metz with him.

The following day, Bassompierre received a letter from Louis XIII, informing him that he was proceeding at once into Normandy to save Rouen, which Longueville was endeavouring to raise against him, and ordering him to assemble all the forces he could muster at Saint-Menehould, leaving Vaubecourt's regiment to garrison what places in Champagne he considered necessary, and then to march with all possible speed to Montereau, where he would receive further orders.

At Verdun Bassompierre received a visit from M. de Fresnel, Governor of Clermont-en-Argonne, who was intimately acquainted with the military resources of that part of France. Fresnel warned him that he would find in every garrison-town the same condition of things as at Verdun, and that, apart from Vaubecourt's regiment, he doubted whether he would be able to muster 2,000 men. The magazines, however, were full and capable of equipping any number of men; and, if he were prepared to offer a bounty to everyone who enlisted, he believed that plenty of recruits would be forthcoming.

Bassompierre readily agreed to give the bounty which Fresnel advised, though he had to find the money out of his own pocket, and in a few days Fresnel had raised 800 men on his estates in the Argonne, with whom and another 120 furnished by the town of Verdun, he filled the ranks of the Regiment of Picardy. The Bailiff of Bar, a personal friend of his, sent him 300, whom he drafted into the Regiment of Champagne; another 300 came from the Valley of Aillant, in the Yonne. The drum was beaten vigorously at Vitry, Saint-Dizier, Châlons, Rheims, Sens and other towns, and each of them furnished its contingent, with the result that he soon found himself at the head of what, for those times, was quite a formidable force, though, as the great majority of the men thus obtained were raw recruits who had never been under fire, their fighting value was not very great. However, he had the consolation of knowing that the rebel forces would undoubtedly be at the same disadvantage.

Bassompierre had the good fortune to have at his disposal a number of experienced commissariat-officers, and the arrangements he was thus enabled to make for the rapid march of his army westwards, notwithstanding that it was then the height of a very hot summer, appear to have left little to be desired, and to have shown a solicitude for the soldier's comfort and well-being most unusual at this epoch.

"After deciding," he says, "upon the routes which my troops were to follow, I decided upon my marches, which I made longer than was customary, to wit, nine or ten leagues per day. I gave orders that each regiment should start at three or four in the morning and march until nine o'clock, by which time it should have covered five leagues. And I arranged that the halting-place should be near some river or brook, where it would find a cart containing wine and another filled with bread awaiting it, to refresh the soldiers. Here they would rest until three of the afternoon, in order to avoid marching during the heat of the day, and then take the road again. And I further arranged that when they reached the village where they were to pass the night, they should find the beasts that were to provide their meal already slaughtered, for which I paid one half of the cost, and the village the other. By this means, the soldier, perceiving the care that I took that he should want for nothing, performed without a murmur these long marches so far as Montereau."

On July 13, towards evening, Bassompierre arrived at Poivre, where he had arranged to pass the night. Shortly afterwards, he received a visit from a Huguenot gentleman named Despence, with whom he had some slight acquaintance, and whom he invited to sup with him. When they rose from table, M. Despence led him into the garden adjoining the house, and there inquired if he might speak to him frankly and "in all security"; by which he meant that whatever the nature of the communication he wished to make might be, Bassompierre would afterwards suffer him to depart in peace.

Bassompierre having given him the assurance he demanded, he informed him that he came from Sedan, on behalf of the Duc de Bouillon, who had charged him to say that while the duke, as a soldier himself, could not help but commend the zeal and energy which M. de Bassompierre was employing in raising and equipping troops and overcoming the difficulties with which he had to contend, he wondered greatly what could be the motive which prompted him to all this activity. Could it be that he entertained some personal animosity against the Queen-Mother, to whom, he had always understood, he was indebted for many benefits, or had M. de Luynes placed him under some great obligation? The duke desired to point out to M. de Bassompierre that the Queen-Mother and the princes and nobles who supported her had not taken up arms to attack the King or the State, but to decide whether both should be governed by her who had ruled so well during his Majesty's minority, or by three robbers who had seized the authority and the person of the King. He praised M. de Bassompierre's resolution to "keep always to the trunk of the tree, and to follow, not the best and most just party, but that which possessed the person of the King and the seal and wax." But to display such fiery ardour, such boundless activity; to exceed even the orders of the King in the rapidity with which he was pushing forward his troops; to employ his own money so profusely as he was doing in the cause of persons who had proved themselves so ungrateful to the Queen, their first benefactress, and would prove no less ungrateful to their friends; to be apparently intent on compassing the ruin of the party of the Queen, the consort of the late King, who had been so much attached to him; to assist "three pumpkins who had sprung up in a night"[132] to trample upon her, and thus to compromise his reputation and his honesty—for all this M. de Bouillon could see neither rhyme nor reason.

After this long-winded preamble, M. Despence came to the point. The duke, he said, had no intention of suggesting to M. de Bassompierre that he should do anything contrary to his honour and duty; nothing was further from his thoughts. But, if he could see his way to delay for three weeks the junction of the army under his command with that of the King, which might be done without disobeying the orders he had received from his Majesty, who did not anticipate that he would be able to join him before then; if he would rest content with such troops as he found in garrison, and cease to amuse himself by levying everywhere at his own expense men to reinforce them, and, in short, abate a little of his ardour and animosity towards the party of the Queen-Mother, M. de Bouillon would without delay deposit the sum of 100,000 crowns in the hands of any banker whom he might be pleased to name, and no one but themselves would be the wiser.

Bassompierre, with growing indignation, heard him to the end, and then told him that he was astonished that he should have taken advantage of the promise of safety he had received to make him so disgraceful a proposition. "I did not think," said he, "that M. de Bouillon knew me so little as to imagine that money or any other advantage would make me fail in my duty or honour. It is not animosity, but ardour and desire to serve the King which has spurred me to these extraordinary exertions. Next to his I am the most devoted servant of the Queen in the world; but, when it is a question of the service of the King, I do not recognise the Queen. I would that I could run or fly to whatever place his service called me, and, as for my money, I would dispense that right willingly to the last sol, provided that his affairs might be placed in a good state. If you had not obtained an assurance of safety from me, I should have had you arrested, and sent you to Châlons; but the promise I have given you prevents me from doing that."

With which he turned on his heel and left M. Despence to return whence he came, marvelling greatly that so shrewd a judge of men as the lord of Sedan professed to be should have sent him on so bootless an errand.

On the 18th, the army reached Montereau, and Bassompierre brought his troops across the Seine and quartered them in and around Étampes. The evening before he had received a letter from the King announcing that Caen and Rouen had opened their gates to him; that Longueville had retired to Dieppe and shut himself up there; while the Grand Prior, who had been assisting him to stir up trouble, had fled to Angers, and that his Majesty was about to begin his march to the Loire.

On the 19th, Bassompierre went to Paris to make arrangements for the provisioning of his army. On going to salute Anne of Austria, her Majesty told him that "she did not know whether to receive him as general of an army or as a courier, seeing the extreme activity he had displayed," while the Council "could not believe that the army was at Étampes and in such strength as he assured them was the case."

As Bassompierre was so much ahead of his time, and there was no need for him to begin his march to join the army of the King for some days, he received orders to make an attempt to reduce Dreux, one of the few places in Normandy still occupied by the rebels. He accordingly returned to Étampes, and was about to set out for Dreux at the head of the regiments of Champagne and Picardy and a detachment of cavalry, when he received a letter from Anne of Austria informing him that she had received intelligence that the Comte de Rochefort, husband of a lady to whom Bassompierre had "offered his service" at the end of the previous year, and who, we may presume, had been graciously pleased to accept it, was in dire peril of his life. It appeared that Rochefort, who was governor of the Château of Nantes, had been arrested at Angers by orders of Marie de' Medici, and that "M. de Vendôme intended to bring him before the Château of Nantes, to force it to surrender; threatening, in case of refusal, to cut off his head." The only way to save M. de Rochefort, wrote the Queen, was to seize Vendôme's mother-in-law, Madame de Mercœur, and his children, who were at the Château of Anet, near Dreux, the palatial country-seat which Henri II had built for his middle-aged inamorata Diane de Poitiers, and bring them as hostages to Paris. "And she recommended to me this affair, which was very important to the service of the King and which would afford infinite satisfaction to Madame de Rochefort, of whom I was so much the servant."

Bassompierre accordingly detached the greater part of his cavalry and sent them to Anet to secure Madame de Mercœur and the little Vendômes, and with the rest of his force presented himself before the gates of Dreux. They were opened to him at once, and the citizens shouted, *Vive le Roi!* with all the strength of their lungs; but Bassompierre informed them that, although he was very gratified to hear such cries, he would prefer to have some practical proof of their loyalty. And he ordered them to assist him in bringing M. d'Escluzelles, the governor of the château, to reason.

M. d'Escluzelles, however, refused to surrender, and, though Bassompierre's troops, with the assistance of the citizens, built a formidable barricade which cut off all communication between the château and the town, he appeared to regard their proceedings with indifference. When, however, on the following day, Bassompierre caused him to be informed that, unless he capitulated forthwith, he proposed to burn his country-seat, which lay a few miles from Dreux, to the ground, cut down every tree on his estate, and carry off his wife and children to Paris, he "had pity upon his property and his family," and sent to demand a parley. Next morning (July 25), the château surrendered, and Bassompierre having placed a garrison there and seen Madame de Mercœur and her grandchildren, whom the cavalry had brought from Anet, off to Paris, returned to Étampes and began his march towards the Loire. On August 2 his army arrived at Connerré, not far from Le Mans, where Louis XIII's headquarters were, and Bassompierre went to pay his respects to his Majesty, who gave him a most flattering reception and "expressed himself very satisfied with the care and expedition which he had shown."

Two days later, the King reviewed Bassompierre's army in the plain of Gros Chataigneraie, near La Flèche. It now consisted of 8,000 infantry and 600 cavalry, and his Majesty pronounced it "very fine and very complete, and beyond what he had expected to find." The two armies were then joined into one corps, and the King having given the command to Condé, with Praslin as his second in command, and appointed four brigadier-generals, of whom Bassompierre was one, the Royal forces advanced on Angers.

The rapid submission of Normandy had deceived all the expectations of Marie de' Medici, for d'Épernon was not yet ready to join her, nor had Mayenne completed the formidable levies of troops which he was making in Guienne. Towards the end of July, her troops had advanced so far as La Flèche, but, on the news of the approach of the Royal army, had fallen back rapidly on Angers. Richelieu endeavoured to stop the King by opening negotiations, but Louis XIII, whose military instincts had been awakened by the life of the camp, continued to advance. On August 6 the Queen-Mother made new proposals, and, though

Condé urged the King to reject them, Luynes, who was still doubtful about the issue of the war, persuaded Louis to return a favourable answer and to grant his mother an armistice until the following morning. Deputies were then despatched to Angers, but, owing to some misunderstanding, they had to wait several hours before being admitted to the town. This delay was attended with disastrous results to the insurgent forces.

The troops of the Queen-Mother, which did not exceed 8,000 men, were spread out along a front of about four miles from Angers to the Ponts-des-Cé, an important position which assured to them the passage of the Loire. Vendôme, who commanded under the youthful Comte de Soissons, the nominal chief of the army, had conceived the fantastic idea of connecting these two towns by a long line of entrenchments, which, however, were not yet half-finished, and which, even if they had been completed, would have required a much larger force than the one at his disposal to defend effectively. The Royal army was encamped in the plain of Trélazé, about a league from the Ponts-des-Cé.

On the morning of the 7th, just about the time when the King's commissioners were entering Angers to conclude peace, Louis XIII was persuaded by Condé, who was determined to do everything in his power to prevent the termination of hostilities before a decisive defeat had been inflicted on the Queen-Mother's party, to consent to a reconnaissance in force of the rebels' position; and the Royal army accordingly advanced to within sight of the unfinished entrenchments. Whether from cowardice or from irritation at the neglect of his interests which Marie de' Medici had shown in the treaty which was about to be signed, the Duc de Retz chose this moment to withdraw from the position assigned to him with his own regiment and another which had been placed under his command, and to retire across the Loire. The disorder consequent on this movement, which was entirely unexpected, was taken by the Royal captains for the beginning of a general retreat, and on their advice the King ordered the bugles to sound the attack.

Bassompierre's troops, with those of the Marquis de Nerestang, formed the left wing of the Royal army. Between them and the entrenchments lay some fields, the hedges of which were lined with musketeers; but they were speedily dislodged, and took refuge behind a body of cavalry, who retreated, in their turn, without making any attempt to charge, so soon as fire was opened upon them, and retired to what shelter the entrenchments afforded. The cannon of the citadel now came into play, but the gunners were quite unable to find the range, and not a man was hit. As they neared the entrenchments, Bassompierre dismounted and, taking a halberd from a sergeant, placed himself at the head of one of the battalions of the Regiment of Champagne. On seeing this, Nerestang rode up, exclaiming: "Monsieur, that is not the place for a brigadier-general; you will be unable to make the other battalions fight if you remain at the head of this one."

"I answered," says Bassompierre, "that he was right; but that these regiments, which were largely composed of new recruits, would fight well if they saw me at their head, and badly if I remained behind; and since I had raised and brought them to this army, I had an interest in their conducting themselves well. Then he said: 'I shall not remain on horseback if you are on foot,' and, dismounting, placed himself on my left."

The entrenchments were carried with but little resistance, for the defenders appear to have been demoralised by the desertion of Retz and his troops and the suddenness of the attack, and fled in disorder towards the town. A flanking-fire, however, from the roofs and windows of some of the houses in the faubourgs caused a few casualties amongst Bassompierre's men; and, as they were crossing some open ground between the trenches and the town, a squadron of cavalry emerged from a field, deployed and seemed about to charge.

"And now," says Bassompierre, "I shall relate a strange thing. A man from one of our storming-companies who had remained behind—I never learned his name—and who was carrying a pike, addressed himself to a chief who was riding some twenty paces in front of the others and gave his horse a thrust in the stomach with his pike. The horse reared, upon which the soldier gave him another thrust; and the rider, fearing to be thrown, wheeled to the left and galloped off. And, at the same moment, the squadron wheeled in the same direction and passed under the arch of the bridge, where the water was very shallow."

The Comte de Saint-Aignan, who, it will be remembered, had accompanied the Comte de Soissons when he left Paris to join the Queen-Mother, was with this squadron, having ridden up to order it to charge. He was on its left flank and tried to rally the fugitives, but without success, and was carried away with them for some little distance. Now, M. de Saint-Aignan was a great dandy, and was wearing gilded armour and a hat that was the *dernier cri* in sumptuous headgear—a hat to marvel at, adorned with great ostrich plumes fastened by diamond-buckles—and when he at last succeeded in getting out of the press and pulling up his horse, he found that his hat had been knocked off. He could not bring himself to abandon it, and accordingly rode back to where it lay and attempted to recover it with the point of his sword. Bassompierre, passing near him, on his way into the town, did not attempt to make him prisoner, and merely shouted: "Adieu, Saint-Aignan!" "Adieu, adieu!" replied the count, without desisting from his efforts to recover his hat. This was no easy matter, as his horse was very restive, but eventually he succeeded and had just replaced it triumphantly on his head, and was about to ride away, when he was stopped and taken prisoner by two carabiniers.

The Royal troops continued their advance through the faubourgs and into the town, the enemy making no attempt to rally, though there was a good deal of desultory firing from the houses, and Nerestang had his right thigh broken by a musket-shot.[133] In less than an hour, however, the town was cleared of the rebels, some of whom took refuge in the château, which surrendered on the following day, while the rest fled towards Angers.

Bassompierre was then sent to report the result of the action to the King and to take him the nobles who had been made prisoners. His Majesty, whom he found in company with Condé, Luynes and Bellegarde, "received him with extraordinary cordiality, and M. de Luynes spoke in praise of him to *Monsieur le Grand.*" But when Louis XIII heard that Saint-Aignan was amongst the prisoners, he looked very grave indeed, as did the others, and they consulted together as to what was to be done with him. Then the King informed Bassompierre that, as M. de Saint-Aignan was, not only an officer of the regular army, but Colonel-General of the Light Cavalry, and had been taken in arms against his sovereign, it had been decided that he was to be tried at once by the Keeper of the Seals, who was, with the army, and, in the event of conviction, to be decapitated that very day. And so it seemed as though poor Saint-Aignan had only succeeded in saving his hat at the cost of his head.

Happily for him, Bassompierre was determined to save him.

"I firmly opposed this decision," he writes, "and told the King and *Monsieur le Prince* that, if they treated him in this way, no man of rank among the enemy would allow himself to be made prisoner, from fear of dying by the hand of the executioner; that M. de Créquy and I had received his surrender, and that he was a prisoner of war; that the rank we held authorised us to give him our assurance that he should be regarded as such, and that we were not provost-marshals to cause our captives to be hanged. At the same time, I sent to warn M. de Créquy, who sent word that he would retire from the Ponts-des-Cé and would abandon everything,[134] if he did not receive a promise that the execution would be suspended. We obtained a respite until the morrow, when, the first indignation against Saint-Aignan having spent itself, it was easy to persuade them to abandon their resolution; and the peace which followed accommodated his affair, by the surrender of his charge, which was conferred upon La Curée."

The engagement of the Ponts-des-Cé was a terrible blow to the Queen-Mother's party; nevertheless, Marie was far from reduced to extremities. If no longer able to make peace on favourable terms, two courses were open to her. She might shut herself up in Angers with what was left of her army, and hold out until Mayenne and d'Épernon were able to come to her assistance, or she might ford the Loire with her cavalry, only a part of which had been engaged at the Ponts-des-Cé, and make her way to Angoulême, where d'Épernon's headquarters were. Thus, although no hope of success now remained, she might succeed in prolonging the war for months.

Luynes was aware of this, and aware too that a continuance of hostilities could not fail to add to his unpopularity; while he was beginning to fear Condé, with whom Louis XIII was now on quite alarmingly friendly terms, almost as much as he feared the Queen-Mother. The High Catholic party, too, were eager for peace, in order that the King might have his hands free to deal with the Protestants of Béarn; and their representations, joined to that of Luynes, decided Louis to abandon any idea of imposing on his mother and her adherents the stringent terms which their recent defeat would otherwise have justified. The treaty, which was signed at Angers on August 10, was, to all intents and purposes, a confirmation of that of the previous year, save for a stipulation that the partisans of the Queen-Mother were not to be restored to the offices and charges of which the King had disposed during the rebellion. Three days later, Marie and her son met at Brissac, and were, to all appearances, on the best of terms; and on the 16th a royal declaration proclaimed the innocence of the intentions of the Queen-Mother and her adherents "during the late disturbances." Mayenne and d'Épernon thereupon laid down their arms, and the powerful faction which for a moment had threatened to subvert the State melted away.

CHAPTER XXI

Refusal of the Protestants of Béarn to restore the property of the
Catholic Church—Louis XIII and Luynes resolve on rigorous
measures and set out for the South—Visit of Bassompierre to La
Rochelle—He joins the King at Bordeaux—Arrest and execution
of d'Arsilemont—The Parlement of Pau declines to register the
Royal edict and Louis XIII determines to march into Béarn—
Bassompierre charged with the transport of the army across the
Garonne, which is accomplished in twenty-four hours—Béarn and
Lower Navarre are united to the Crown of France—Coldness of
the King towards Bassompierre—Bassompierre learns that this is
due to the ill offices of Luynes, who regards him as a rival in the
royal favour—He is informed that Luynes is "unable to suffer him
to remain at Court"—Bassompierre decides to come to terms with
the favourite, and it is arranged that he shall quit the Court so
soon as some honourable office can be found for him—The
Valtellina question—Bassompierre appointed Ambassador
Extraordinary to the Court of Spain—Birth of a son to Luynes.

No sooner had peace been signed than Louis XIII, urged on by Luynes, who was above all things anxious to conciliate the High Catholic party, determined to deal with the recalcitrant Protestants of Béarn.

The re-establishment of the Catholic religion in Béarn had been one of the conditions on which Clement VIII had consented to grant absolution to Henri IV; but that monarch had only half kept his word, and had limited himself to nominating bishops to the sees of Lescar and Oleron, and paying them their salaries; re-establishing the Mass in a good many places, and admitting Catholics to charges and dignities. The two new bishops demanded the restoration of the ecclesiastical property formerly attached to their offices;[135] but the Government turned a deaf ear to their appeals, and it was not until Luynes rose to power that they had a chance of being listened to.

Besides his desire to gain the support of the *dévots*, Luynes saw in the affair of Béarn an opportunity of ridding himself of the possible rivalry of the young Marquis de Montpouillan with the King, as Montpouillan's father, the Marquis de la Force,[136] was governor of Béarn and chief of the Protestants of that country. He thereupon pressed Louis XIII to carry out the engagements which Henri IV had sought to evade, and, by a decree of the Council of June 25, 1617, the King ordered the restitution of Church property in Béarn. The Estates of Béarn, supported by La Force, remonstrated vigorously; but in September the King confirmed his decision of June.

The Protestants of Languedoc and Guienne embraced the cause of the Béarnais, and the Parlement of Pau, in which the Reformers were in a great majority, refused to register the edict. The troubles with the Queen-Mother prevented Louis XIII and Luynes from taking any rigorous measures, but now that their hands were free, they were resolved to lose no more time.

Before Louis XIII began his march to the South, Bassompierre obtained permission to pay a visit to his brother-in-law Saint-Luc at Brouage, of which town the latter was governor, and to travel by way of La Rochelle. He set out on September 13, accompanied by Créquy, La Rochefoucauld and a great number of other gentlemen, who, in view of the possibility of a renewal of the Wars of Religion in the near future, had gladly embraced the opportunity of visiting the great Huguenot stronghold.

The party stopped to dine at Surgères, a château belonging to La Rochefoucauld, from which the count sent a letter to the mayor of La Rochelle, "to warn him of the good company who were coming to see him, in order that he might not be alarmed at the sudden arrival of so many people." He received a most cordial response, for the authorities of La Rochelle were probably far from displeased to learn that the Colonel of the French Guards and the Colonel-General of the Swiss were on their way to visit their famous town, before whose stubborn walls, forty-six years earlier, nearly 20,000 Catholics had laid down their lives, and all to no purpose. Certainly, M. de Créquy, M. de Bassompierre and their friends should be afforded every facility for seeing all that was worth seeing, and particularly the defences; and when the King questioned them about their visit, as, of course, he would do, they would probably tell his Majesty that if, as seemed only too probable, he were determined to drive his Protestant subjects to take up arms once more in defence of their faith, he would do well to let La Rochelle severely alone.

And so M. le Maire came to meet them at the gates of the town, and bade them right welcome to La Rochelle, and took them to see the harbour, in which, if the Rochellois were obliged to summon foreign aid, an English fleet might one day be seen riding at anchor.

And then, as the hour was late, he escorted them to the best inn in the town, which for some hours past had been in a state of ferment, since it was not often that preparations for the reception of so many distinguished guests had to be made at such short notice, where, having invited them, in the name of the

Président, Jean Pascaut, to dine at the Présidial next day, he took leave of them.

Early on the morrow, the mayor returned and conducted the party round the fortifications; after which he took them to visit the Tour de la Chaîne, one of the two towers which defended the entrance to the harbour. Then they all repaired to the Présidial, where, with appetites sharpened by the sea air, they did full justice to "a magnificent banquet, at which sixty covers were laid."

In the afternoon, Bassompierre and his friends left La Rochelle, little imagining in what tragic circumstances they were to tread its streets again, and proceeded to Brouage, where they were very hospitably entertained by Saint-Luc. During their stay at Brouage they paid a visit to the neighbouring château of Marennes, ostensibly to pay their respects to the count of that name, but really to see his three daughters, "who were very beautiful." But, unfortunately, Bassompierre does not give us any further information about these ladies.

On leaving Brouage, they spent a night at the château of the Baron de Pons, whose family claimed to be descended from the House of Albret, a claim which was to cause an infinity of trouble at the Court during the regency of Anne of Austria, and to lead to the affair known as *"la guerre des tabourets."* Next day, they dined with d'Épernon at Plassac, a country-seat of his near Jonzac, and then set out for Bordeaux.

On September 19, Louis XIII arrived at Bordeaux, where he met with a great reception, and on the following day was entertained by Mayenne to a great banquet at the Château-Trompette. An unpleasant incident, however, cast a shadow over the rejoicings.

A gentleman named d'Arsilemont, who commanded the Châteaux of Fronsac and Caumont on behalf of the Comte de Saint-Paul, brother of Longueville, and had taken advantage of his position to levy unauthorised taxes on the people living along the Dordogne, and committed other illegal acts in defiance of the decrees of the Parlement of Bordeaux, had the imprudence to come and salute the King. The Parlement, learning of d'Arsilemont's arrival, sent to complain of him to his Majesty, who caused him to be arrested forthwith; and within forty-eight hours he was condemned to death and executed, "notwithstanding the entreaties of MM. de Mayenne and de Saint-Paul."

On October 4, La Force, Governor of Béarn, and Cazaux, First President of the Parlement of Pau, came to Bordeaux, bringing with them, not the ratification of the edict re-establishing the Catholic clergy in possession of their property, but a fresh remonstrance against it. The King was extremely angry, but on La Force and Cazaux assuring him that this remonstrance was intended to be the last one, and that, on their return to Béarn, they would use every endeavour to persuade the Parlement to ratify the edict without further delay, he decided to postpone military action for the present, and sent them away, accompanied by La Chesnaye, one of his gentlemen-in-ordinary and a Huguenot himself, who was instructed to keep his Majesty informed of the progress of the affair. At the same time, in order to show the Parlement that he was determined that they should submit to his will, he left Bordeaux with his army, and advanced to Preignac, on the left bank of the Garonne.

Some days later La Chesnaye returned, and informed the King that, notwithstanding the efforts of La Force and Cazaux, the Parlement still persisted in their refusal to ratify the edict, an action which Bassompierre ascribes to their belief that Louis XIII would not care to venture into so barren and difficult a country at that advanced season of the year, and to a rumour which had reached them that a great part of the baggage of the Court was already on its way back to Paris.

The King, however, was determined to be obeyed, and, on this occasion at any rate, showed none of the weakness and irresolution so conspicuous in later years. "Since my Parlement," said he, "wishes to give me the trouble of going in person to ratify the decree, I will do it, and more fully than they expect." And he summoned the Ministers who were with him and his chief officers to a council of war, for, says Bassompierre, "though he was resolved to go, he, nevertheless, wished to ascertain everyone's opinion on the matter."

Mayenne sought to dissuade the King from advancing into Béarn, representing that while his Majesty was engaged in imposing his will on the Huguenots at one extremity of his realm, their co-religionists in other parts of the country might seize the opportunity to rise in arms; that twelve days would probably be required to transport the army across the Garonne; that the difficulty of provisioning the troops in the inhospitable Landes at that season of the year would be very great, and so forth. The other members of the council, however, aware that the King had made up his mind on the matter—or that Luynes, who was anxious to secure the support of the High Catholic party, had made it up for him—and that nothing was to be gained by opposing his resolution, urged him to undertake the expedition, upon which he tinned to Mayenne and said:—

"I do not trouble myself about the weather or the roads; I am not afraid of those of the Religion, and, as for the passage of the river, which, you say, will take my army twelve days, I have a means of having it accomplished in eight. For I shall send Bassompierre here to conduct it, who has already raised me an army, with which I have just defeated a powerful party, in half the time that I had expected."

"I confess," observes Bassompierre, "that I felt my heart elated by such praise and by the good opinion that the King entertained of me; and I replied that he might rest assured that the hope that he had conceived of my diligence would not be vain, and that he would shortly have news that would gratify him."

In those days, when the engineers were not yet organised as a distinct branch of the army, and the difficulties of transport were very great, pontoons were seldom carried, unless before the campaign opened it was certain that they would be required; and the army which Bassompierre had undertaken to pass across the Garonne was unprovided with any. Consequently, he had either to wait until a sufficient number could be constructed, which would, of course, entail a considerable delay, or to obtain the best substitutes he could in the towns and villages along the Garonne, and trust that his fortunate star would be in the ascendant during the passage of the river to avert any disaster. He chose the latter alternative, and having established himself at Langon, on the left bank of the Garonne, sent parties of soldiers along both banks to collect every boat of suitable size which they could find.

"I caused two boats to be joined into one," he says, "and laid platforms over them, on which, on October 10, I placed two pieces of artillery, and had two others joined together without platforms, on which I placed the gun-carriages; and in four journeys I passed all the artillery across. And, by the expenditure of a great deal of money, I so contrived matters that in the course of the following day the munitions and provisions were passed across, and the whole army likewise; and we advanced to a town a league beyond the river, where we halted for the night."

A two days' march brought the army to Saint-Justin d'Armagnac, on the borders of the Grandes Landes and Armagnac. Here Bassompierre received a despatch from Louis XIII, who had left Preignac on the 10th and was now at Roquefort, in which the King expressed himself "extremely pleased with his diligence, by which he had reduced the twelve days allowed by M. de Mayenne for the passage of the Garonne to twenty-four hours." His Majesty ordered him to send him the Regiment of Champagne and some other troops, which he intended to place in garrison in Béarn, but not to enter the country with the rest of the army, since he feared it would be impossible to provision it.

With the force which Bassompierre had sent him, Louis XIII marched rapidly on Pau. At the news of his approach, the Parlement hastened to ratify the edict; but it was too late. The King continued his march and entered the town on the 15th. He re-established the Catholic bishops and clergy in possession of their churches and property, disbanded the national militia, and replaced the governor of Navarreins, the strongest fortress in the country, by a Catholic. Finally, by letters-patent of October 18, he united Béarn and Lower Navarre to the Crown of France, and fused the sovereign courts of these two countries into one single Parlement, sitting at Pau. Then, having sent the Maréchal de Praslin to Bassompierre, with orders to distribute the troops under his command amongst various garrisons and to rejoin him at Bordeaux, he took his departure, to the profound relief of the Béarnais.

Bassompierre reached Bordeaux on the 24th. The King arrived the following day, and Bassompierre went at once to pay his respects and compliment him on his victory over the Parlement of Pau.

"I expected a good reception," he says, "but, on the contrary, he did not even look at me, at which I was a little astonished. However, I approached him and said: 'Sire, are you displeased with me in good earnest, or are you making game of me?' 'I am not looking at you,' he answered coldly, and with that turned away.

"I was unable to imagine what could be the reason for this coldness, after the complimentary letters I had received from him. I went to salute M. de Luynes, and was received so coldly by him, that I saw plainly that my situation had undergone some great change. I returned to the gallery of the archbishop's palace, where I found the Cardinal de Retz and MM. de

Schomberg and de Roucelaï, who drew me aside and told me that M. de Luynes complained infinitely of me, saying that I had neglected his friendship and believed that without it I could maintain myself in the good graces of the King; and that he had declared that people should see which of us two had the power to overthrow the other; that the favour of the King could not be shared, and that, since I had offended him, he could no longer suffer me at the Court."

Bassompierre, more and more astonished, begged his friends to tell him "what wind could have developed into this tempest," since he had never had any quarrel with M. de Luynes, but, on the contrary, had been of service to him on many occasions and had contributed not a little to his advancement at Court, insomuch that the latter had "promised and sworn to him the closest friendship." He was therefore at a loss to comprehend how M. de Luynes desired, not only to break with, but to persecute, nay, even ruin, him, if it were in his power to do so. To this they replied that M. de Luynes had given them to understand that he had no less than five grievances against him:—

In the first place, when, at the Ponts-des-Cé, the King had shown M. de Bassompierre the draft of the articles of peace which had been drawn up by M. de

Luynes, who was himself present, M. de Bassompierre had expressed the opinion that they were far too lenient as regards the rebels, and that it would be as well to make an example of one of these gentlemen, in order to strike terror into the others and make them a little less ready to take up arms against their sovereign in the future. This was to cast a serious reflection upon M. de Luynes, and to suggest that he had been negligent of his Majesty's interests in drafting the treaty.

Secondly, when the King was at Poitiers, awaiting a visit from the Queen-Mother, whose coming was unavoidably delayed, M. de Bassompierre had suggested that this delay was "an artifice of her partisans to prevent his Majesty's journey to Guienne"; and this most uncalled for observation had made so great an impression upon the King's mind, that M. de Luynes had experienced a thousand difficulties in persuading him to remain at Poitiers until the Queen-Mother's arrival.

Thirdly, although, while the Court was at Bordeaux, M. de Luynes had on several occasions invited M. de Bassompierre to dine with him, that gentleman had always declined, thereby showing that he held his friendship of but little account.

Fourthly, when the King was at Preignac, awaiting the ratification of his edict by the Parlement of Pau, M. de Bassompierre had remarked to his Majesty that, if these gentlemen gave him the trouble of going to Béarn, he counselled him to make them pay dearly for his journey. This was to incite the King to cruelty, and was most reprehensible.

And, finally, M. de Bassompierre had so preoccupied the mind of the King, that his Majesty did not believe that anything could be done well unless it were done by him, as was proved by the fact that, without even troubling to consult his Council, he had "dethroned" the other brigadier-generals and placed M. de Bassompierre in command of his army. This M. de Luynes was unable to suffer, being aware that he had still sufficient influence to put a stop to the progress which the other was making daily, to his prejudice, in the good graces of the King.

When Bassompierre heard this, he "judged well that M. de Luynes was seeking pretexts to ruin him, and, since he could not find any legitimate ones in his actions, he had maliciously perverted the sense of his words." His friends, on their side, "did not disguise from him that it was nothing but pure jealousy of his favour which possessed that gentleman, and that, being in the position he was, he kept always a watchful eye on those who might divert from him the affection of the King, and that, observing the great inclination of the King for him (Bassompierre), he looked upon him as the dog who intended to bite him." They then begged Bassompierre to furnish them with his reply to the charges brought against him by the jealous favourite, which they promised to report faithfully to the latter, and endeavour by every means in their power to bring about an amicable settlement.

Bassompierre thereupon proceeded to deal in detail with the different causes of complaint which Luynes had against him, and concluded by requesting his friends to inform him that, if he would be pleased to prescribe some rules of conduct for him, he would undertake to follow them so exactly, that in future M. de Luynes should have no cause to believe that he aspired in any fashion whatsoever to usurp the good graces of the King, except by his services to the Crown; and to add that "he esteemed so little, and feared so much, favours that were not the reward of merit that, if they were lying on the ground at his feet, he would not condescend to stoop and pick them up."

Next day, the Cardinal de Retz and his fellow-mediators came to Bassompierre and told him that they had duly carried his answer to Luynes, who had informed them that M. de Bassompierre had so deeply offended him, that he could only repeat what he had said to them before, namely, that he was unable to suffer him at the Court. If, however, M. de Bassompierre were willing to withdraw with as little delay as possible, he would see that the salaries of his various appointments were promptly paid him during his absence, and that within a certain period—which, however, he had refused to define—he would cause him to be recalled with honour, when he would do all in his power to advance his interests.

On receiving this proposal, Bassompierre could not contain his indignation, and requested his friends to return at once to Luynes and inform him that "he (Bassompierre) was not the kind of man who could be treated as a scoundrel and driven ignominiously away in this fashion"; that, if his honesty or his loyalty were suspected, he could be imprisoned and punished, if found guilty; but that to drive him from the Court merely to gratify a caprice was outrageous, and he defied him to do it.

His friends, however, deprecated such strong language and begged him to seek to compose, rather than to embitter, this most unfortunate affair. They then suggested, if he were willing, that they should inform the favourite that M. de Bassompierre desired them to say that he was indeed astonished that M. de Luynes had treated his enemies with such magnanimity after the action at the Ponts-des-Cé, when it was in his power to punish them as they deserved and avenge himself upon them; while for M. de Bassompierre, who had hazarded his life in his service—since there could be no question that the object of the recent rebellion was not to dispossess the King of his crown, but to separate him from M. de Luynes—and, by his own admission, had acted so worthily in these disturbances—he had nothing but ingratitude. He felt assured, however, that if M. de Luynes would but reflect upon the obligations under which he had placed him, he would decide that he was deserving of reward, and not at all of such a punishment as to be driven with infamy from the Court, to which M. de Bassompierre could never bring himself to submit.

Bassompierre, aware that he could trust his friends to do their best for him in the very awkward predicament in which he was placed, told them that he left the matter entirely to their discretion, and they went away.

From Bordeaux the Court proceeded to Blaye, where the King remained three days, and was magnificently entertained by the new Duke of Luxembourg-Piney, who was governor of that place. At table, Louis XIII, who, before this trouble arose, had been in the habit of talking and jesting incessantly with Bassompierre, did not speak a single word to him, "which gave him pain." However, on the evening before the King's departure for Saintes, where he was to pass the following night, he ordered Bassompierre to precede him with the Swiss, who were to furnish the guard at Saintes; and when the latter approached him to receive the password, which was, of course, always given in a very low voice, his Majesty said: "Bassompierre, my friend, do not worry, and do not appear to notice anything." "I made no reply," writes Bassompierre, "from fear lest someone might perceive something, but I was not sorry that the source of the King's kindness had not dried up, so far as I was concerned."

After supper that night, he received a visit from Roucelaï, who said that the Cardinal de Retz and Schomberg, who were then with Luynes, had sent him to say that the favourite had pronounced his final decision, which was that Bassompierre must leave the

Court so soon as possible after the King returned to Paris. At the same time, he desired to deal honourably with him and that his departure should be free from any appearance of disgrace, and if Bassompierre would suggest some way by which this could be contrived, he would be prepared to give it his favourable consideration.

Bassompierre, recognising that the all-powerful favourite was determined to drive him from the Court, and that the only course open to him was to make the best terms he could, replied that if Luynes were willing to procure for him a government, an important military post, or an embassy extraordinary, which would enable him to quit the Court with honour, and to render the King more useful service than he could by remaining there, he would take his departure so soon as he pleased. Roucelaï then returned to his friends with Bassompierre's answer, which was duly communicated to Luynes. The latter expressed his approval of it, and told them that in the course of the next day's journey he would come to an arrangement with him on these conditions.

"This he did with a good grace," says Bassompierre, "and told me frankly that the esteem which he perceived that the King entertained for me gave him umbrage, and that he was like a man who feared to be deceived by his wife, and who did not like to see even a very honest man paying attention to her; that, apart from that, he had a strong inclination for me, as he intended to show me, provided that I did not cast loving glances at his mistress. And that same evening he took me to speak to the King, who received me very cordially and told me to make ready to travel post on the morrow."

The King journeyed in this fashion from Saintes to Paris, accompanied only by thirty or forty attendants. As they were nearing Châtellerault, Bassompierre, learning that it was proposed to spend the night there, warned Luynes that the town contained a large proportion of Huguenots, and that if these, incensed by the King's forcible re-establishment of the Catholic faith in Béarn, were to summon their co-religionists from La Rochelle to their aid, which they could easily do, and make an attempt upon his Majesty's person, he would be in great danger. On hearing this, Luynes was much alarmed and begged the King not to stop at Châtellerault; but Louis XIII, whose physical courage presented a striking contrast to his moral flabbiness, refused to alter his arrangements, and told him that he would answer for his own safety and that of his attendants.

On November 6, the King reached Paris, and his first act was to visit the Queen-Mother, who had now been permitted to return to the capital. On the following day he went to Saint-Germain, and subsequently visited Luynes at Lesigny, returning to Paris towards the end of the month. Bassompierre does not appear to have been in attendance on the King during these visits, nor was he commanded to accompany him when, early in December, he set out with Luynes to inspect the fortresses of Picardy. It was evidently the favourite's policy to keep his rival as much as possible at a distance from the King, until some post away from the Court could be found for him.

An act of aggression on the part of Spain furnished Luynes with what he was seeking.

The Spaniards, masters of the Milanese, had long coveted the Valtellina, or Upper Valley of the Adda, which had been ceded to the Grisons by the last of the Sforza. The possession of this valley would be of immense strategic importance to them, since it would link the Milanese with the Tyrol and Austria, and, at the same time, intercept the communications of the

Venetians with the Grisons, the Swiss and France. Since France had an exclusive treaty with the Grisons, the Valtellina was an open door for her into Italy, and Spain desired to close this door at any cost. Successive governors of Milan had industriously fomented the religious quarrel between the Protestant Grisons and the Catholics of the Valtellina, and these intrigues at length bore fruit. One Sunday in July, 1620, the Valtellina Catholics rose, massacred all the Protestants of their country, to the number of several hundred, and then appealed to the Spaniards to defend them from the vengeance of the Grisons. The response, as may be supposed, was prompt and effective; the Spaniards immediately entered the valley and took possession of all the strong places, and, though the cantons of Berne and Zurich came to the assistance of the Grisons, their united efforts proved powerless to dislodge them.

This bold stroke of the Spaniards was a direct menace to Venice and Savoy, and an indirect act of aggression against France; and the French Government resolved to send an Ambassador Extraordinary to Madrid to demand the evacuation of the Valtellina by Spain. Luynes had no difficulty in deciding who that Ambassador Extraordinary ought to be, and one day, towards the end of December, a courier from Picardy drew rein before Bassompierre's door and handed him a letter from the King, informing him of his appointment, and directing him to be in readiness to start for Madrid immediately after his Majesty returned to Paris.

A few days after Luynes had succeeded in finding so admirable a pretext for ridding himself, for some months at least, of the only man whom he considered capable of disputing with him the favour of the King, another piece of good fortune befell him. On the night of Christmas Day, 1620, the Duchesse de Luynes gave birth to a son.[137]

No sooner was the news of this great event noised abroad than the bells of every church in Paris rang out a joyous peal, and several couriers started to carry the glad tidings to Calais, where the King and Luynes had arrived a day or two before to inspect the fortifications of the harbour, which had been greatly damaged by a recent gale. Louis XIII was the first to receive the news, and so delighted was he that he gave the bearer a present of 4,000 crowns and undertook to announce it himself to his favourite. Before doing so, however, he ordered all the guns of the citadel to be discharged, and when Luynes inquired the meaning of this, embraced him and exclaimed: "My cousin, I am come to rejoice with you, because you have a son!"

Truly, as Contarini, the Venetian Ambassador, observed, in announcing the event to his Government, "the Duc de Luynes seemed to have enchained Fortune."

CHAPTER XXII

An alliance with Luynes's niece, Mlle. de Combalet, proposed to Bassompierre—His journey to Spain—His entry into Madrid—He is visited by the Princess of the Asturias, the grandees and other distinguished persons—His meeting with the Duke of Ossuña—His audience of Philip III postponed owing to the King's illness—Commissioners are appointed to treat with Bassompierre over the Valtellina question—Death of Philip III—His funeral procession—An indiscreet observation of the Duke of Ossuña to one of Bassompierre's suite is overheard and leads to the arrest of that nobleman.

LOUIS XIII and Luynes returned to Paris on January 12, 1621, and Bassompierre was "extremely pressed to take his departure." But, as may be supposed, he was in no hurry to go, and, by raising all kinds of difficulties in regard to his instructions, succeeded in gaining a respite of three weeks; and it was not until the beginning of February that his despatches were handed to him. Even then, on one pretext or another, he contrived to postpone his departure for another week, though his suite, which numbered no less than 140 persons, including forty gentlemen whose expenses he had undertaken to defray himself, were sent on ahead in batches to await him at Bordeaux.

Just before he left Paris, what was regarded at the time as a most advantageous marriage was proposed to him.

It happened that, some weeks before, the Duc de Retz, the nobleman who had played such a sorry part at the Ponts-des-Cé, had lost his wife, upon which his uncle, the Cardinal de Retz, and his friend, the Comte de Schomberg, decided to counsel him to demand the hand of Luynes's niece, Mlle. de Combalet. Condé and Guise, learning what was in the wind, and fearing that this marriage might divert all the good things which were in the favourite's power to bestow from themselves and their relatives to the Retz family, thereupon determined to put Bassompierre forward as a rival candidate. For Bassompierre had no near relatives to provide for—at least none who were French subjects, with the exception of his natural son by Marie d'Entragues—and, so far as courtiers went, he was neither ambitious nor greedy. They judged, too, that Luynes would welcome the opportunity of attaching Bassompierre to his interests, which he might serve in many ways. However, they were a little doubtful as to how that gentleman himself might be inclined to regard the matter, for, since the day when his matrimonial aspirations had been so rudely dashed by the intervention of Henri IV, he had shown a most marked disinclination to enter the "holy estate." But since, notwithstanding this, the ladies had great influence over him, Condé proposed that he should depute his wife, and Guise his sister, the Princesse de Conti, "to persuade him to embrace the match." With the former Bassompierre had always remained on the friendliest terms; for the latter he was known to entertain a warmer feeling than friendship.

On February 9—the day before he left Paris—Bassompierre attended a grand ball given by Luynes, to which he had apparently gone with the intention of taking leave of the Comtesse de Rochefort, of whom he was still the very devoted servant.

"As I was ascending the stairs," he says, "*Madame la Princesse* and the Princesse de Conti, who were laughing very much, drew me into a window, but, instead of speaking, came nigh to splitting their sides with laughter. At last they told me that formerly I had spoken of love to many fair ladies, but that never had ladies of good family spoken to me of marriage, which now they were going to require of me. I was a long time in deciphering the meaning of what they said, but, finally, they told me that the husband of one and the brother of the other had charged them to seduce me, but that it was to enter into an honourable marriage; and that I must empower *Monsieur le Prince* and M. de Guise to negotiate and conclude the affair of Mlle. de Combalet while I was Ambassador Extraordinary in Spain."

To this proposal Bassompierre gave a not very cordial consent. Since a man must marry some time or other, as well the niece of the favourite as any other lady, and he did not quite see how otherwise he was to disarm the jealousy of Luynes.

On the following day Bassompierre set out on his long journey to Madrid, and on the 17th arrived at Bordeaux, where he remained a couple of days "for love of MM. d'Épernon and de Roquelaure." On reaching Belin, nine leagues from Bordeaux, on the evening of the 19th he found a courier awaiting him with a letter from Du Fargis d'Angennes, the ordinary French Ambassador at Madrid, begging him to delay his arrival there until he heard from him again, as a most unpleasant incident had occurred, in consequence of which the greater part of his staff and servants were now in prison, while he himself had been obliged to leave the city, as his life was no longer safe there.

It appears that Du Fargis, whom Tallemant des Réaux describes as "a man of courage, intelligence, and learning, but of a singular levity," not finding the French Embassy a sufficiently-commodious residence, desired to remove to a larger one, and had cast his eye upon a very fine house near by, which appeared in every way suited to his requirements. Now, in those days, there were at Madrid certain State officials called *aposentadores*, part of whose duty it was to find suitable accommodation for ambassadors and other distinguished foreigners, and who were empowered to requisition any house which these important personages might desire to have. Du Fargis accordingly went to the *aposentadores* and informed them that he wished to remove to this house, and the *aposentadores* immediately assigned it to him. But just as he was on the point of taking possession, the owner of the house appeared upon the scene, and produced a document bearing the King's signature which expressly exempted his property from being requisitioned for State purposes. The Ambassador angrily replied that the house had been assigned to him by the *aposentadores* and that he should insist on having it, upon which the owner told him that he should appeal to the Council of Castile. This he did, and the Council at once decided in his favour.

Meantime, however, Du Fargis, with the idea of stealing a march upon his adversary, had sent two of his valets to the house with part of the ambassadorial wardrobe, and when the decision of the Council was communicated to him, he replied that, as some of his property was already in the house, he was in possession, and could not be turned out. And so resolved was he to have his way that he forthwith sent all his staff and servants there, together with some of the people of the Venetian Ambassador, who was a particular friend of his, with instructions to resist by force any attempt to dislodge them.

The exasperated owner went to complain to the Council, who sent orders to the invaders to leave the house and take their master's clothes with them, and two *alguazils* to see that they did so; because, never dreaming that the Ambassador intended to resist the law—"a thing unheard of in that country"—they did not think it necessary to send any more. But the French and their Venetian allies fell upon the unfortunate officers and killed them, after which, in derision, they hung their *vares*, or wands of office, from the balcony of the house.

The townsfolk, on learning of this outrage, were infuriated, and soon an armed mob more than two thousand strong besieged the house and the Ambassador, "who had gone in by a back door." The garrison, on their side, prepared for a desperate resistance, and a sanguinary affray seemed inevitable, when, happily, an *alcalde*, Don Sebastian de Carvajal, arrived on the scene, persuaded the mob to disperse and the Ambassador and his people to evacuate their fortress, and carried off Du Fargis in his carriage to the French Embassy.

Although Du Fargis had only himself to blame for this affair, he had the presumption to seek an audience of Philip III and "demand justice for the outrage which had been committed against him, contrary to the Law of Nations." The King promised to give him every satisfaction and appointed a commission to inquire into the matter. But when he was informed of what had actually occurred, he was very angry, and gave orders that, while the sacred persons of the Ambassadors of France and Venice were to be scrupulously respected, every one of their people who could be found outside the Embassies, unless he happened to be in attendance on his master at the time, and therefore covered by the ægis of his presence, was to be promptly arrested and hauled off to prison. The *alguazils*, burning to avenge their murdered comrades, went to work with right good will, and rounded up secretaries of legation, attachés, lackeys, and chefs so effectively, that in a day or two their Excellencies could hardly find anyone to copy their despatches or prepare their meals. "The Ambassador himself," says Bassompierre, "not feeling himself safe from the fury of the people, withdrew from the town, and wrote to the King to warn him of the situation to which he was reduced, and to me to delay my arrival."

Bassompierre, however, had no desire to kick his heels about dirty Spanish inns until Du Fargis could persuade Philip III to set his people at liberty; besides which he knew that the affair of the Valtellina was a pressing one and that he had already wasted a good deal of time. He therefore decided to continue his journey, but wrote to the Duke of Monteleone and Don Fernando Giron, two grandees of his acquaintance, begging them to endeavour to accommodate the affair. These noblemen spoke to the King and informed Bassompierre that his Majesty desired to see him as soon as possible, and had promised that, on his arrival, he would find everything settled to his satisfaction.

On February 21 Bassompierre reached Bayonne, where he remained for four days as the guest of the

Comte de Gramont, who was governor and hereditary mayor of the town, and then set out for Saint-Jean-de-Luz, accompanied by the count. On the way he had the unusual experience for a landsman of witnessing a whale-hunt:—

"As we were coming from Bayonne to Saint-Jean-de-Luz, we saw out at sea more than fifty little sailing-boats giving chase to a whale, which had been sighted going along the coast, accompanied by a little whale. And at eleven o'clock that evening we had news that the little whale had been captured, which we saw the next morning lying on the beach, where it had been stranded during the high tide."

While at Saint-Jean-de-Luz, some of the inhabitants danced a ballet for the diversion of their distinguished guests, "which," says Bassompierre, "was, for the Basques, as fine as could be expected." Before leaving the town they learned of the death of Pope Paul V, which had occurred on January 28, and of the election of his successor, Alessandro Ludovisio, Cardinal Archbishop of Bologna, who took the name of Gregory XV.

Gramont accompanied his friend so far as the Bidassoa, which divided France from Spain, and then took leave of him; and Bassompierre and his suite crossed the little river and entered Spain, under the guidance of the *coreo mayor*, or post-master, of the province of Guipuzcoa, who escorted the party to a *venta* near Irun, where they passed the night. The next day's journey brought them to Segura, and on the 28th they crossed the barren limestone heights of the Sierra de San Adrian, and proceeded, by way of Vittoria and Miranda de Ebro, to Burgos, where they arrived on March 3.

At Burgos Bassompierre went to visit the cathedral, one of the marvels of Gothic architecture in Spain, which he pronounces "*bien belle*," and saw "*el santo crucifisso*," by which presumably he means the much-revered image of Our Saviour known as the "Christo de Burgos."

The following day he arrived at Lerma, and went to see the magnificent mansion which that old rascal the Cardinal Duke de Lerma had recently built for himself with a portion of the immense sums of which he had robbed his unfortunate country. He afterwards went to hear Mass at a convent which had also been built by Lerma, where the music, he tells us, was excellent.

On the 8th, Bassompierre reached Alcovendas, a few miles to the north of Madrid. Here he received a visit from Du Fargis, who came to inform him of the arrangements for his entry into Madrid. Du Fargis's staff and servants, and those of his friend the Venetian Ambassador, were still in prison, but they were to be set at liberty next day, in time to assist at Bassompierre's reception.

On the following afternoon, Bassompierre made his entry into the capital of Spain, and had no cause to complain of the way in which he was received:—

"The Ambassador [Du Fargis] and all the families of the other Ambassadors came to meet me. The Count of Barajas[138] came to receive me with the carriages of the King, in one of which I seated myself. He was accompanied by many of the nobility; and a very great number of women in carriages came out of the town to see my arrival. I alighted at the house of the Count of Barajas, which had been sumptuously prepared for my accommodation. There I found the Duke of Monteleone, Don Fernando Giron, Don Carlos Coloma and a great number of other noblemen whom I had known in France or elsewhere, waiting to greet me. I went to pay my respects to the Countess of Barajas,[139] who had invited a number of ladies to assist her in receiving me, and afterwards I supped at a table where fifty covers were laid, which was kept for me all the time I was at Madrid. In the course of the evening, the Duke of Uceda sent one of his gentlemen to greet me on his behalf."

Bassompierre spent the following day in receiving the visits of a great number of distinguished persons. An early arrival was the wife of the heir to the throne (Élisabeth of France) who was accompanied by a large party of ladies of the palace, "both old and young." She was followed by grandees and their wives, dignitaries of Church and State, members of the Corps Diplomatique, and so forth, whom we need not particularise, though Bassompierre's account of the arrival of one of the chief grandees in Spain at that time cannot be omitted:—

"The Duke of Ossuña[140] was the next who came to greet me, with extraordinary pomp; for he was carried in a chair; he wore an Hungarian robe furred with ermine and a number of jewels of great value; and was followed by more than twenty carriages, filled with Spanish nobles, his relations and friends, or Neapolitan nobles; while his chair was surrounded by more than fifty captain-lieutenants or *alferes reformados*, Spanish or Neapolitan. He embraced me with great affection and cordiality, and, after calling me Excellency three or four times, he reminded me that, at a supper at Zamet's, at which the King[141] was present, we had made an alliance, and that I had promised to call him father and that he should call me son; and he begged me to continue to do this. So that we afterwards treated one another without any ceremony. After this he was pleased to greet all who had accompanied me from France, speaking to them in French and saying so many extravagant things that I was not astonished at the disgrace into which he shortly afterwards fell."

Next day came more grandees, more ladies, more prelates, and more ambassadors, including those of England and the Emperor; and no sooner had the unfortunate Bassompierre got rid of one batch, than another appeared upon the scene, until by the time the last of his visitors had taken his departure he was quite worn out. However, he was not to be allowed much rest, for in the evening he received a visit from the auditor of the Nuncio, who was conducting the affairs of the Holy See at Madrid during the absence of his chief, who had gone to Rome to receive a cardinal's hat. This ecclesiastic came to talk politics, and showed Bassompierre the copy of a brief which he had received from Gregory XV on the subject of the Valtellina, in which his Holiness demanded the restitution of the country, "for the sake of the freedom of Italy," and threatened his Catholic Majesty with the employment of both spiritual and temporal weapons if the latter's troops were not promptly withdrawn. Altogether, it was quite a courageous letter for a new Pope to write to a King of Spain, and pleased Bassompierre mightily; and he was still more gratified to learn that the demands of France and the Vatican were to be supported by the representatives of England, Venice, and Savoy. However, when once the Spaniard of those days got his claws into anything he coveted, it was no easy matter to induce him to release his prey; and, though very ready to promise, he was exceedingly slow to perform.

The Papal representative was followed by Don Juan de Serica, one of the Secretaries of State, who came to visit Bassompierre on behalf of Philip III, and who informed him, "after several flattering observations, touching the satisfaction that the King felt at his arrival and the good opinion that he entertained of him," that he would be accorded an audience so soon as his Majesty's health would permit.

"He was indeed ill," says Bassompierre, "though everyone believed that he feigned to be so, in order to delay my audience and my despatches."

And then he goes on to relate how the unfortunate monarch had fallen a victim to those inexorable rules of Spanish Court etiquette, of which he was the central object:

"His illness began on the first Friday in Lent (February 26). He was engaged on some despatches, and the day being cold, an excessively hot brazier had been put in the room where he was working. The reflection of this brazier fell so strongly on his face, that drops of sweat poured from it; but, as he was of a character never to find fault or complain of anything, he said nothing. The Marquis of Povar,[142] from whom I heard this, told me that, perceiving how the heat of the brazier was annoying him, he told the Duke of Alba,[143] who, like himself, was one of the Gentlemen of the Chamber, to take it away. But since they are very punctilious about their functions, he replied that it was the duty of the *sommeiller du corps*, the Duke of Uceda. Upon that the Marquis de Povar sent for him; but, unhappily, he had gone to look at a house which he was having built. And so, before the Duke of Uceda could be brought, the poor King was so broiled, that on the morrow he fell into a fever. The fever brought on an erysipelas, and the erysipelas, sometimes subsiding and sometimes increasing, at length ended in a petechial fever, which killed him."

During the next three days Bassompierre continued to receive visits from distinguished persons of the Court, the most important of whom was the old Duke del Infantado,[144] the mayor-domo mayor,[145] who came to see him in great state, with the four mayor-domos walking before. This old grandee, Bassompierre tells us, took a great fancy to him and rendered him many services while he was at Madrid.

If poor Philip III was too unwell to grant Bassompierre an audience, he seemed anxious to make his stay in his capital as agreeable as possible. For, not only did he obtain from the Patriarch of the Indies, "who was like a Legate at the Court," a Bull permitting him and one hundred members of his suite to eat meat in Lent, but authorised him to have plays performed at his house by the two companies of Royal players, which were amalgamated, in order to secure a stronger cast. The King paid the actors 300 reals for each performance, to which the munificent Frenchman added 1,000 out of his own pocket.

Theatrical representations in Lent had never been seen before in Spain, and, though the more bigoted were doubtless very scandalised, and thought that his Catholic Majesty's illness must be of the brain rather than of the body, the majority of people were delighted at the innovation, and invitations were eagerly sought for.

"The first performance," says Bassompierre, "took place on March 14, in a great gallery in my house, which was beautifully decorated and illuminated, and a great number of ladies and nobles were present. During the play I had sweetmeats and *aloja* brought in for the ladies who had come. The ladies were of two kinds: those who had been invited by the Countess of Barajas, who remained on the high dais and had their faces veiled; and those who sat on the steps of the dais or in the *salle*. These last were covered by their mantillas. The men also came, some covered and some not. All the ambassadors were invited. After the play was over, I gave a supper in private, prepared *à la Française* by my people, at which seven or eight of the grandees, or chief nobles, of Spain were my guests."

After this, plays were performed almost every evening up to the time of the King's death.

On the 15th, Don Juan de Serica was sent by Philip III to inform Bassompierre that he feared that his illness would prevent him from giving him audience for some days longer. Since, however, he had learned that there was a rumour afloat to the effect that he was feigning illness with the object of retarding the important affairs upon which his Excellency had come to see him, he had decided, in order to give the lie to this rumour, to nominate forthwith commissioners to treat with his Excellency. Bassompierre begged Don Juan to convey his very humble thanks to his Majesty for the favour which he was doing him; and next day the King nominated four commissioners, one of whom was Don Balthazar de Zuniga, who was to play a prominent part at the beginning of the next reign. At Don Balthazar's suggestion, Bassompierre consented to Giulio de Medici, Archbishop of Pisa, the Ambassador of Tuscany, being associated with them as mediator, "to make us agree and to readjust matters, if there were any hitch or rupture in the negotiations."

A day or two later, Serica came to see Bassompierre and informed him that the King was better, and had decided to give him audience on the following Sunday (March 21). On the Sunday, however, while Bassompierre was awaiting the arrival of the Duke of Gandia, who had been charged to conduct him to the palace and present him to the King, he learned that, as Philip III was dressing in order to receive him, he had been suddenly taken ill and had been obliged to return to bed, and that the audience must therefore be postponed to another day.

In point of fact, it never took place at all, for the King grew rapidly worse. Bassompierre has left us some details about his last days:—

"On the 23rd, the King had a great increase of fever, and they began to fear the result. He was very melancholy from the persuasion that he was going to die.

"On the 27th, he told his physicians that they understood nothing about his complaint, and that he felt he was dying. He commanded processions and that public prayers should be offered for him.

"On, Sunday, the 28th, the image of Nuestra Señora de Attoches was carried in solemn procession to Las Descalzas reales.[146] All the counsellors attended, with a great number of penitents, who whipped themselves cruelly for the King's recovery. The body of the blessed St. Isidore was carried to the

King's chamber, and the Holy Sacrament laid on the altars of all the churches.

"On the 29th, the physicians despaired of his life, upon which he sent to summon the President of Castile, and his confessor Alliaga[147] to whom he spoke for a long time, and to the Duke of Uceda, who sent for the Prince[148] and Don Carlos.[149] He gave them his blessing, and begged the Prince to employ his old servants, amongst whom he recommended the Duke of Uceda, his confessor, and Don Bernabe de Vianco. Then he ordered the Infanta Maria and the Cardinal Infant[150] to be admitted, to whom he also gave his blessing. The Princess was unable to come, by reason of a faintness which seized her as she was entering the King's chamber. The King next divided his relics amongst them, after which he communicated.

"On Tuesday, the 30th, at two o'clock in the morning, Extreme Unction was administered to the King. He then signed a great number of papers. About noon he had the body of St. Isidore brought and placed against his bed, and he vowed to build a chapel to the saint. He then sent to summon the Duke of Lerma, who was at Valladolid.

"On Wednesday, the 31st and last day of March, he yielded up his soul.

"The King's death was officially communicated to the ambassadors at noon, and we, at the same time, received permission to despatch couriers at five o'clock to carry the news to our masters.

"The Queen[151] went with the Infanta Maria to the Descalzas, and the new King left in a closed carriage to go to San Geronimo.[152] On the road he met the body of Our Lord, which was being carried to a sick man, and, according to the ancient custom of the House of Austria, wished to alight and accompany it. The Count of Olivarez[153] said to him: '*Advierta V. Md. que anda tapado.*' ('Your Majesty should recollect that you ought to be covered.') To which he answered: '*No ayque taparse delante de Dios.*' ('It is never right to be covered before God.')

"This was thought a very good omen at Madrid."

On April 1 the body of Philip III lay in state at the palace, the face being uncovered, and Bassompierre went with the other ambassadors to sprinkle it with holy water. On the following day it was removed to the Escurial for burial.

"At five o'clock in the afternoon," says Bassompierre, "they removed the body of the late King from the palace to carry it to the tomb of his fathers in the Escurial. I went to see it pass over the Puente Segoviana, with nearly all the grandees and ladies of Madrid. In my opinion, it was a rather sorry funeral procession for so great a King. First came a hundred or a hundred and twenty Hieronymite monks, wearing their surplices and mounted on fine mules. They rode two and two, following their leader, who carried the Cross. Then came thirty Guards, led by the Marquises de Povar and de Falsas; and following them the King's Household, the *mayor-domos* last, with the Duke del Infantado, *mayor-domo mayor*, preceding the body of the King, which was borne on a litter drawn by two mules, which were covered, as was the litter, with cloth-of-gold. The Gentlemen of the Chamber walked behind the litter, and twenty archers of the Burgundian Guard brought up the rear. They halted for the night at Pinto, and rather early on the morrow arrived at the Escurial, where the funeral service was celebrated, after which the company returned to Madrid."

Bassompierre's "father," the Duke of Ossuña, was one of the grandees who witnessed the procession from the Puente Segoviana; and he ascribes to some injudicious remarks made by the duke on this occasion to two gentlemen of his suite the fact that he was shortly afterwards arrested and imprisoned:—

"The Duke of Ossuña was on the bridge to see the body of the King pass by, and happening to stop opposite a carriage which contained some of the gentlemen who had accompanied me to France, he inquired if they knew when I was to have audience of the new King. M. de Rothelin and the Marquis de Bussy d'Amboise[154] answered that I had been informed that it would be on the following Sunday. 'I am rejoiced to hear that,' said he, 'for I am promised the next audience, in which I propose to say to the King that there are now three great princes who govern the world, of whom one is aged sixteen, another seventeen, and the third eighteen; that they are himself, the Grand Turk, and the King of France; that whichever of the three will have the longest sword will be the bravest; and that one must be my master.' These words were reported by a person in his coach, who had been charged to spy upon his discourse and actions, and, together with his previous conduct, were the cause of his being thrown into prison, where he ended his days."

CHAPTER XXIII

Bassompierre's audience of the new King, Philip IV—The Procession of the Crosses—An old flame—Good Friday at Madrid—Anxiety of the Queen's ladies-in-waiting to see Bassompierre—His visit to them—He is commissioned by Louis XIII to present his condolences to Philip IV—He is informed that etiquette requires him to leave Madrid as though to return to France and then to make another formal entry—Revolution of the palace at Madrid: fall of the late King's Ministers—The Count of Saldagna ordered by Philip IV to marry Doña Mariana de Cordoba, on pain of his severe displeasure—Bassompierre offers to facilitate the escape of Saldagna to France, but the latter's courage fails him at the last moment—Negotiations over the Valtellina—Treaty of Madrid—Bassompierre's pretended departure for France—He visits the Escurial, returns to Madrid and makes a second ceremonious entry—The audience of condolence—State entry of Philip IV into Madrid—Termination of Bassompierre's embassy—He returns to France.

ON Palm Sunday, April 4, Bassompierre had an audience of the new King at the Convent of San Geronimo.

"Twenty carriages were brought," says he, "in which the Ambassador [Du Fargis] and I and the whole of our respective suites placed ourselves. We were conducted only by the Count of Barajas, because it was not a solemn audience, but a private one, at San Geronimo, to which the King had retired, and he was only admitting me as a favour in order to pay honour to the King [of France] his brother-in-law, and to show the promptitude with which he desired to conclude the affair upon which I had come. We all wore mourning according to the Spanish fashion, with the *loba*, the *caperuza* and *capirote*,[155] which I did for two reasons: first, because, since all the grandees present at the audience, and the King himself, were wearing it, I should have been uncovered, while they were not, which would not have been seemly on my part; secondly, because the sight of me wearing deep mourning for the death of their late King was very agreeable to the Spaniards, who would not have felt thus had I been dressed in our fashion. I made my obeisance to the King and offered him the *pesame*, which is the compliment of condolence upon the death of the King his father, after which we offered him the *parabien*, which is the compliment of felicitation upon his happy accession to the Crowns.[156] This we did also in the name of the King [of France], while awaiting the despatch by him of some prince or great noble expressly to pay this compliment. I then spoke to the King about our affairs, to all of which things he answered very pertinently; and, after having paid my respects to the prince,[157] who was with him, I retired."

On the Wednesday in Holy Week, Bassompierre and Du Fargis witnessed the Procession of the Crosses from the balcony of a house in the Calle Mayor, which had been reserved for them:

"There were," says Bassompierre, "more than five hundred penitents, who walked barefooted, drawing large crosses, like that of Our Lord, and, at intervals, were movable theatres, on which divers representations of the Passion were exhibited in a very lifelike manner."

Bassompierre pronounces this spectacle "*très belle*"; nevertheless, he soon appears to have had enough of it, and on being joined by the Ambassador of Lucca and two Spanish nobles, he rose, protesting that he could not remain seated and leave three such distinguished persons standing—for there were only two chairs on the balcony—but would resign his seat to one of them, leave M. du Fargis to represent France, and go and beg of a party of ladies whom he perceived below the favour of occupying one of their footstools. This he did, and the ladies were most kind and did him the honour to allow him to sit at their feet, and, we fear, paid more attention to his Excellency than to the procession. Nor was this all; for Fortune willed it that he should discover amongst them a flame of the days of his youth, a certain Doña Aña de Sanasara, whom he had known twenty-five years before at Naples, and who was now the wife of the Secretary of the Council of Finance. "They recognised each other with joy," and Doña Aña, who was very rich, sent her old admirer handsome presents and invited him to her house, where she entertained him most sumptuously.

On the following day—Maundy Thursday— Bassompierre witnessed another procession, that of the Penitents, "in which there were more than two thousand men who belaboured themselves with whips." Afterwards he went to hear the *Tenebræ* at Nuestra Señora de Constantinopoli and spent the night in visiting different churches.

On Maundy Thursday and Good Friday Madrid was a city of mourning:

"The bells of the churches were silent; the carriages ceased to pass through the town; no one rode on horseback; no one carried a sword; no one was accompanied by his servants; and all the women were veiled."

On Easter Monday, Bassompierre went to pay his respects to the new Queen at the Carmelite convent, where she was still in retreat. Her Majesty told him that all her ladies-in-waiting were longing to make his acquaintance—evidently, the fame of his successes amongst the fair had preceded him to Madrid—and that he ought to have compassion upon them and demand *lugar* [158] of every one of them. Bassompierre replied that, if he were to do that, it would occupy more time than he would require to conclude the affair of the Valtellina, and asked, as a favour, that he might be allowed to interview the whole posse of them at the same time, promising to do his best not to confound one lady with another. The Queen said that such a proceeding would not be in accordance with etiquette; but Bassompierre observed that whenever their Majesties granted favours they authorised some breach of etiquette, and that he did not see why they could not do so in this case. The Queen smiled and said that she would be quite willing, but that she dared not take so important a step without first consulting the King. However, she would speak to his Majesty, and inform him of the result.

A few days later, Bassompierre was informed that the King had been graciously pleased to consent that the rules of etiquette should be waived in his Excellency's favour, for which his Excellency "rendered very humble thanks to the King." Then he wrote to demand audience of all the Queen's ladies-in-waiting, and, this having been accorded, proceeded to the Alcazar and was conducted to her Majesty's ante-chamber, where he was presently joined by a bevy of fair and intensely curious ladies, in charge of a duenna, all eager to behold this redoubtable *vainqueur de dames*. And when they found that, in addition to his good looks and fascinating manners, he was able to pay them the most charming compliments in irreproachable Castilian, their delight knew no bounds, and it was more than two hours before they would allow him to depart.

On April 16, Bassompierre received a despatch from Louis XIII commissioning him to present his condolences to the new King on the death of his father. When, however, he informed Zuniga of this and inquired when Philip IV could give him audience to enable him to acquit himself of his new duty, that old gentleman shook his head and declared that it was quite contrary to the etiquette of the Spanish Court for an Ambassador Extraordinary charged with the duty of concluding a treaty to represent his sovereign in a different matter, unless he were to absent himself from the capital for some days and then make a second public entry. He therefore advised his Excellency to say nothing about the matter at present, but, on the conclusion of the treaty which he was then negotiating, to take leave of the King as though he were returning to France, and to go so far as Burgos on his homeward journey. From that town he would send a courier to Madrid to announce that, having on the way received a new commission from his sovereign, he was returning to discharge it; and, on his arrival, he would, of course, be received with the same ceremony as on the previous occasion.

Bassompierre, though greatly annoyed at these exasperating formalities, which would not only delay his return to France, but involve him in a great deal of unnecessary expense and inconvenience, had no alternative but to promise compliance. He succeeded, however, in obtaining the concession that his fictitious departure for France need not be preceded by fictitious farewells of anyone besides the King and the Royal family, and that, so long as he left the capital with his whole suite and remained away for two or three days, the Escorial might be the limit of his journey.

The death of Philip III was followed by a revolution of the palace almost as sweeping as that which had succeeded the assassination of Concini in

France. The new King's favourite, Olivares, who, with his uncle Don Balthazar de Zuniga, now assumed the direction of affairs, bore a bitter grudge against the Sandoval family, who, on more than one occasion, had endeavoured to get rid of him by assassination, and he proceeded to take vengeance both upon them and their creatures. The Duke of Uceda was arrested and thrown into prison, where, like the Duke of Ossuña, he ended his days. His father, the Duke of Lerma, who, in obedience to the dying summons of Philip III, was hastening to Madrid, was met on the road by an officer of the Guards and informed that he was to return to Valladolid, on pain of immediate arrest; while, shortly afterwards, the greater part of his ill-gotten wealth

PHILIP IV., KING OF SPAIN.
From the painting by Velasquez.

was confiscated, under a clause in the late King's will by which he revoked the immense gifts he had made during his lifetime. The confessor Alliaga was deprived of his post of Grand Inquisitor and relegated to the obscurity of the monastery from which he had emerged; and several other highly-placed personages lost their charges and were banished from Court.

The Count of Saldagna,[159] Lerma's younger son, thanks to his having had the good fortune to marry a daughter of the old Duke del Infantado,[160] who was held in general esteem, was more leniently dealt with than his father and elder brother, and was merely deprived of his office of *cavalerizzo mayor* (Grand Equerry) and ordered to go and fight the Dutch in the Netherlands. But, a day or two later, "one of the Queen's maids-of-honour, Doña Mariana de Cordoba, presented to the King a promise of marriage which the Count of Saldagna had given her,[161] and the King commanded the said count to prepare to accomplish it."

The royal command appears to have been accompanied by an intimation that, in the event of the count's refusal to do the lady justice, most unpleasant things would happen to him. Anyway, Saldagna appears to have been greatly alarmed, and promised the King to lead Doña Mariana to the altar "on the first day after the octave of Easter" (April 21).

Now, when Bassompierre was setting out for Spain, Anne of Austria, who was much attached to the Sandoval family, "had pressingly recommended to him all that concerned the Duke of Lerma"; and, aware of this, Saldagna's aunt the Countess of Lemos[162] and other relatives and friends of his, who were in despair at the prospect of his contracting a *mésalliance*, to which, in their opinion, death itself would almost be preferable, went to the ambassador and besought him, with tears in their eyes, "to aid in preventing this marriage by every means he was able to devise." The recollection of his own troubles with Marie d'Entragues naturally inclined Bassompierre to view Saldagna's with a sympathetic eye, and, apart from this, he had a decided weakness for meddling in other people's affairs in a benevolent kind of way. He knew, too, that, by helping the Sandovals, he would establish a claim upon the gratitude of Anne of Austria, who, though she had little or no influence at present, might one day possess a great deal. He accordingly promised them to do what he could to deliver their relative from the sad fate which threatened him, and proceeded to San Geronimo—

where Saldagna had gone into retreat on the plea of illness, to escape the remonstrances of his friends and the mocking felicitations of his enemies—with the resolution to screw that nobleman's courage up to what Shakespeare calls the sticking-place, and then to propose to smuggle him out of Spain, disguised as one of his servants.

"After we had exchanged compliments," he says, "I told him that I knew not whether to give him the *parabien* or the *pesame* on his approaching marriage,[163] since, although it might be a great satisfaction for him, nevertheless a gallant of the Court, such as he was, could not without sorrow abandon the pleasant existence he had led up to the present to accept a lonely life, full of anxiety and care, as was marriage.

"He answered that he must perforce obey the master, who commanded him to execute what he had promised the mistress; and that, although it was a hard condition which he was placing on his shoulders, it was an ill for which there was no remedy.

"It appeared to me, from his discourse, that the pack-saddle galled him, and that he would be very willing to find some alleviation. And this encouraged me to tell him that there were more remedies than he thought of, if he desired to be cured, and that the express command which I had received from the Infanta-Queen to assist in every way I could the duke-cardinal his father, as her own person, obliged me, when I perceived the palpable displeasure with which he and all his family regarded this forced marriage, to offer him, on this occasion, my aid and assistance to extricate him from it, if he so desired.

" 'And what aid and assistance can you bring me,' said he, 'when neither I myself nor my relatives are capable of doing anything?'

"Then I told him that, if he were willing to believe me and to trust himself to me, I would extricate him from this difficulty with honour and glory; that the Duke of Alba, grandfather of the present duke,[164] had preferred to commit the crime of rebellion, in delivering his son Fadrigue de Toledo,[165] in the midst of peace, by the use of petards, from a château in which he had been shut up in order to force him to espouse a maid-of-honour, than to allow him to espouse a very wealthy girl, of a family equal to his own; and that I myself had been at law for eight years with a powerful family, who had threatened me with certain death if I did not espouse a maid-of-honour of the Queen [of France] by whom I had had a child, and to whom I had given a promise of marriage to serve her as a blind; that, in case his honour and that of his House was dear to him, as I believed it to be, he ought without regret to quit for a time the Court of Spain, in which he was out of favour, since he had been deprived of the charge of *cavalerizzo mayor*, while his relatives and friends were disgraced and persecuted; that the remedy I offered him was to leave the town at nightfall by post, and go to await me at Bayonne, where I would join him at a month at furthest; that the Comte de Gramont would entertain him there in the meantime in such fashion that his stay would not be disagreeable; that, in case he had not the money at hand to take him there, I would furnish him with 1,000 pistoles to defray his expenses until my arrival; that I would answer that, when he reached the Court, the Queen would give him—until, by her intervention, his peace was made here—1,000 crowns a month, and that, if she did not, I would do so out of my own purse and give him the word of a *caballero* for it.

"He assured me that he was deeply grateful both to the Queen and to myself, and then said: 'But what means have I of leaving Spain without being stopped? And, if I were stopped, they would undoubtedly have my head struck off.'

"I answered that I never proposed impossible things to those whom I desired to serve, and that I would be responsible for his departure, his journey and his safety; that I had been given a passport for a gentleman whom I was sending that same day to the King, and that he was travelling with two attendants; that he would serve him on the road as valet, although this gentleman ought to be his; that he would not take his departure until an hour of the night when he [Saldagna] might come to me unperceived, and that he might leave the other arrangements to me.

"He told me that he was resolved to do as I proposed, and would be all his life under a profound obligation to me; that he wished to speak first to two of his friends; and that he begged me to have everything in readiness at the hour I had named."

Not a little elated with his success, Bassompierre left him and returned to Madrid to finish the despatch which Saldagna's supposed master was to carry that night to France. This task accomplished, he placed the thousand pistoles he had promised the count in two purses, summoned his equerry Le Manny, whom he had decided to send, told him of the distinguished personage who was to accompany him and gave him his instructions what to do in the event of their being stopped, though of that there was little or no danger, as he would indeed be a bold man who, without authorisation, would venture to detain the couriers of an Ambassador Extraordinary.

The fateful hour arrived, but no Saldagna. Instead, there came a message from that nobleman informing Bassompierre that, to his profound regret, he found himself unable to carry out what they had decided upon together, "for reasons which he would tell him when he had the happiness of seeing him."

"I know not," says Bassompierre, "whether the friends to whom he had spoken had dissuaded him, if he lacked the resolution to undertake it, or if the love which he bore this girl had decided him to espouse her."

Anyway, espouse her he did on the day which he had promised the King. The marriage took place in the church of the Carmelite convent, where the Queen was still in retreat. The King led the bridegroom, and the Queen the bride, to the nuptial Mass, and then brought them with the same ceremony to the door of her Majesty's ante-chamber. Here certain officers of the Court appeared upon the scene, took charge of bride and bridegroom, conducted them, "without even giving them time to dine," to the gates of the town, where a travelling-carriage was in waiting, told them to step in and informed them that they were banished from Madrid.

Meantime, the negotiations on the Valtellina question, which had been interrupted by the death of Philip III, had been resumed. At first, the Spaniards suggested that if France would guarantee the protection of religion in the Valtellina, refuse to Venice the right of passage for her troops, and compensate Spain for the expense to which she had been put in occupying the country, she would withdraw. Bassompierre promptly declined. They then offered to waive the question of compensation, in return for the right of transit for Spanish troops, the very privilege which they had just endeavoured to deny to France's old ally Venice. This proposition, as may be supposed, was likewise declined. It was impossible for the Spanish commissioners to persist in such demands, as the influence of Gregory XV, greatly alarmed by visions of Spain's supremacy throughout Italy, had been thrown into the French scale. And so Zuniga proposed that the Grisons should receive compensation for the Valtellina, and the district be ceded to the Pope. Bassompierre curtly replied that he had been sent to Madrid to recover, not to sell, the Valtellina. Zuniga and his colleagues brought forward other schemes: that the Valtellina should be erected into a fourth League; that it should be constituted into a fourteenth canton of the Swiss Confederation, and so forth. But, finding that Bassompierre stood firmly by his instructions, they at length gave way, and on April 26, 1621, the Treaty of Madrid was signed.

This treaty stipulated that Spain should withdraw her troops from the Valtellina; that the Grisons should grant a general amnesty to the Valtellinas; that "the novelties prejudicial to the Catholic religion should be removed," and that the Grisons should ratify the treaty, which was to be guaranteed by the King of France and the Swiss Cantons.

The Cabinet of Madrid hoped that, in the interval between the conclusion and the execution of the treaty, some incident might arise which would furnish them with a pretext for not keeping their word; and in this, as we shall see, they were not disappointed.

On April 28, Bassompierre, having taken leave of Philip IV, left Madrid, accompanied by his whole suite, as though he were returning to France. He spent the night at Torreladones, and on the following morning reached the Escorial, "where he saw everything in this wonderful building and all the rare things which it contained." Early on the 30th, he left the Escorial and proceeded to El Pardo, a pleasure-house belonging to the King, where he dined, and then went on to Alcovendas. Here he passed the night, and on May 1, dressed in deep mourning, as became one who had been charged with an embassy of condolence, made his second ceremonious entry into Madrid.

On the 4th, he had an audience of the King to offer the *pesame*, and appeared, according to his own account, before the bereaved monarch "with a countenance which, apart from the absence of tears, presented every indication of grief and sadness."[166] Afterwards, by Philip IV's invitation, he accompanied him to the funeral service in honour of the late King at San Geronimo.

On the following day Bassompierre began to pay his farewell visits to the grandees and other important persons whose acquaintance he had made at Madrid, a task which was to occupy him several days, as there were so many to visit and so many formalities to be observed. His adieux were interrupted on May 9 by Philip IV's solemn entry into Madrid, which he witnessed from a balcony at the Puerta Guadalaxara, which the King had ordered to be prepared for him:

"The King," he says, "set out from San Geronimo and came to his palace by way of the Calle Mayor. Before him marched the kettle-drummers; then came the gentlemen of the King's table; then, the *titulados*;[167] after them the mace-bearers; then the four mayor-domos; then the grandees; and then the Duke del Infantado, *cavalerizzo mayor*, bareheaded, and carrying a drawn sword. He preceded the King, who followed under a canopy, supported on thirty-two poles, which were borne by the thirty-two *regidores* of Madrid,[168] habited in cloth of silver and crimson. Then came the *corregidor*,[169] surrounded by the King's equerries, and the Counsellors of State and Gentlemen of the Chamber closed the procession."

In a despatch to Louis XIII, dated the following day, Bassompierre describes the entry as "very magnificent for Madrid, but not equal to the least of those which take place in France."

On the 12th, Bassompierre had his farewell audience of the King, who gave him a letter in his own hand for Louis XIII and another for Anne of Austria. He then took leave of Don Carlos, and, on leaving the Alcazar, went to bid adieu to Olivares and Zuniga.

In the afternoon "the executors of the late King's will placed in his hands a great reliquary, which must have been worth 500,000 crowns," and charged him to present it to the Queen of France, to whom Philip IV had bequeathed it.

On the 15th—the day he was to leave Madrid—Don Juan de Serica came to present him, on behalf of Philip III, with "an ensign of diamonds worth 6,000 crowns."[170] The Countess of Barajas sent him "a very beautiful present of perfumes," and he begged the countess's acceptance of a diamond chain worth 1,500 crowns. Shortly before his departure, he received another gift from the King, in the shape of a very fine horse from his Majesty's stud.

In the afternoon he left Madrid, "the King ordering him to be escorted on his departure in the same fashion as when he had made his entry," and was accompanied so far as Alcovendas, where he was to pass the night, by Du Fargis, the Prince of Eboli and a number of Spanish nobles. His journey to the frontier was uneventful, and on May 24 he reached Bayonne.

CHAPTER XXIV

A new War of Religion breaks out in France—Luynes created Constable—Louis XIII and Duplessis-Mornay—Bassompierre joins the Royal army before Saint-Jean d'Angély—Capitulation of the town—Bassompierre returns with Créquy to Paris—He is "in great consideration" amongst the ladies—Apparent anxiety of Luynes for the marriage of his niece to Bassompierre—The King and the Constable resolve to lay siege to Montauban—Bassompierre decides to rejoin the army without waiting for orders from the latter—He arrives at the King's quarters at the Château of Picqueos—Dispositions of the besieging army—Narrow escape of Bassompierre while reconnoitring the advanced-works of the town—A gallant Swiss—Death of the Comte de Fiesque—Heavy casualties amongst the besiegers—The Seigneur de Tréville—Bassompierre and the women of Montauban—Death of Mayenne—The Spanish monk—An amateur general—Disastrous results of carrying out his orders—Furious sortie of the garrison—Bassompierre is wounded in the face—An amusing incident—The Cévennes mountaineers endeavour to throw reinforcements into Montauban—A midnight *mêlée*.

BASSOMPIERRE would probably have found the Spaniards more difficult to deal with, had it not been that they were anxious to free Louis XIII, for the moment, from foreign embarrassments in order that he might commit himself fully to a war with his Protestant subjects, which could not fail to weaken

France and render it unlikely that she would be willing to engage in hostilities beyond her borders.

The drastic measures adopted by Louis XIII towards the Protestants of Béarn had aroused bitter resentment amongst their co-religionists throughout France; and towards the end of December, 1620, a general assembly of the party was held at La Rochelle to decide upon the policy to be adopted in view of this menace to their faith. Of the great Huguenot chiefs, Bouillon, Sully, and Lesdiguières did not respond to the summons or send anyone to represent them; but La Force, Châtillon, La Trémoille and Rohan sent delegates.

The Assembly authorised the raising of troops and a general levy on the funds of the party; and then proceeded to divide France into eight departments—veritable military districts on the model of the German "circles"—each being placed under the command of a general-in-chief. Although these measures were intended to be purely defensive, nothing more calculated to provoke hostilities could have been devised; the Protestants were at once accused by the Government of having established a republic within the State, and in April a new War of Religion began.

It differed from the old wars, however, inasmuch as neither the chiefs nor the rank and file of the Huguenots were unanimous in supporting it. Lesdiguières, who had been won over by the Court, deserted the common cause, as did most of the Protestant nobles; Rohan, his younger brother Soubise and La Force alone remained faithful. Outside the nobility, the same division of opinion manifested itself; the great majority of the warlike Calvinists of the South took up arms; but the rest of Protestant France did not move.

At the moment of entering upon the campaign against the Protestants, Luynes demanded the sword of Constable of France, which Louis XIII bestowed upon him with the utmost pomp, although he had already promised it to Lesdiguières, on condition that he should abjure the Protestant faith, which the marshal had engaged to do. That the sword which had been borne by such warriors as Du Guesclin, Clisson, Buchan, Saint-Pol, the Duc de Bourbon, and Anne de Montmorency should be conferred upon the hero of an assassination, who could not drill a company of infantry, aroused universal astonishment and disgust; and Luynes's exchange of the *rôle* of statesman for that of general was, as one might anticipate, attended with disastrous results for the forces under his command.

However, the campaign opened auspiciously enough. The King and Luynes advanced to Saumur, of which the latter succeeded in getting possession by a characteristic act of bad faith. The Governor of Saumur was that grand old veteran Du Plessis-Mornay, the companion-in-arms and counsellor of Henri IV. Mornay had refused to support a rebellion which, in his eyes, was unjustified, and when Luynes assured him that the King had no intention of depriving him of a post which had been conferred upon him by his father more than thirty years before, he opened the gates of town and château to the royal troops. No sooner were they in possession, than he was informed that prudence would not permit the King to leave a Huguenot in charge of so important a link in his communications. He was offered a bribe of money, and even a marshal's bâton, in return for the resignation of his government, which he indignantly refused, but accepted the royal promise that in three months' time he should be reinstated. On various pretexts, however, Louis XIII succeeded in evading this engagement until Mornay's death, two years later.

At the end of May, the Royal army laid siege to Saint-Jean-d'Angély, called the "bulwark of La Rochelle," to the possession of which great importance was attached; and it was here that Bassompierre, who, after remaining a day at Bayonne, had hastened northwards, joined it. The town, which was defended by Soubise, held out for nearly a month, and at times there was some pretty sharp fighting in the faubourgs, in which Bassompierre appears to have distinguished himself. But on June 23 it capitulated, and d'Épernon and Bassompierre marched in with the French and Swiss Guards.

On the 26th, Bassompierre accompanied the King to Cognac, from which town he was despatched to Paris, to ratify with the Chancellor and the Spanish Ambassador Mirabello the treaty which he had made at Madrid. He was accompanied by Créquy, who had received a musket-ball through the cheek at the siege of Saint-Jean-d'Angély, and to whom Luynes had suggested the advisability of a short sojourn in the capital for the benefit of his health. About the same time, another brigadier-general, Saint-Luc, was appointed lieutenant-general of the western seaboard of France, and sent by Luynes to Brouage, "to make the King powerful at sea." The reason, however, why the new Constable felt able to dispense simultaneously with the services of three of the most distinguished officers in the army was not made apparent until some weeks later, as, on taking leave of him, each was assured that he would be recalled so soon as any important operations were contemplated.

Bassompierre's reception by his friends of both sexes in Paris left nothing to be desired:

"It is impossible to say," he writes, "how I passed my time during this visit. Everyone entertained us in turn. The ladies congregated or came to the Tuileries. There were few gallants in Paris, and I was in great consideration there, and in love in divers directions. I had brought back from Spain rarities to the value of 20,000 crowns, and these I distributed amongst the ladies, who gave me a most cordial reception."

Bassompierre had not been long in Paris when he received a visit from his friend Roucelaï, who came on behalf of Luynes to interview him on the question of his marriage with the Constable's niece, Mlle. de Combalet, which had been proposed to the favourite by Condé and Guise during Bassompierre's absence in Spain. Luynes was anxious to conciliate these two princes, who had been far from pleased at his assumption of the office of Constable, and, aware that

Bassompierre had strengthened his position at Court by the success of his embassy to Madrid and his services at Saint-Jean-d'Angély, he appears to have been anxious to remove all difficulties in the way of the match.

"He had sent Roucelaï," says Bassompierre, "to ascertain what I desired for my advantage and my fortune, if this marriage were made. For he imagined that I should demand offices of the Crown, dignities and governments, and that it was my intention to be bought. But I answered Roucelaï that the honour of marrying into the family of the Constable was so dear to me, that he would offend me by giving me anything except his niece, and that I demanded nothing beyond that, although afterwards I should not refuse the benefits of which he might deem me worthy when I was his nephew. He [Luynes] was delighted at my frankness, and caused me to be informed that he would place me in the perfect confidence of the King, who had a very strong inclination for me, of which in future he would no longer be jealous, as he had been the previous year."

All this was no doubt very gratifying, but, at the same time, the Constable, notwithstanding that active operations had long since been resumed, showed no inclination to recall either Bassompierre, Créquy, or Saint-Luc to the army; and presently they learned that he had appointed three other brigadier-generals—creatures of his own—in their places, having persuaded the King that, though they were very capable officers, "they were not persons who would stick to their work or give the necessary attention to it." The real reason seems to have been the favourite's fear that "they might eclipse his glory and that of his brothers," and that they might be disinclined to carry out the orders of one whom they knew to be entirely ignorant of military matters.

Towards the middle of August, Bassompierre learned that the King and Luynes, encouraged by the taking of the little town of Clairac and some minor successes, had resolved to lay siege to Montauban, the great citadel of the Huguenots of the South, and were marching towards that town. About the same time, he received a letter from Marie de' Medici, who had returned to Tours, informing him that the Constable had demanded of her Marillac, who was in her service,[171] as the only man capable of reducing Montauban, "and had begged her to send him to the King at once," in order not to delay his Majesty's conquest by his absence.

Notwithstanding the formal reconciliation, Marie still hated the man who had taken her son from her, and subjected her to so many humiliations, as bitterly as ever; and her object in writing was, of course, to animate Bassompierre against the Constable and put an end to the good understanding at which they now seemed to have arrived. By this means she would, so to speak, kill two birds with one stone, since she had probably not forgiven Bassompierre for the activity which he had displayed in the King's cause during the last war, which had contributed materially to the defeat of her party. Bassompierre, however, had no intention of quarrelling with his prospective uncle to gratify the Queen-Mother or anyone else. At the same time, he was deeply mortified to learn that a mediocre officer like Marillac, who had nothing to recommend him but his subservience to the favourite, was to be appointed to a high command, while he himself was left unemployed; and he felt that to remain inactive while such important operations were in progress was impossible. He therefore decided to rejoin the army without waiting for orders from the Constable, trusting, by the exercise of a little tact, to succeed in disarming the annoyance which his return might occasion that personage.

The Royal army had encamped before Montauban on August 18. If the town fell, all the South would fall with it; and Luynes, elated by recent successes, believed that victory was assured. The most prudent officers did not share the optimism of the favourite; to them the siege of Montauban seemed a very difficult undertaking. La Force had retired into the place with three of his sons, the Comte d'Orval, younger son of Sully, and a number of Huguenot gentlemen; from 3,000 to 4,000 picked soldiers, supported by more than 2,000 armed citizens, formed a truly formidable garrison; the Duc de Rohan, still master of a great part of the Albigeois and Rouergue, would, they knew, make every effort to revictual the place and harass the siege operations; and he could command the services of the Protestant mountaineers of the Cévennes. Several generals and members of the Council had expressed the opinion that they should begin by clearing Upper Guienne and Upper Languedoc of the rebels, and postpone operations against Montauban until the spring. But the King and Luynes had refused to listen to them.

Bassompierre arrived in the Royal camp on the 21st, just as the trenches were about to be opened, and at once proceeded to the Château of Piquecos, to the north of the town, on the right bank of the Aveyron, where Louis XIII had taken up his quarters. Having excused his return without orders on the ground of his zeal for the service of the King, he hastened to disclaim any desire to serve as brigadier-general and declared that "he should content himself with being in this siege Colonel-General of the Swiss." Luynes thereupon became quite cordial, and the King told Bassompierre that, when the siege was over, and he and the Constable had returned to Paris, he would give him the command of the army.

Lesdiguières had advised Luynes to employ against Montauban all the resources of the military art, and to enclose the town in lines of circumvallation protected by forts. But the presumptuous Constable was unwilling to waste time in what he was pleased to regard as superfluous precautions; and the siege of this formidable stronghold, defended by several thousand resolute men, prepared to die sword in hand in defence of their religion rather than surrender, and with strong reinforcements under an able general hovering in the background, was embarked upon as lightly as if its reduction had presented no more than ordinary difficulty.

The besieging army was divided into three divisions. One division, composed of the French and Swiss Guards, with the regiments of Piedmont and Normandy, and commanded by the Maréchaux de Praslin and de Chaulnes, under the orders of the Constable, was to assail the advanced works of Montmirat and Saint-Antoine, to the west and north-west of the town, on the right bank of the Tarn, in front of the faubourg of Ville-Nouvelle. The second, of which Mayenne had the command, with the Maréchal de Thémines under him, was to attack Ville-Bourbon, a faubourg situated on the left bank of the Tarn,[172] and connected with the town by an old brick bridge, dating from the early part of the fourteenth century. The third, commanded by Joinville—or the Duc de Chevreuse, as he had now become—who had Lesdiguières and Saint-Géran to assist him, was entrusted with the attack on Le Moustier, a fortified suburb to the south-west of the town. Two bridges which had been thrown across the Tarn maintained communication between the three divisions, to the first of which Bassompierre, as Colonel-General of the Swiss, was attached.

On leaving the King, Bassompierre returned to the camp, and he and Praslin crossed the river to visit Mayenne. The Lorraine prince offered to show them the fortifications of Ville-Bourbon, and took them as close to the walls as he could persuade them to go, "with the intention of drawing upon us some musket-shots." This kind of bravado appears to have been a favourite amusement of Mayenne, but, as we shall presently see, he was to indulge in it once too often.

On their return to the Guards' camp, they began preparations for opening the trenches, and Bassompierre, accompanied by an Italian engineer named Gamorini, who had been sent to the army by Marie de' Medici, in whose service he was, went out to reconnoitre the advance-works of the town. They succeeded in getting quite close to them without being observed; but, as they were returning, they lost their way and were suddenly confronted by an advanced guard-house of the enemy. The sentries fired upon them point-blank, and one ball went through Bassompierre's coat; but both he and Gamorini succeeded in effecting their escape unharmed. They brought back with them some useful information, and that evening the first trench was opened, the work being entrusted to the Regiment of Piedmont.

On the following day, Luynes came to their camp and summoned Bassompierre and the other leaders to a council of war. While this was proceeding, the enemy brought one of their cannon to bear upon the men working on the trench, the first shot blowing a captain of the Regiment of Piedmont to pieces and mortally wounding two other officers, one of whom, a lieutenant named Castiras, was in Bassompierre's service. The bombardment was followed by a furious sortie, and the Piedmonts were obliged to abandon the unfinished trench and fall back. Bassompierre, leaving the council, hurriedly collected reinforcements, and drove the enemy back into the town; but the Piedmonts had suffered severely.

Work proceeded without interruption during the next three days, and considerable progress was made; but, during the night of August 26-27, the enemy sallied out again, their attack on this occasion being directed against a sunken road, which the Royal troops were fortifying, with the intention of placing a battery there. They were again repulsed, but not before they had succeeded in over-turning the gabions which had been placed there. Some of these they carried off with them, but abandoned between the road and the fortifications, well within musket-shot of the latter.

"The following night," writes Bassompierre, "one of the Swiss named Jacques told us that, if I were willing to give him a crown, he would bring back the gabions which the enemy had removed from the road; and what astonished us the more, was that this man brought back the gabions on his back, so strong and robust was he. The enemy fired two hundred arquebus-shots at him, without wounding him. After he had brought back six, the captains of the Guards begged me not to permit so brave a man to risk his life again for the one that still remained. But he told them that he wished to bring it back to complete his bargain; and this he did."

On the 27th, Lesdiguières and Saint-Géran attacked the counterscarp of the bastion of Le Moustier, and carried it after a desperate struggle of more than three hours. This success, which cost the besiegers some 600 casualties, was not followed up, chiefly owing to the opposition of Marillac, who was of opinion that, if they descended into the fosse to attack the bastion, they would find themselves exposed to a murderous flanking-fire from masked batteries.

On the 29th, the Guards' trenches had been sufficiently advanced to allow of a battery of eight guns being established, and Schomberg, who was acting as Grand Master of the Artillery, came to inspect it. Bassompierre warned him that the park of powder was too near the battery for safety, and that, with a high wind blowing in its direction, the sparks from the cannon might be carried to the powder. The Sieur de Lesine, the officer in charge of the munitions, however, protested that there was no danger, and Schomberg did not order their removal.

They continued to push forward their trenches, and on the 31st Bassompierre, "to reconnoitre how far they had advanced, came to the head of the trench and advanced eight or ten paces from it." He got back again in safety, the enemy not having had time to train their muskets upon him. But when, shortly afterwards, his friend, the Comte de Fiesque, attempted to do the same, they were ready for him, and he received a musket-ball in the abdomen, from which he died two days later. "He was a great loss to us," writes Bassompierre, "and more particularly to me, for he was greatly attached to me. He was a brave noble, an honourable man and an excellent friend."

By the evening of that day they had got another battery of four guns into position, and on the following morning a furious bombardment of the enemy's advanced works began, Schomberg and Praslin superintending the work of the larger battery and Bassompierre of the smaller.

"They both made a fine noise," writes Bassompierre; "but, after firing for an hour or more, what I had predicted two days before happened: the sparks from the cannon were carried into the park of powder and fired five tons of it, with the loss of Lesine and forty men."

In the course of the afternoon, a similar disaster occurred in Mayenne's camp before Ville-Bourbon, amongst the killed being that prince's uncle the Marquis de Villars and a son of the Comte de Riberac, a young man of great promise. Worse misfortunes, however, were in store for Mayenne's division.

In the night of September 2-3, the Lorraine prince advanced to the assault of a crescent-shaped outwork which had been constructed by La Force, and was defended by his sons and other Huguenot nobles and some of the best soldiers in the garrison. The attack failed; but on the following afternoon the attempt was renewed. After a furious hand-to-hand conflict, Mayenne was again repulsed, with heavy loss. On that day died the gallant Marquis de Thémines, eldest son of the marshal, La Frette, the governor of Chartres, "who yielded to no man of his time in courage and ambition," and more than fifty Catholic gentlemen. The siege of Montauban, so lightly undertaken by Luynes, seemed likely to cost France dear.

On September 4, the King and the Constable called a council of war to discuss the advisability of endeavouring to carry the bastion of Le Moustier by assault. Bassompierre strongly urged that the attempt should be made, and was supported by Lesdiguières; but the other generals opposed it, and Marillac declared that to descend into the fosse meant certain death. Luynes asked Bassompierre to step into his cabinet, where the King presently joined them. Louis XIII informed them that Marillac and the others had said to him that it was easy for M. de Bassompierre to advocate this hazardous undertaking, as all the danger would be left to them, and he would have no share in it; and had accused him of wishing to expose them to butchery. Bassompierre, in high indignation, thereupon declared that, if the King would give him leave, he himself would lead the assault on the bastion, and pledged his word that, if he did not fall, "in three weeks he would have three cannon in position there against the town."

"The King, who always had a rather good opinion of me, said to the Constable: 'Take Bassompierre at his word and let him go; I will answer for him. Send the three brigadier-generals from Le Moustier to the camp of the Guards, and place him at Le Moustier. I am sure that he will do as he promises us, and we shall be the gainers.'"

The Constable objected that the change would not be agreeable to either division, and declared that the Guards would not obey the orders of the brigadier-generals from Le Moustier. Finally, Luynes asked Bassompierre to go and reconnoitre the bastion. This he did, in company with the Italian engineer Gamorini and two other officers from his division, and reported that an attack would not present more than ordinary difficulty. Luynes thereupon proposed that it should be undertaken; but Marillac and his colleagues persisted in their objections, and assured him that Montauban would soon be theirs, without any need for such sacrifice of life as this attack must entail. And they succeeded in bringing him round to their opinion.

On the 9th, the Guards, after some fierce fighting, succeeded in getting a footing in the advanced-works of Ville-Nouvelle. In this attack a poor gentleman of Béarn, Henri de Peyrac, Seigneur de Tréville, who had served for four years as a private soldier, greatly distinguished himself; and Bassompierre brought his gallantry to the notice of the King, and recommended him for an ensigncy in the Regiment of Navarre. This Louis XIII granted him, and Bassompierre told Tréville that he must accompany him to Piquecos to thank his Majesty. Tréville, however, refused the commission offered him, saying that he did not wish to leave his regiment, and that he "intended to conduct himself so well in future that the King would feel obliged to give him one in the Guards." This he not long afterwards obtained, and eventually rose to be captain of the company of Musketeers of the Guard and to be governor of the district of Foix.

A few days later, 1,200 of the Cévennes mountaineers succeeded in eluding the vigilance of the covering force and throwing themselves into Saint-Antonin, a town eight leagues north-east of Montauban, obviously with the intention of marching through the Forest of Gréseigne and reinforcing the beleaguered garrison. The folly of Luynes in refusing to listen to the advice of Lesdiguières to enclose the town within lines of circumvallation was now apparent to all. The Constable's ineptitude, however, was already a by-word in the army; and "both he and his brother the Maréchal de Chaulnes showed such ignorance of the military art, that the King, who, at any rate, understood the rudiments, perceived it and made game of them."

In consequence of this disconcerting move on the part of the enemy, it was necessary to send out a strong force of cavalry every night to guard the roads between the forest and Montauban, which Bassompierre and the other generals commanded in turn.

On the 13th, Mayenne delivered another assault on the outworks of Ville-Bourbon, with the same result as had attended his previous efforts. "This," says Bassompierre, "put great heart into the enemy and disheartened his troops. As for him, he was beside himself with rage."

A day or two later, there was a comic interlude in the siege, of which Bassompierre was the hero. We shall allow him to describe it in his own words:—

"It had been resolved some days before to break by cannon-shot the bridge of Montauban,[173] in order to stop the reinforcements which those in Montauban were sending to Ville-Bourbon. The Maréchal de Chaulnes, who was newly returned from Toulouse, where he had been lying ill, had charged me to bring a battery to bear upon the bridge. But, since it was a great way off and five hundred shots caused but little damage, which could easily be repaired with wood, I remonstrated against the little utility and great expense of this bombardment; and I was told not to persist in it. At the same time, two hundred women who were in the habit of washing linen and kitchen-utensils under or near this bridge, and who were incommoded by the cannon-shot, aware that I was in command in the quarter from which the firing came, and that I had always made war upon women in kindly fashion, sent me a drummer to beg me, on their part, not to incommode their washing. This request I granted them readily, since I had already received an order to that effect; and so pleased were they with me, that they demanded a truce in order to see me, and a great number of the principal women of the town came on to the top of the ramparts to look at me. And I, on that day alone, during the whole of the siege, dressed myself with care and adorned myself, so that I might go and talk with them."

All this was very charming, but, a few days later, Bassompierre was to meet the women of Montauban in much less agreeable circumstances.

On the 17th, Guise, who had arrived in the camp some days earlier, accompanied by a great number of gentlemen from his government of Provence, came to see Bassompierre and persuade him to go and dine with Mayenne. Bassompierre, however, who had to attend a council of war which Praslin had summoned, excused himself and, at the same time, warned the duke to be on his guard against Mayenne, "who had no greater pleasure than to make the enemy fire on him or on those whom he took to view his works, and was burning his fingers in order to burn others."

"To my great regret," he continues, "my prophecy was in a certain fashion a true one, for, after dinner, as he [Mayenne] was showing them his works, a ball from an arquebus, which had first pierced M. de Schomberg's hat, struck him in the eye and killed him."

Mayenne had possessed amiable qualities, and had enjoyed in Paris a popularity which recalled that of the great Guises. The news of his death caused a riot in the capital, where an infuriated mob fell upon the Huguenots one day when they were returning from their temple at Charenton. The Huguenots were armed, and several persons were killed on both sides, while the temple was burned.

The King and the Constable had recourse to a singular expedient to avenge Mayenne and take the town. The famous Spanish Carmelite monk Domingo de Jesu Maria, who had marched at the head of the Imperial army on the day of the Battle of Prague, and to whom the devout attributed the victory, was passing through France on his way from Germany. Luynes sent for him to come to the camp, and asked him what he ought to do to reduce this heretic stronghold, upon which the monk assured him that if he caused four hundred cannon-shots to be fired into the town, the terrified inhabitants would undoubtedly surrender. The King thereupon sent for Bassompierre and ordered him to fire the four hundred shots, which were to deliver Montauban into his hands. "This I did," says Bassompierre; "but the enemy did not surrender for all that."

Matters continued to go badly with the besiegers, which is scarcely surprising, having regard to the gross ineptitude of the amateur warriors who commanded them. At Ville-Nouvelle, where alone any real progress had been made, a mine had been prepared which was intended to demolish the inner face of the advanced-work of which the Guards had carried the outer. On the day before it was to be fired,

Ramsay, the officer in charge of the mine, came to the Maréchal de Chaulnes to inquire how he wished it to be charged. Chaulnes, who was entirely ignorant of such matters, turned to the officers about him for information; but he misunderstood what they said and ordered the charge to be made four times as large as that which they had suggested. The astonished engineer remonstrated, but was curtly told to carry out his orders. On the following day, however, Chaulnes appears to have discovered his mistake, and told Bassompierre to go and have the mine charged as he judged best. It was too late; for, just as he reached the entrance to the gallery, Ramsay came rushing out and shouted to him to run for his life, as he had ignited the fuse and feared that the explosion would be terrible.

"I needed no second bidding," writes Bassompierre, "and ran back forty paces as fast as I could to get away. The mine exploded with a greater violence than I have ever seen, and all the entrenchment under which it was laid was carried into the air. It was a long time in descending, when it came pouring down into the trench upon us."

Bassompierre, who had had the presence of mind to thrust his head and the upper portion of his body into an empty barrel which happened to be lying near him, was fortunate enough to escape injury, though he had considerable difficulty in extricating himself, as there were "more than a thousand pounds of earth upon his loins, his thighs and his feet." When he at last succeeded, he found that the effect of the explosion had been most disastrous, more than thirty men having been killed by the falling débris, amongst them being the unfortunate engineer Ramsay. The mine had also demolished a great part of their own defences, and placed them in a most dangerous position.

The enemy did not fail to seize their advantage, and, having discharged a storm of grenades and fire-balls at them, sallied out and fell upon two companies of the Guards on the left of the line. Bassompierre, with a body of gentlemen-volunteers, hurried to their assistance, and the assailants were repulsed. But, as he was returning, he met Praslin, who begged him to go at once to their four-gun battery, which was being heavily attacked. As he approached the battery, he saw that it was on fire, and that while some of the fifty Swiss who guarded it were engaged in extinguishing the flames, the rest were defending themselves with their pikes and halberds against a large force of the enemy, who were evidently determined to capture the battery at all costs.

"I saw, for the first time in my life," he says, "women in a fight, throwing stones against us with far more strength and animosity than I should have conceived possible, or handing them to the soldiers to throw."

He arrived only just in time, for the Swiss, many of whom had already been killed or wounded, were being desperately hard-pressed, and in a few minutes the battery must have been taken. But he placed himself at their head with his volunteers, and led a charge which drove the enemy back a little distance. They continued, however, to assail them with missiles of every description, and a large stone striking Bassompierre in the face—let us hope it was not thrown by one of the ladies with whom he had been conversing so amiably a few days before!—brought him to the ground insensible. Some of the Swiss raised him up, and carried him out of the *mêlée*, when he soon came to himself and returned to the fight. Finally, Praslin came up with two companies and forced the enemy to retire.

Their troubles, however, were not yet over, for meantime the enemy had made a sally in another quarter. Bassompierre and his noblesse again went to the rescue, and taking the assailants in the rear, obliged them to retreat, leaving several prisoners behind them.[174]

Bassompierre was certainly a person of extraordinary energy, for after this strenuous day he volunteered to take command of the force which was detached each evening to watch for the approach of the enemy's reinforcements from Saint-Antonin, in place of Praslin, who was suffering from the effects of a slight wound, and spent the whole night in the saddle.

"Next morning," he says, "as I was returning with my thousand men to camp, the King sent for me to come to him at Picqueos. I did not alight from my horse, and, in the dirty and disordered condition in which I was, after having been on the watch all night, and with the clotted blood from the wound on my head spread all over my face and round my eyes, I was unrecognisable. On my arrival, the King and the Constable told me that M. de Luxembourg,[175] who had command of 600 horse who went out every night to watch for the arrival of the reinforcements, had fallen ill, and that I must take charge of them, until the reinforcements had either made their way into the town or had been defeated. This I accepted willingly. While I was talking to them, the Queen arrived from Moissac.[176] The King sent the Constable to receive her and remained talking to me. As she entered, she asked who was that frightful man talking to the King. He told her that it was a nobleman of that part of the country called the Comte de Curton. 'Jesus!' she exclaimed, 'how ugly he is!' The Constable said to the King as he approached the Queen: 'Sire, present M. de Bassompierre to the Queen, and tell her that he is the Comte de Curton.' And this the King did. I kissed the hem of her gown, after which the Constable presented me to the Princesse de Conti, Mlle. de Vendôme, Madame de Montmorency and Madame la Connétable, his wife. I saluted them and heard them say: 'This is a strange-looking man, and very dirty; he does well to stay in the country.' Then I began to laugh, and, from my laugh and my teeth, they knew me, and had great pity upon me, and still more after dinner, when, on an alarm being raised that the enemy's reinforcements were coming, we went out to fight."

The alarm proved to be a false one; but in the night of September 26-27, just as Bassompierre was looking forward to the enjoyment of the first night's rest he had had for more than a week, his equerry Le Manny came in with the news that the reinforcements from Saint-Antonin were approaching. There could be no doubt about the matter this time; the officer who had arrived with the news had seen them marching through the forest.

Bassompierre awoke the Duc de Retz and Créquy's son Canaples, who slept in his room, and told them that the enemy were at hand; "but they thought he was playing a jest on them, as they had been up ten successive nights watching and waiting." And they positively refused to accompany him. Leaving them, he went into a gallery near his room, where some thirty gentlemen slept, but could only persuade two of them to go with him. "The cry of 'Wolf!' had been raised so often without any justification that they vowed they would answer it no more." But the wolf from the Cévennes was really coming this time, and a very fierce wolf he proved to be.

Hurriedly getting together some 1,200 men, of whom 200 were Swiss, Bassompierre marched away and took up his position in a sunken road intersecting the plain of Ramiers, which lies between the Forest of Gréseigne and Montauban, where it had been decided to await the enemy. Learning that they were approaching in three bodies, he detached the Baron d'Estissac with 400 men to his right; the Comte d'Ayen, who was in command of the cavalry that night, was already in position on his left.

It was a very dark night, and when presently the forms of men began to loom out of the blackness ahead, he was uncertain whether they were the enemy or a party of the Royal troops. But he shouted, "*Vive le Roi!*" and the answering cry of "*Vive* Rohan!" settled the question.

His position was protected by a barricade, but the agile mountaineers quickly swarmed over it and jumped down into the road, where a furious struggle began. So intense was the darkness there that it was often impossible to tell friend from foe, and not a few must have died by the weapons of their comrades. Bassompierre, lunging with a halberd at one of the enemy, stumbled and fell; the Huguenot, killed by the Swiss, fell on top of him, as did two other men who had shared his fate; and he was pinned down and unable to rise. At length, Le Manny and one of his servants, hearing his cries for help, came and extricated him; but scarcely was he on his feet again, than he narrowly escaped being run through the body by a Swiss, who mistook him for an enemy. The *mêlée* continued for some time, but at length numbers prevailed, and practically all the brave mountaineers were either killed or made prisoners. The dead had not died in vain, however, for, though their comrades on the right had been routed by d'Ayen, those on the left, to the number of some 600 men, had contrived in the darkness to elude d'Estissac, and throw themselves into Montauban.

Among the prisoners taken by Bassompierre[177] was the Sieur de Beaufort, the commander of the Cévennais. He was treated as a prisoner of war and imprisoned in the Bastille, from which he was released on the conclusion of peace. His humble comrades, however, were less fortunate, and those who recovered from their wounds were sent to the galleys.

END OF VOL. I.

FOOTNOTES:

[1] Most of the places of the German part of Lorraine had two names, of which one was the approximate translation of the other. The future marshal's family would not appear to have adopted definitely the French form of the name until the end of the sixteenth century; but, for the sake of convenience, we propose to use it throughout this work.

[2] Agrippa d'Aubigné, in his *Histoire universelle*, cites a letter from Guise to Christophe de Bassompierre, dated May 21, 1588, which is signed "l'amy de cœur."

[3] She was the daughter of George le Picart de Radeval and Louise de la Motte-Bléquin.

[4] Of Bassompierre's two brothers, the elder, Jean, Seigneur de Removille, after serving as a volunteer in Hungary against the Turks, entered the service of France, and took part in the invasion of Savoy, in 1600. In 1603, having quarrelled with Henri IV, he quitted his service for that of Philip III of Spain, and died the following year of a wound received at the siege of Ostend. The younger, George African, was destined for Holy Orders, but renounced

this intention on learning of his brother's death, and assumed the title of Seigneur de Removille. He married in 1610 Henriette de Tornelle, daughter of Charles Emmanuel, Comte de Tornelle, by whom he had six children. He died in 1632, on his return from the campaign of Leipsic, on which he had accompanied Charles IV of Lorraine.

[5] See the author's "The Brood of False Lorraine," Vol. II., p. 545.

[6] Don Cesare d'Este, grandson of Alphonso I and Laura Eustachia, had caused himself to be proclaimed Duke of Ferrara on October 29, 1597. Pope Clement VII claimed the duchy as devolving on the Holy See by the extinction of the legitimate line of Este.

[7] Pietro Aldobrandini, nephew of Clement VII. He had been created cardinal in 1593 and subsequently became Archbishop of Ravenna. He died in 1621.

[8] By a capitulation, signed on January 13, 1598, Don Cesare renounced the duchy of Ferrara in favour of Clement VIII and remained only Duke of Modena and Reggio.

[9] The Archduke Albert, who had taken Holy Orders and been created a cardinal, had renounced that dignity in order to marry the Infanta.

[10] Peter Ernest, Count von Mansfeld. He was subsequently created a Prince of the Empire by Maximilian II. He died in 1604.

[11] Daughter of René, Vicomte de Rohan, and Catherine de Parthenay, Dame de Soubise. She married in 1604 Johann of Bavaria, Duke of Zweibrücken.

[12] Claude de Lorraine, younger son of Henri I de Lorraine, Duc de Guise, and Catherine de Clèves. He bore at first the title of Prince de Joinville, but in 1606 became Duc de Chevreuse, in consequence of his elder brother having resigned that duchy to him. He died in 1657.

[13] Charles, Comte d'Auvergne (1573-1650), natural son of Charles IX and Marie Touchet. He was created Duc d'Angoulême in 1620; but before this period Bassompierre, in his *Mémoires*, frequently speaks of him as M. d'Angoulême.

[14] The Grand Equerry, the Duc de Bellegarde.

[15] Charles Auguste de Saint-Lary, brother of Bellegarde, whom he succeeded in the post of Grand Equerry.

[16] Annibal de Schomberg, second son of Gaspard de Schomberg.

[17] In April, 1599, this boy was legitimated by letters-patent, which were duly registered by the complaisant Parlement of Paris.

[18] But she had, nevertheless, condescended to ask favours of "the woman of impure life," and to regard her as a sister. "I speak to you freely," she writes to Gabrielle, on February 24, 1597, "as to one whom I wish to keep as a sister. I have placed so much confidence in the assurance that you have given me that you love me, that I do not desire to have any protector but you near the King; for nothing that comes from your beautiful mouth can fail to be well received." She had also, shortly before signing the procuration, transferred to Gabrielle her duchy of Étampes.

[19] See the excellent work of Desclozeaux, *Gabrielle d'Éstrées, Marquise de Monceaux* (Paris: 1889).

[20] Alphonse d'Ornano (1548-1610), son of the celebrated Corsican patriot. He was colonel-general of the Corsicans in the service of France, and had been created a marshal of France in 1596.

[21] Gabrielle, as we have just stated, survived until the following day (Saturday, April 10); but La Varenne, either to spare the King the sight of his mistress, whom, Bassompierre tells us, he himself had seen on the Thursday afternoon, "so changed that she was unrecognisable," or to prevent a scandal, had taken upon himself to announce in advance the event which he knew to be inevitable and close at hand.

[22] The Parlement of Paris also sent a deputation to condole with the grief-stricken monarch.

[23] Bassompierre says "a few days"; Tallemant des Réaux "three weeks." In point of fact, it was not until the following June that Henri IV., while on his way from Fontainebleau to Blois, broke his journey at the Château of Malesherbes, where resided François de Balsac d'Entragues, governor of Orléans, who had married as his second wife Marie Touchet, mistress of Charles IX, and mother of Charles de Valois, Comte d'Auvergne, and there saw Henriette, then a girl of eighteen, for the first time.

[24] Although so young, Mlle. de Entragues was very much alive to her own interests, and, counselled by her parents, determined that the brilliant destiny of which fate had deprived her predecessor in the royal affections should be hers. The enamoured monarch loaded her with costly gifts and employed every persuasion he could think of to overcome her resistance; but the damsel was adamant, until, in despair, he placed in her hands the following remarkable document, which Henriette carried about in her pocket and triumphantly exhibited to all her friends:—

"We, Henri, by the Grace of God, King of France and Navarre, promise and swear by our faith and kingly word to Monsieur François de Balsac, Sieur d'Entragues, etc., that he, giving us to be our consort (*pour compagne*) demoiselle Henriette Catherine de Balsac, his daughter, provided that within six months from the present date she becomes pregnant and bear us a son, that forthwith we will take her to wife and publicly espouse her in the face of Holy Church, in accordance with the solemnities required in such cases."

Once more, however, the unexpected came to save the situation. One night, the room in which the sultana—now become Marquise de Verneuil—lay, was struck by lightning. The shock caused a miscarriage, and the King, whose marriage with Marguerite de Valois had been solemnly annulled, on December 29, 1599, by the commission appointed by the Pope, holding himself released from his promise, thereupon decided to send a formal demand to the Court of Tuscany for the hand of Marie de' Medici.

[25] Charles de Lorraine, Duc d'Elbeuf (1566-1605).

[26] The Prince de Joinville was, or had been, in love with Henriette d'Entragues, who, until the King appeared upon the scene, had been far from insensible to his admiration, and he believed that the Grand Equerry was endeavouring to prejudice his Majesty's mind against him on that account.

[27] Achille de Harlay. He was First President of the Parlement of Paris from 1583 to 1611.

[28] The brother, mother, and sister of the Prince de Joinville.

[29] Henri, Duc and Maréchal de Montmorency (1534-1614).

[30] Yolande de Livron, demoiselle de Bourbonne, daughter of Erard de Livron, Baron de Bourbonne,

and Yolande de Bassompierre, and cousin-german of the future marshal, who tells us that he would probably have married the young lady and "might not have lived unhappily with her," had it not been for the opposition of his mother, whom he did not wish to displease.

[31] Mlle. Quelin. She was the mother of Nicolas Quelin, counsellor to the Grande Chambre of the Parlement of Paris, who claimed, wrongly it is said, to be the son of Henri IV.

[32] Marie Babou de la Bourdaisière, daughter of Georges Babou, Seigneur de la Bon, Comte de Sagonne. She was one of Queen Louise's maids-of-honour.

[33] La Côte-Saint-André, on the road from Vienne to Grenoble.

[34] The cause of this quarrel was in all probability the famous promise of marriage which Henri IV had given to Madame de Verneuil and the approaching arrival of Marie de' Medici—"*la grosse financière*," as Henriette disrespectfully called her—who was to become Queen of France.

[35] Basing House, Hampshire.

[36] William Pawlet, Marquis of Winchester.

[37] Madame de Verneuil gave birth to a son a month later, and, in the pride of her motherhood, scoffed at "*la grosse financière*," who, said she, had indeed got a son, but not the Dauphin. For the King was her husband—she had his written promise—and it was SHE who held the Dauphin in her arms.

[38] Jacques de la Guesle, procurator-general to the Parlement.

[39] The Comte d'Auvergne showed the most craven terror, and offered—king's son though he was—to play the part of a spy and to continue to communicate with his confederates, in order to disclose their plans to the Government.

[40] The Prince de Joinville, having become the lover of Madame de Villars, who had aspired to succeed Gabrielle d'Estrées in the affections of Henri IV, and was bitterly hostile in consequence to Madame de Verneuil, had been cajoled by that lady into handing over to her the love-letters which he had received from Henriette, some of which contained expressions of great tenderness and had been written at the very time when the King was paying the damsel his addresses. These letters Madame de Villars had the meanness to send to Henri IV, who was naturally furious at the discovery that his mistress had had two

strings to her bow. Eventually, however, his Majesty allowed himself to be persuaded by Madame de Verneuil and her friends that the letters were forgeries, the work of one Bigot, whom Joinville had suborned; and Henriette was forgiven, while the prince received orders to leave France.

[41] Rossworm had distinguished himself in 1601 at the capture of Stuhl-Weissemburg, and in 1602 had taken by assault the lower town of Buda and the town of Pesth.

[42] Presumably, Ladislaus's Hall, or the Hall of Homage, constructed towards the end of the fifteenth century by Rieth.

[43] Lorraine, though its independence had been recognised in 1542, still contributed its share to the charges which had for their object the peace and security of the Empire; and, as the troops which Bassompierre proposed to raise were intended for service in Hungary against the Turks, it was on this fund, called the *landsfried*, that the order was drawn.

[44] Jacqueline de Bueil was an orphan who had been brought up by Charlotte de la Trémoille, widow of Henri I, Prince de Condé. She was a very astute young lady indeed, and demanded, as the price of her surrender, a large sum of money, a pension, a title, and

a husband, all of which the amorous monarch conceded. The husband chosen for her was a needy and complaisant noble, Philippe de Harlay, Comte de Cess, a nephew of Queen Margaret's old lover, Harlay de Chanvallon, who raised no objection to his sovereign exercising *le droit de seigneur.* Subsequently, the King created the lady Comtesse de Moret in her own right.

[45] Henri de Lorraine, Duc d'Aiguillon, eldest son of the Duc de Mayenne, and brother of the Comte de Sommerive.

[46] Among the members of Queen Marguerite's suite, was a youth of some twenty summers, the son of one Date, a carpenter of Arles, whom her Majesty ennobled, *"avec six aunes d'étoffe,"* and who forthwith blossomed into a Sieur de Saint-Julien. This Saint-Julien, if we are to believe the chroniclers of the time, was passionately beloved by his regal mistress, though perhaps, as a charitable biographer of Marguerite suggests, her affection for him may have been "merely platonic and maternal." However that may be, he stood on the very pinnacle of favour, and was regarded with envy and hatred by his less fortunate rivals. One of these rivals, Vermont by name—not Charmont, as Bassompierre calls him—

either because he was jealous of the privileges which Saint-Julien enjoyed, or, more probably, because he believed that the favourite had used his influence with the Queen to procure the disgrace of certain members of his family, suspected of having aided the intrigues of the Comte d'Auvergne, swore to be avenged. Nor was his vow an idle one, for one fine morning in April, 1606, at the very moment when Saint-Julien was assisting Marguerite to alight from her coach, on her return from hearing Mass at the Célestines, he stepped forward, and, levelling a pistol, shot him dead. The assassin endeavoured to escape, but was pursued and captured; and the bereaved princess, beside herself with rage and grief, vowed that she would neither eat nor drink until justice had been done, and wrote to the King "begging his Majesty very humbly to be pleased that the assassin should be punished." The King sent orders for Vermont to be brought to trial without an hour's delay; and he was condemned to death and executed the following morning in front of Marguerite's hôtel, "declaring aloud," writes L'Estoile, "that he cared not about dying, since he had accomplished his purpose."

[47] Although he had resumed his relations with Madame de Verneuil, and seemed more infatuated

with her than ever, his Majesty continued his attentions to Madame de Moret, and had also fallen in love with a certain Mlle. de la Haye, with whom he spent a honeymoon at Chantilly, obligingly placed at his disposal by the Connétable de Montmorency, under the pretext of enjoying the fine hunting which the neighbourhood afforded. This affair, however, only lasted a short time. The young lady, it appears, had persuaded his Majesty that he was the first who had gained her heart, but, in point of fact, she had begun her career of gallantry by a *liaison* with M. de Beaumont, the late French Ambassador in England, who, however, had soon broken off his relations with her. Mlle. de la Haye had not forgiven him for this rupture, and, believing herself more in favour than she was, she endeavoured to prejudice the King's mind against him. Beaumont, learning of this, promptly sent his Majesty the letters which Mlle. de la Haye had written him when she was his mistress; and Henri IV, indignant at having been deceived, broke with her in his turn.

[48] Tallemant des Réaux, in his *Historiettes*, gives some details concerning this *liaison* of Bassompierre and the part played therein by Henri, who appears to have been made a fool of, as in several analogous

circumstances. "Bassompierre," he writes, "had the honour to have for some time the King as rival. Testu, Chevalier of the Watch, assisted his Majesty in the affair. One day, when this man came to speak to Mlle. d'Entragues, she hid Bassompierre behind a tapestry, and said to Testu, who reproached her with being less cruel to Bassompierre than to the King, that she cared no more for the former than for the latter, at the same time striking with a switch which she held in her hand the place where her gallant was concealed."

[49] Men whose duty it was to remove the bodies of persons who had died of the plague or other contagious maladies. During several months of that year Paris was ravaged by an epidemic, which was either plague or a virulent form of typhus.

[50] Nearly two centuries later, this adventure of Bassompierre so impressed the romantic imagination of Chateaubriand, then a young man of twenty, that he made a pilgrimage to the Rue Bourg-l'Abbé and "the third door on the side of the Rue Saint-Martin." But, to the great disappointment of the future author of *René*, he found himself confronted, not by the old gabled house which Bassompierre must have entered and quitted so abruptly, but by a hopelessly modern residence, the ground-floor of which was occupied by

a hairdresser's shop, with "a variety of towers of hair behind the window-panes." And "no frank, disinterested, passionate young woman" was to be seen, but only "an old crone, who might have been the aunt of the assignation."

"What a fine story, that story of Bassompierre!" he writes. "One of the reasons which caused him to be so passionately loved ought to be understood. At that time, France was divided into two classes, one dominant, the other semi-servile. The sempstress clasped Bassompierre in her arms as though he were a demi-god who had descended to the bosom of a slave: he gave her the illusion of glory, and Frenchwomen alone amongst women are capable of intoxicating themselves with that illusion. But who will reveal to us the unknown causes of the catastrophe? Was the body which lay upon the table by the side of another body that of the pretty wench of the Two Angels? Whose was the other body? Was it the husband or the man whose voice Bassompierre had heard? Had the plague (for the plague was raging in Paris) or jealousy reached the Rue Bourg-l'Abbé before love? The imagination can easily find matter for exercise in such a subject as this. Mingle with the poet's inventions, the chorus of the populace, the approaching grave-diggers, the 'crows' and Bassompierre's sword, and a magnificent melodrama springs from the adventure."—*Mémoires d'Outre Tombe*, Vol. I.

[51] Louise Pot, second wife of Claude de l'Aubespine, Seigneur de Verderonne.

[52] Mlle. de la Patière, daughter of Georges l'Enfant, Seigneur de la Patière, and of Françoise du Plessis-Richelieu. The La Patières were friends and neighbours of Bassompierre.

[53] Jean Louis de Nogaret de la Valette, born 1554; created Duc d'Épernon, 1581; died 1642.

[54] The Duc de Montpensier died on February 27, 1608; the ballet appears to have been danced about the middle of January.

[55] Charlotte de Montmorency, daughter of the Connétable Henri de Montmorency, by his second wife, Louise de Budos. She was born in 1594 and was at this time only fourteen. By his first wife, Antoinette de la Marck, the Constable had two daughters: (1) Charlotte de Montmorency, married in 1591 to Charles de Valois, Comte d'Auvergne, died in 1636, at the age of sixty-three; (2) Marguerite de Montmorency, married in 1593 to Anne de Lévis, Duc de Ventadour, died December 3, 1660, aged eighty-three.

[56] Jean du Fay, Baron de Pérault, lieutenant of the King in the Bresse. He was married to Marie de Montmorency, a natural daughter of the Constable.

[57] See the author's "The Fascinating Duc de Richelieu" (London, Methuen; New York, Scribner, 1910).

[58] The exception was Renée de Lorraine, Mlle. de Mayenne, daughter of Charles, Duc de Mayenne.

[59] Charles de Montmorency. He was at first known under the title of Seigneur de Méru, then as Baron de Damville, and, in 1610, was created Duc de Damville. He died in 1612, after having filled the offices of Colonel-General of the Swiss troops in the French service and Admiral of France.

[60] Henri II, Duc de Montmorency and de Damville, only son of the Constable by his second wife, Louise de Budos; born August 30, 1595; beheaded for high treason at Toulouse, October 3, 1635.

[61] Gabrielle Angélique, legitimated daughter of Henri IV and the Marquise de Verneuil, married December 12, 1622, to Bernard de Nogaret, Duc de la Valette; died December 24, 1627.

[62] Diane de France, Duchesse de Montmorency and d'Angoulême, legitimated daughter of Henri II by a Piedmontese girl called Filippa Duc, whom he had met during the campaign of 1537 in Italy. Born in 1538, she was brought up at the Court of France, and married in 1553 to Orazio Farnese, Duke of Castro, who was killed a few months later, whilst defending Hesdin against the troops of Charles V. In 1559 the young widow married François, Duc and Maréchal de Montmorency, elder brother of the Constable, who died in 1579. A beautiful, accomplished and highly intelligent woman, and a singularly loyal friend, Diane was greatly esteemed by the last Valois sovereigns and also by Henri IV. Her half-brother, Henri III, gave her the duchies of Angoulême and Châtellerault, the county of Ponthieu, and the government of the Limousin; and it was she who in 1588 brought about the reconciliation between that monarch and Henri of Navarre. She died in 1619, at the age of eighty, having seen no less than seven kings on the throne of France.

[63] As son of Éleonor de Montmorency, a sister of the Connétable Henri de Montmorency.

[64] Henri II de Bourbon, Prince de Condé, son of Henri I, Prince de Condé, by his second wife, Catherine Charlotte de la Trémoille. He was officially

styled *Monsieur le Prince*, and as such is always referred to in Bassompierre's *Mémoires*.

[65] Catherine Charlotte de la Trémoille, Princesse de Condé, was a daughter of Jeanne de Montmorency, sister of the Constable, who was therefore Condé's great-uncle.

[66] Anne de Lorraine, Duchesse d'Aumale, daughter and heiress of Charles de Lorraine-Guise, Duc d'Aumale, and of Marie de Lorraine-Elbeuf; married in 1618 to Henri de Savoie, Duc de Nemours; died in 1638.

[67] The favour which Henri IV was offering Bassompierre consisted, strictly speaking, not in the re-establishment of the duchy of Aumale, of which the title remained by right to Mlle. d'Aumale, but in uniting once more the peerage to the duchy, the old peerage having become extinct through the failure of male heirs.

[68] Although the King always alluded to the Prince de Condé as his nephew, he was really only a nephew *à la mode de Bretagne*, a first cousin once removed.

[69] Pierre de Beringhen, Seigneur d'Armainvilliers et de Grez, first *valet de chambre* to the King.

[70] Jeanne de Scepeaux, Comtesse de Chemillé, Duchesse de Beaupréau, only daughter and heiress of Guy de Scepeaux, Comte de Chemillé, Duc de Beaupréau. She had married early in that year Henri de Montmorency (Monsieur de Montmorency, as he was officially styled), only son of the Constable; but Henri IV, being desirous of marrying the heir of the Montmorencys to his daughter Mlle. de Vendôme, caused this union to be declared null and void a few months later. In May, 1610, Mlle. de Chemillé married Henri de Gondi, Duc de Retz.

[71] On March 25, 1609, John William, Duke of Clèves, Juliers and Berg, had died childless. The question of the succession to his dominions was of vital importance, as they connected the bishoprics of Münster, Paderborn, and Hildesheim, with the Spanish Netherlands, and, during the reign of the late duke, who was a Catholic, had interrupted the communications of the Protestants of Central Germany with the Dutch. Their transference to a Protestant prince would be a fatal blow to the North German Catholics and would threaten the security of

the Spanish Netherlands. A number of claimants appeared, the most prominent of whom were two Protestant princes, the Elector of Brandenburg and the Count Palatine of Neuberg, who claimed through the two elder sisters of John William. They came to an agreement to occupy part of the country and establish a provisional government; but the Emperor maintained that the duchies were male fiefs which could only descend in the direct male line, pronounced them sequestrated, and called upon the two princes to submit their claims to him as "feudal lord and sovereign judge." On their refusal to do this, he placed them under the ban of the Empire, and ordered the Archduke Leopold to take possession of the territory as Imperial Commissioner (July, 1609). Henri IV protested vigorously against the Emperor's action, declaring that he was determined not to permit any such addition to the power of the House of Austria, and that, if it came to war, he would prosecute it with all the resources of his kingdom.

[72] Alexandre d'Elbène, gentleman of the chamber-in-ordinary to the King, colonel of the Italian infantry in the service of France, and first *maître d'hôtel* to the Queen. It was he who, with the Captain

of the Watch, had been the first to break the news of the flight of the Condés to Henri IV.

[73] Damian de Montluc, Sieur de Balagny. He was governor of Marle.

[74] Brulart de Sillery.

[75] Henri IV had meanly stopped the payment of Condé's pensions.

[76] For a full account of this episode, see the author's "The Love Affairs of the Condés." (London; Methuen. New York: Scribners. 1912.)

[77] The Queen's entry was to have taken place on May 16.

[78] Bassompierre carried at the *Sacre* the train of the Princesse de Conti, who herself carried that of the Queen.

[79] But, according to a contemporary account of the ceremony, Henri IV was in an unusually sombre mood, and, on entering the church and beholding the vast silent assemblage, observed: "It reminds me of the great and last judgment. God give us grace to prepare well for that day!" (*Cérémonial français*, Tome I., p. 570.)

[80]   Pierre   Fougeu,   Seigneur   d'Escures, Quartermaster-General of the camps and armies of the King.

[81] Bernard Potier, Seigneur de Blérencourt. He was Lieutenant-Colonel of the Light Horse of which Bassompierre was Colonel.

[82] Méry de Vic, Seigneur d'Ermenonville. He was appointed Keeper of the Seals in 1621.

[83] This was no idle threat, for Madame de Bassompierre's will contains a clause providing that, in the event of her son espousing the demoiselle Marie Charlotte de Balsac, "she disinherited him and deprived him of all her property, having expressly forbidden him to contract a marriage with her."

[84] "Five giants took part in the procession, of the race of those whom Hercules slew in the war which they waged against the gods, in the valley of Phlegra, in Thessaly."—Laugier de Porchères, *le Camp de la Place-Royale* (Paris, 1612).

[85] "The five challengers styled themselves the Knights of Glory. M. de Bassompierre made his entry among them under the name of Lysander. He had for his device a lighted fuse, with these words: *Da l'ardore l'ardire* (*De l'ardour la hardiesse*), in

allusion to a love avowed."—*le Camp de la Place-Royale.*

[86] The Prince de Conti's troupe called themselves the Knights of the Sun; the Duc de Vendôme's the Knights of the Lily.

[87] François de Noailles, Comte d'Ayen (1584-1645). He was governor of Rouergue, Auvergne and Roussillon.

[88] Jacques du Blé, Baron, afterwards Marquis d'Huxelles. Bassompierre, conforming without doubt to the pronunciation, writes the name sometimes d'Ucelles and at others Du Sel.

[89] Henri II, Duc de Longueville, Comte de Dunois (1595-1643). He married in 1642, as his second wife, Anne Geneviève de Bourbon-Condé, who was the celebrated Duchesse de Longueville, of the Fronde.

[90] Under the name of the Knight of the Phœnix.

[91] The Nymphs were: the Comte de Schomberg, hamadryad; Colonel d'Ornano, wood-nymph; Créquy, dryad; Saint-Luc, naiad; and the Marquis de Rosny, oread.

[92] Antoine Coeffier, called Ruzé, Marquis d'Effiat, who was created a *maréchal* de France in 1631. He was the father of the ill-fated Cinq-Mars.

[93] This entry is called, in *le Camp du Place-Royale*, that of the illustrious Romans. According to this relation, there were but seven of them: Trajan, Vespasian, Paulus Æmilius, Marcellus, Scipio, Coriolanus and Marius. There also entered on this day a troupe of Knights of the Air, which, however, was incomplete, owing to one of the "Knights," the Seigneur de Balagny, having been wounded in a duel.

[94] The young Duc de Mayenne, son of the old chief of the League, who had died in October, 1611.

[95] Saint-Paul, a soldier of fortune, was one of the four marshals created by the Duc de Mayenne in 1593. He was lieutenant of Charles, Duc de Guise in his government of Champagne, and rendered himself intensely unpopular with the inhabitants of Rheims by various acts of oppression. Guise killed him with his own hand, in the Place de la Cathédrale there, on April 25, 1597. For a full account of this incident and also of the affair of the Chevalier de Guise and the Baron de Luz, see the author's "The Brood of False Lorraine" (Hutchinson, 1919).

[96] The Duc de Guise was Governor of Provence.

[97] After the death of his elder brother, the Cardinal de Bourbon, the Prince de Conti had been placed in possession of the Abbey of Saint-Germain-des-Prés, which had been one of the cardinal's benefices. The Queen was offering to the Princess de Conti, in the event of her widowhood, the reversion of these revenues.

[98] *Histoire de France jusqu'en 1789.*

[99] They did not fail of their reward, Bassompierre tells us, for one of them, Masurier, was presently appointed First President of the Parlement of Toulouse, while the other, Mangot, became First President of that of Bordeaux, and was afterwards made Keeper of the Seals.

[100] "This dignity, formerly so respected, had been conferred lavishly since the Wars of the League, but it had not been degraded to this point. Concini having never borne arms, they were obliged to renounce in his case the ancient custom of the new marshal of France presenting himself to the Parlement, accompanied by an advocate, who expounded his claims and his valiant deeds. There is a limit to everything, even to the impudence of flatterers."—Henri Martin.

[101] Malherbe's letters contain some interesting observations concerning the Queen and Bassompierre: "20 October [1613]. I am told that 51 [the Queen] has not spoken to him [Bassompierre] for a week. It is believed that 65 [Concini] has done him a bad turn. The affair is patched up to some extent, to which 59 [Guise] has contributed much. I have seen him [Bassompierre] to-day in the cabinet, but much less impudent than he usually is, and 51 [the Queen] never spoke to him at all. It will pass.

"27 October. The disfavour of 66 [Bassompierre] continues visibly; the cause is the alliance of 55 [Concini] and 69 [Villeroy], who have both told 51 [the Queen] that, when they were on bad terms, 66 [Bassompierre] betrayed them both, and, besides, had given her to understand that he boasts of her favour.

"24 November 66 [Bassompierre] is in less disfavour; but I fear that he will never be again as he has been.

"27 November. I have seen 66 [Bassompierre], so that I believe the disagreement is patched up, or will be patched up."

[102] The Duc de Rohan was not a prince, but he was descended on his mother's side from two sovereign houses, those of Navarre and Scotland.

[103] Gaspard Gallaty had fought as a captain at Moncontour and as a colonel at Arques and Ivry. He was ennobled in 1587.

[104] The Duc de Guise and his brother the Prince de Joinville.

[105] Gabriel de la Vallée-Fossez, Marquis d'Everly. He was governor of Montpellier.

[106] The Commandeur de Sillery, *chevalier d'honneur* to Marie de' Medici, had been disgraced shortly before his brother, the Chancellor, was dismissed.

[107] Créquy was Colonel of the French Guards.

[108] He was Captain-Lieutenant of the Gensdarmes of the King's Guard.

[109] La Curée was Captain-Lieutenant of the company of Light Cavalry of the Guard instituted by Henri IV in 1593.

[110] In response to the summons he had received from the Queen-Mother, Condé was making his way along a narrow passage which led from her Majesty's chamber to her cabinet, when he was suddenly confronted by Thémines, at the head of several of the King's Guards "Monseigneur," said the old noble to the astonished prince, "the King having been informed

that you are giving ear to sundry counsels contrary to his service, and that people intend to make you engage in designs ruinous to the State, has charged me to secure your person, to prevent you falling into this misfortune." "What?" cried Condé, "do you purpose to arrest me? Are you then captain of the Guards?" And he laid his hand upon his sword. "No, Monseigneur," rejoined Thémines, "but I am a gentleman and obliged to obey the command of the King, your master and mine." His followers forthwith surrounded the prince and led him into an adjoining room, where he found d'Elbène and a party of soldiers, each of whom held a pistol in his hand. Never remarkable for his courage, though in his youth he had once been provoked into challenging the Duc de Nevers to a duel, Condé believed that his last hour had come. "Alas," cried he, "I am a dead man. Send for a priest. Give me time at least to think of my conscience!" His captors, however, assured him that his life was in no danger, and conducted him to an upper apartment of the palace, where it had been arranged that he should be confined, until it had been decided what should be done with him.

[111] In the Rue de Chaume, at the corner of the Rue de Paradis.

[112] Charles Alexandre, Duc de Cröy, Marquis d'Havré. He was related to Bassompierre through his mother, Diane de Dommartin.

[113] Enrico Concini, who was at this time a boy of thirteen. Arrested after the tragic end of his father, he remained five years in prison, and then returned to Florence, where he lived until 1631, under the name of the Count della Penna.

[114] This refers to the manifesto issued by Condé in July, 1615, in which he had stigmatised Concini, the Chancellor Sillery, his brother the Commandeur de Sillery, and the Counsellors of State, Bullion and Dolet, as the authors of the evils which afflicted the realm.

[115] The word is, of course, here used in the sense of a man who owed his fortune to him, and not in its vituperative sense.

[116] Fedeau appears to have been a banker or usurer of the time, the terms being often synonymous.

[117] Lavisse, *Histoire de France*.

[118] Probably Gilles de Souvré, Marquis de Courtenvaux, who was also Baron de Lézines.

[119] Charles de Lameth, Seigneur de Bussy. He was killed at the siege of La Capelle in 1637.

[120] Richelieu assures us that Luynes showed Louis XIII forged letters purporting to have been written by Barbin, "full of designs against the person of the King," and, considering the position occupied by Déageant, this appears very probable.

[121] Vitry had been created a marshal of France the day after the assassination of Concini. "Thémines had recently been given the bâton of marshal for having adopted the trade of a bailiff; Vitry had it as his reward for plying that of a bravo. Who would have thought that this high dignity, after having been abased to Concini, would have descended yet lower still?"—Henri Martin.

[122] François de l'Hôpital, Seigneur du Hallier. He was created a marshal of France in 1643, under the name of the Maréchal de l'Hôpital.

[123] Luynes had two younger brothers: (1) Honor d'Albert, Seigneur de Cadanet, afterwards Duc de Chaulnes and Marshal of France; (2) Léon d'Albert, Seigneur de Brantes, afterwards Duc de Piney-Luxembourg.

[124] *Journal historique et anecdotique de la Cour et de Paris.* MSS. of Conrart, cited by Victor Cousin, *la Jeunesse de Madame de Longueville.* The chronicler speaks frequently of the prince's ill-

treatment of his wife, for which he appears to think there was no justification.

[125] Bournonville was brought to trial and condemned to death, while Persan was sentenced to be banished from France; but both were subsequently pardoned.

[126] *Journal historique et anecdotique de la Cour et de Paris.*

[127] It would appear, from an anecdote related by Bassompierre, in March, 1618, that Luynes had not hesitated to falsify history in his efforts to inspire the King with fear of his mother:

"At that time, the King, who was very young, amused himself with many little occupations of his age, making little fountains in imitation of those of Saint-Germain, with pipes of quill, and little inventions for hunting, and playing on the drum, in which he succeeded very well. One day I told him that he was clever at everything which he undertook, and that, although he had never been taught, he played the drum better than the master of that instrument. 'I must begin to blow the hunting-horn again,' said he, 'which I do very well, and will blow it for a whole day.' 'Sire,' said I, 'I do not advise your Majesty to blow it too often, for it causes ruptures, and is very injurious for the lungs; and I have heard that, through blowing the horn, the late King Charles broke a blood-vessel in his lungs, and that caused his death.' 'You are mistaken,' he rejoined; 'it was not blowing the horn that killed him; it was because he quarrelled with the Queen Catherine, his mother at Monceaux, and left her and went to Meaux. But, if he had not been persuaded by the Maréchal de Retz to return to the Queen-Mother at Monceaux, he would not have died so soon.' As I answered nothing to this, Montpouillan, who was present, said to me: 'You did not think, Monsieur, that the King knew so much about these matters, but he does, and about many others besides.' This convinced me that he had been inspired with great apprehension of the Queen, his mother, whom I took care never to mention to him in future, not even in common discourse."

[128] Asked what spell she had employed to make herself mistress of the Queen-Mother's mind, the prisoner is said to have replied: "Only those which a clever woman employs towards a dunce."

[129] The Duc de Mayenne quitted the Court, which was then at Saint-Germain, on March 29, 1620, and went to Guienne, of which he was lieutenant-general.

[130] Louis de Bourbon, son of Charles de Bourbon, Comte de Soissons and Anne de Montafié. Born May 4, 1604; killed at the battle of la Marfée, on July 6, 1641. He was called *Monsieur le Comte*, as his father had been.

[131] There were two kinds of regiments in the French Army at this period: permanent regiments, which usually bore territorial designations, Champagne, Picardy, and so forth, and temporary regiments, which might be disbanded in time of peace, and which bore the names of their commanding officers.

[132] Luynes and his two brothers.

[133] Nerestang died some ten days later, a victim, if we are to believe Bassompierre, to the professional jealousy of the surgeons:—

"The King went to visit M. de Nerestang, who, seeing how severely he had been wounded, was not doing badly, and would have been cured if they had left him in the hands of the surgeon Lion. But the other executioners of surgeons importuned the King so much, when he was at Brissac, that seven days after he was wounded, when he was going on well, they took him out of Lion's hands to place him in those of the King's surgeons; and he only lived two days longer."

[134] Créquy was colonel of the French Guards, and in this action was in command of a brigade.

[135] The property of the Catholic Church in Béarn and Lower Navarre had been confiscated by Jeanne d'Albret in 1569, and applied to the maintenance of pastors of the Reformed faith and works of public utility.

[136] Jacques Nomper de Caumont (1558-1652). He greatly distinguished himself in the Thirty Years' War, and was made a marshal of France and subsequently duke and peer.

[137] This son, who received the names of Louis Charles and to whom Louis XIII stood godfather, became the second Duc de Luynes, and enjoyed some celebrity in the latter part of the seventeenth century through his connection with Port-Royal. He translated into French the *Méditations* of Descartes, wrote under a *nom de guerre* several books of devotion, and was the father of the pious Duc de Chevreuse, the friend of Fénelon.

[138] Don Diego Zapata.

[139] Doña Maria Sidonia, second wife of the count.

[140] Don Pedro Acunha y Tellez-Giron, third Duke of Ossuña (1579-1624). He had been Viceroy of Naples, and one of the three chiefs of the conspiracy against Venice which was to have delivered the city into the power of Spain on Ascension Day, 1618. Suspected of having aspired to make himself King of Naples, he was recalled in 1620. He died in prison in 1624.

[141] The late King, Henri IV.

[142] Enrico de Avila y Guzman.

[143] Antonio de Toledo, fifth duke of Alba, grandson of the celebrated Duke of Alba.

[144] Rodriguez de Mendoza, second son of Diego de Mendoza, Count of Saldagna. He became sixth Duke del Infantado by his marriage with Anna de Mendoza, Duchess del Infantado, daughter of his elder brother.

[145] The office of mayor-domo mayor was equivalent to that of Grand Master of the King's Household in France.

[146] A convent of the barefooted Carmelites in the centre of the town.

[147] He was a Dominican monk and filled the office of Grand Inquisitor.

[148] Philip III's eldest son, afterwards Philip IV. Born on April 8, 1605, he had not yet completed his sixteenth year.

[149] The King's second son; born September 14, 1607; died in 1632.

[150] Fernando, Cardinal Archbishop of Toledo, third son of Philip III; born May 17, 1609; died in 1641.

[151] The new Queen, Élisabeth of France.

[152] A convent of Hieronymite monks, situated a little way from Madrid.

[153] Gaspard de Guzman, third count, and afterwards Duke, of Olivarez. Favourite of the new king, he shared power with his uncle, Don Balthazar de Zuniga, until the latter's death in 1623, from which time up to 1643 he was Prime Minister. He died in 1645.

[154] Charles de Clermont d'Amboise, Marquis de Bussy. He was killed in a duel in the Place-Royale in Paris, in April, 1627.

[155] The *loba* was a long sleeveless robe; the *caperuza* a hood; and the *caperote* a short cloak fitted with a hood.

[156] The Crowns of Spain and Naples, etc.

[157] Don Carlos.

[158] To demand *lugar* of a lady was to request permission to pay one's respects to her at a time and place to be named by her.

[159] Diego de Sandoval y Rojas.

[160] Aloysia de Mendoza. She was Countess of Saldagna in her own right, and her husband assumed the title of Count of Saldagna.

[161] Saldagna had been a widower since 1619.

[162] Catherine de Zuniga y Sandoval, widow of Fernando de Portugal y Castro, sixth Count of Lemos.

[163] See p. 287, *supra*.

[164] The celebrated Duke of Alba.

[165] The fourth Duke of Alba.

[166] "I have paid the compliment of condolence with which the King charged me, so well, that, save that I did not weep, my countenance presented every indication of grief and sadness. Now it lays aside this false mask, since nothing can further retard my return

to France, whither I am going with infinite joy, and infinite desire to serve my master well in war, or my mistress, if we have peace."—Bassompierre to Puisieux, May 10, 1621.

[167] Titled persons; that is to say, noblemen who were not grandees of Spain.

[168] Municipal officials.

[169] The principal magistrate of the town.

[170] In July, 1639, during his captivity in the Bastille, Bassompierre was obliged to part temporarily with Philip IV's gift, which is described as "the diamond of the King of Spain," as security for a loan of 6,300 livres. He redeemed it in May, 1641, but as, after his death, it does not figure in the inventory of his jewels, he would appear to have pledged it again, or perhaps have sold it.

[171] Louis de Marillac, Comte de Beaumont-le-Roger. He was created a marshal of France in 1629, and was executed for high treason on May 10, 1632.

[172] This faubourg had been called Ville-Bourbon, since Henri IV had surrounded it with fortifications.

[173] This was the old fourteenth-century bridge already mentioned.

[174] Bassompierre received next day a letter from the King, complimenting him on the courage and resource he had shown.

[175] The Duc de Luxembourg, the Constable's youngest brother.

[176] The Queen had established herself at Moissac, on the right bank of the Tarn, where she remained during the greater part of the siege.

[177] Louis XIII., in a letter to Noailles, bears testimony to Bassompierre's services in this affair: "In this defeat and action we may recognise, as I have told you, the Providence of God, Who has so fortified the courage of my men that they have performed wonders, and *notably the Sr. de Bassompierre*, the colonel, and the Swiss and the Regiment of Normandy, who have boldly sustained the charge."

Printed in Great Britain
by Amazon